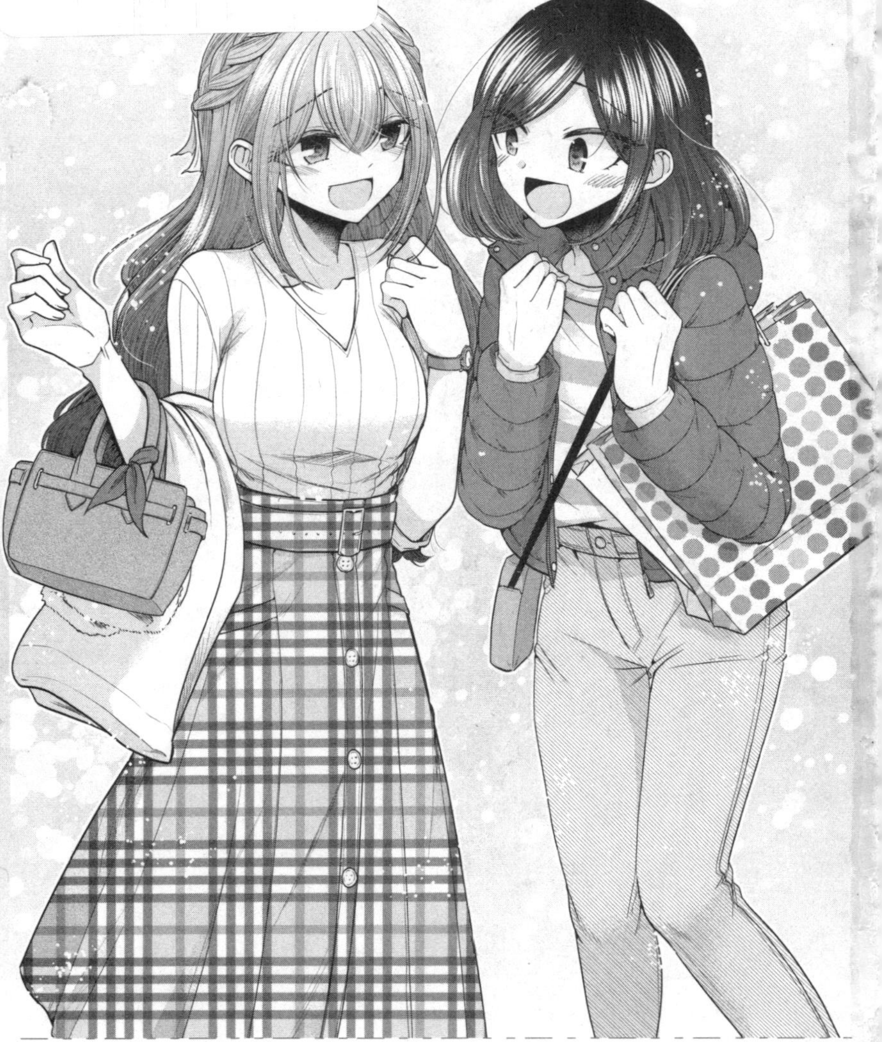

failed princesses volume five

contents

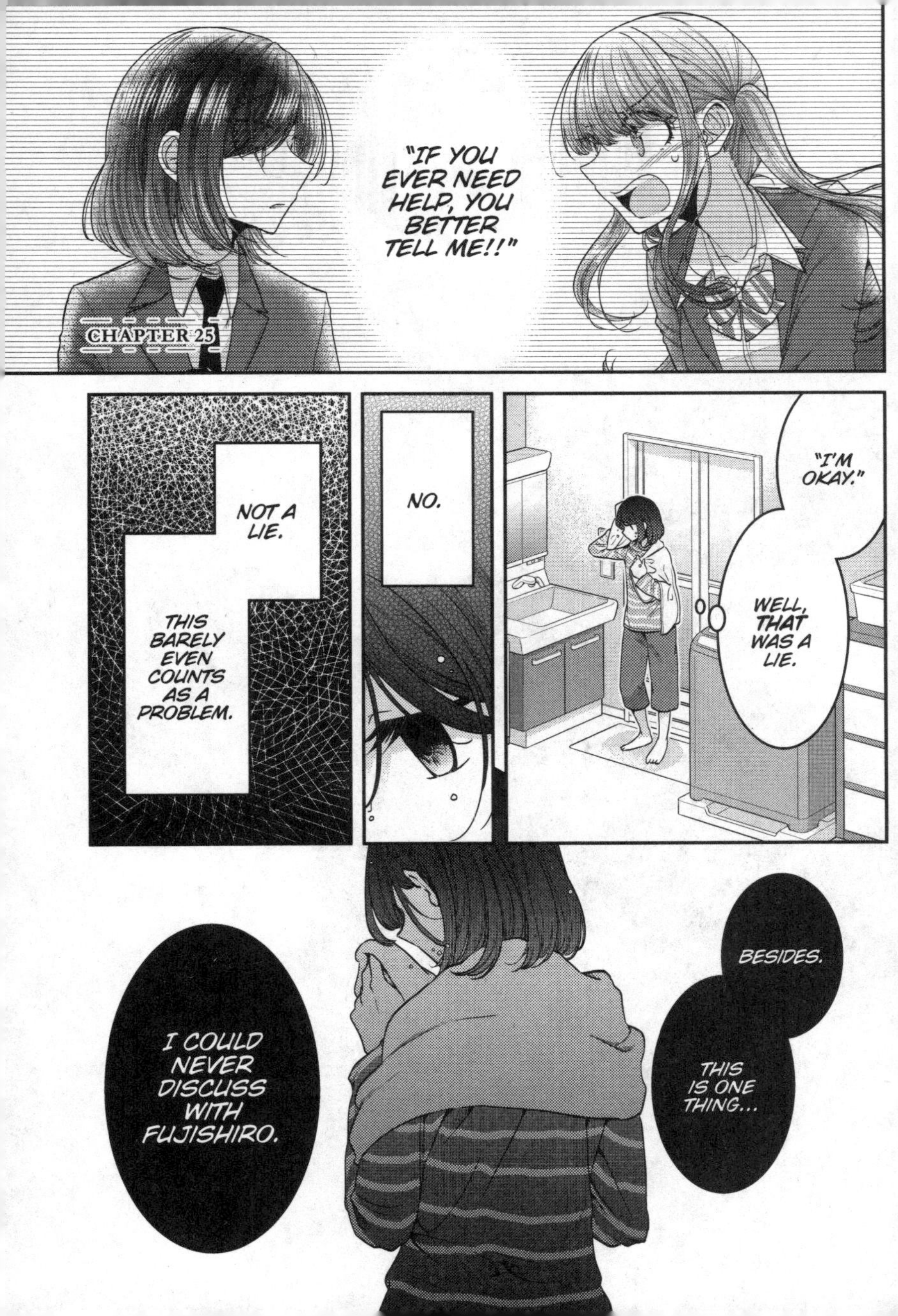
"IF YOU EVER NEED HELP, YOU BETTER TELL ME!!"
CHAPTER 25
"I'M OKAY."
WELL, THAT WAS A LIE.
NO.
NOT A LIE.
THIS BARELY EVEN COUNTS AS A PROBLEM.
BESIDES.
THIS IS ONE THING...
I COULD NEVER DISCUSS WITH FUJISHIRO.

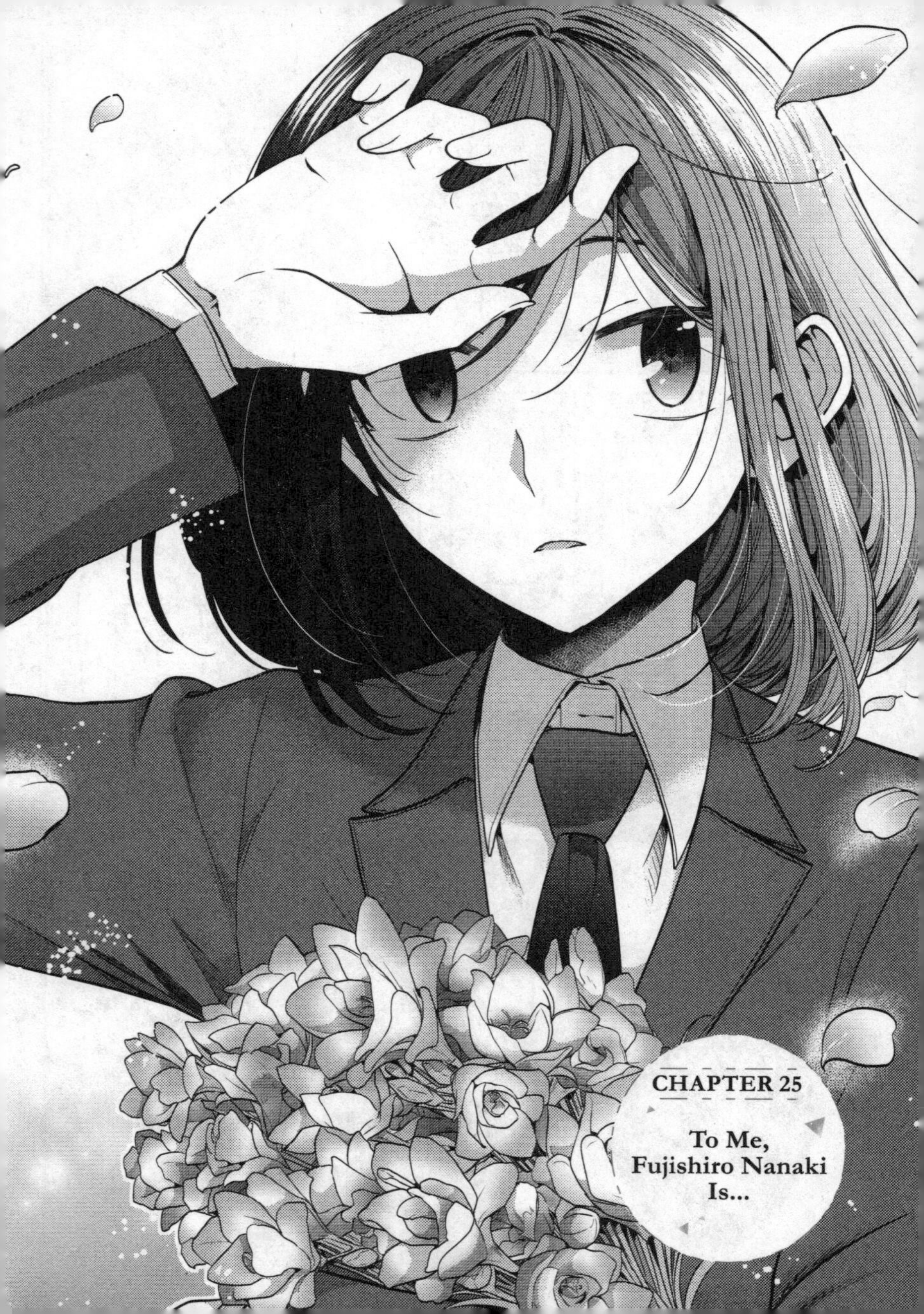
CHAPTER 25
To Me, Fujishiro Nanaki Is...

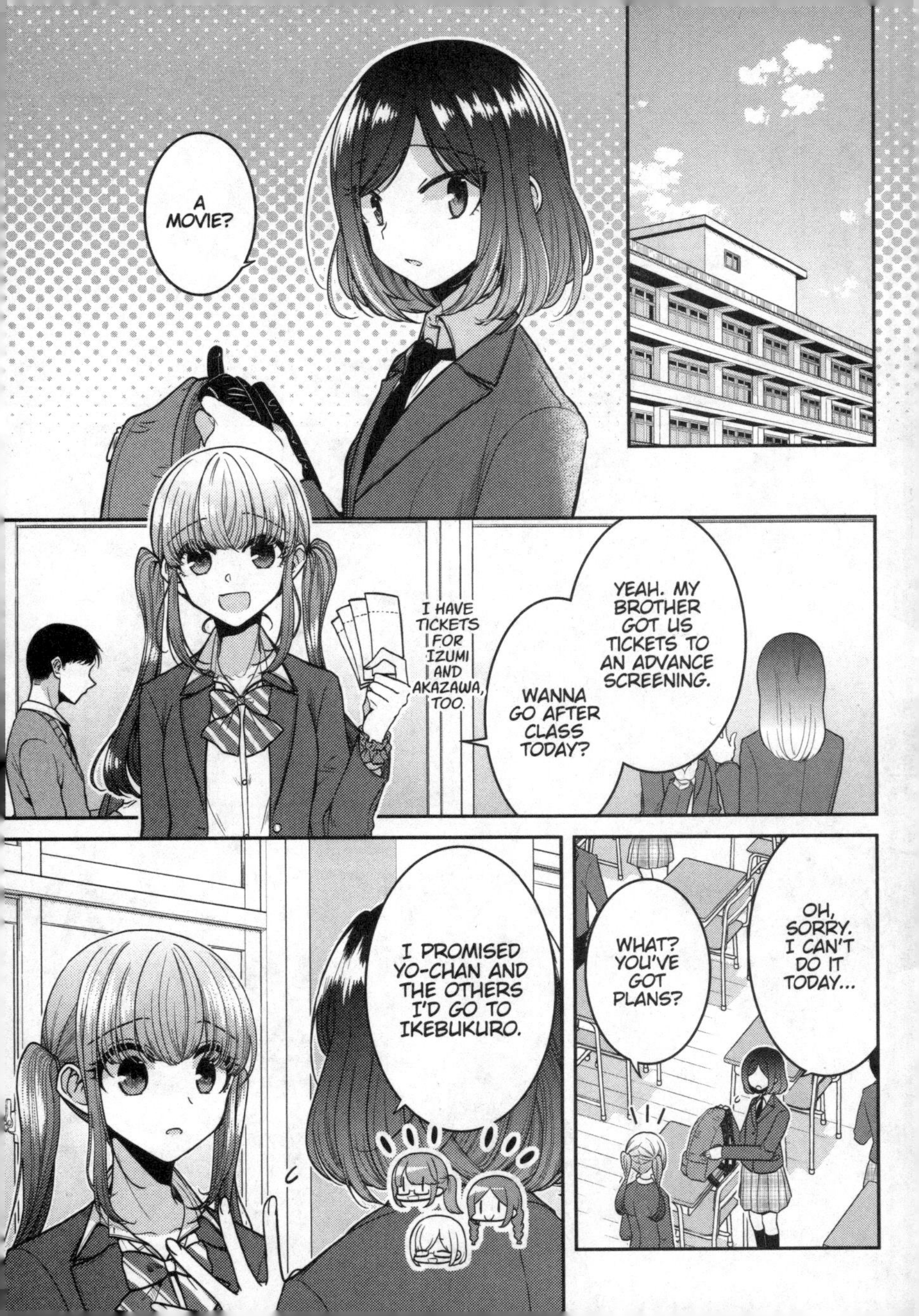
A MOVIE?
YEAH. MY BROTHER GOT US TICKETS TO AN ADVANCE SCREENING.
WANNA GO AFTER CLASS TODAY?
I HAVE TICKETS FOR IZUMI AND AKAZAWA, TOO.
OH, SORRY. I CAN'T DO IT TODAY...
WHAT? YOU'VE GOT PLANS?
I PROMISED YO-CHAN AND THE OTHERS I'D GO TO IKEBUKURO.

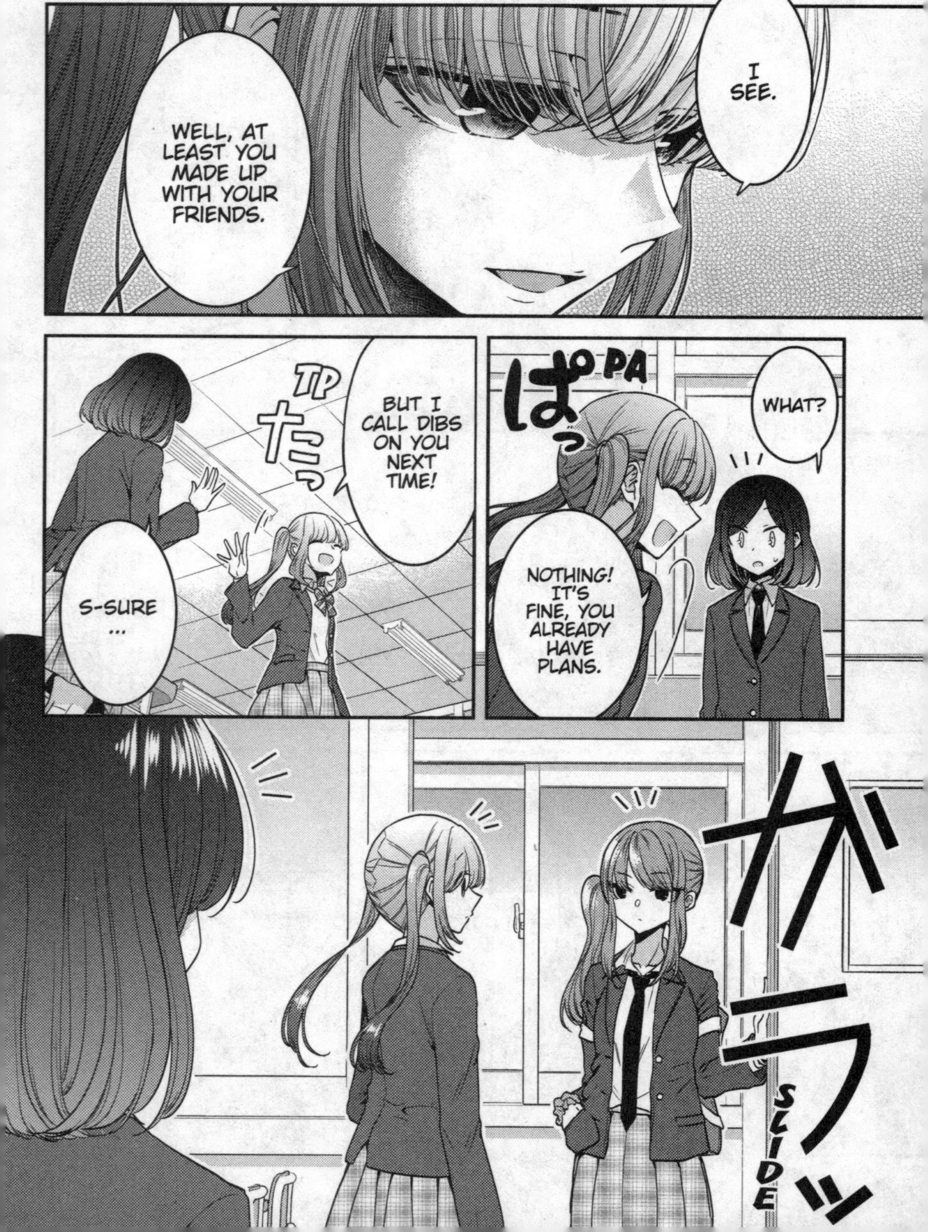
I SEE.
WELL, AT LEAST YOU MADE UP WITH YOUR FRIENDS.
ぱっ
PA
WHAT?
NOTHING! IT'S FINE, YOU ALREADY HAVE PLANS.
BUT I CALL DIBS ON YOU NEXT TIME!
たっ
TP
S-SURE ...
ガラッ
SLIDE

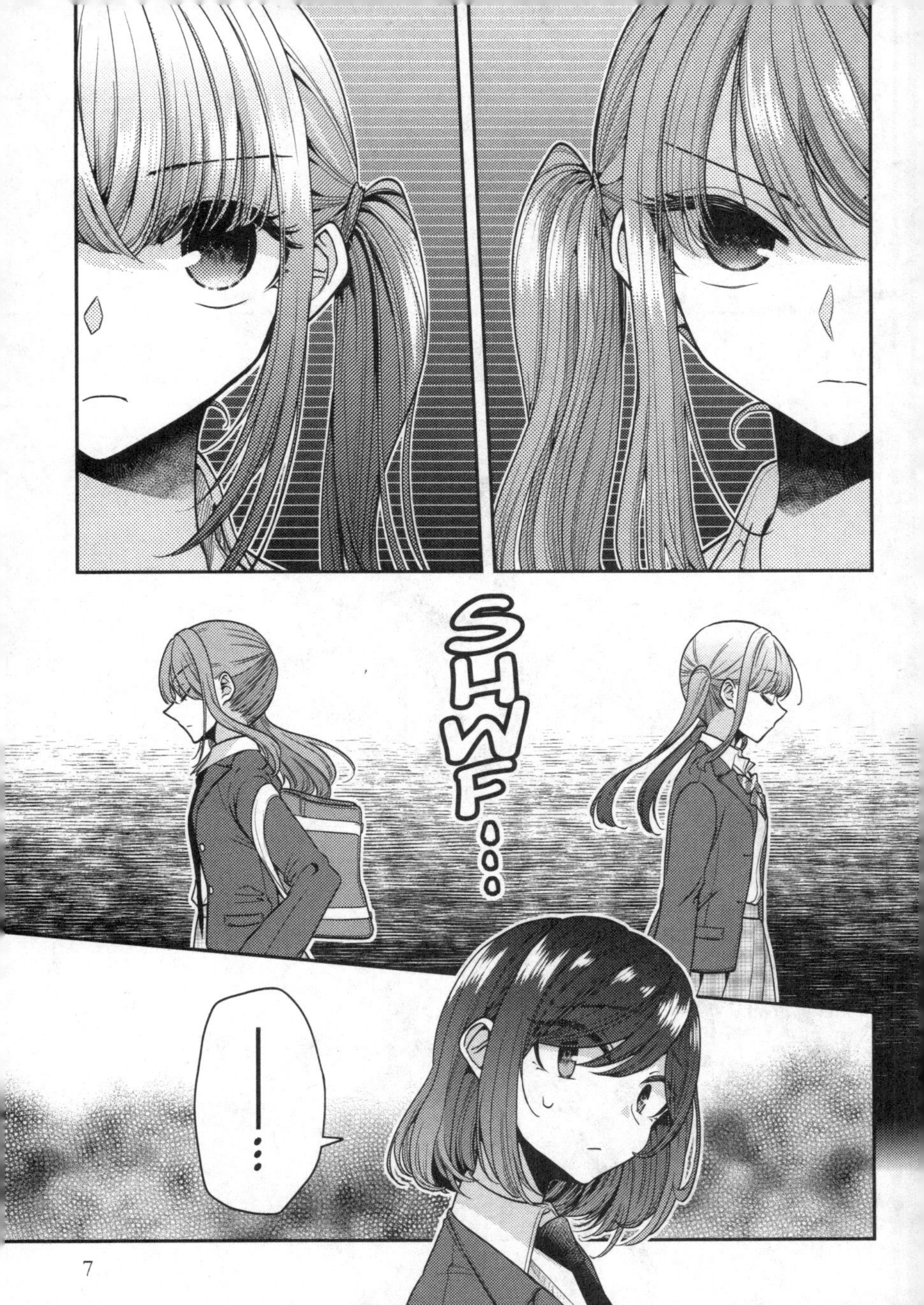
SHWF...
—...

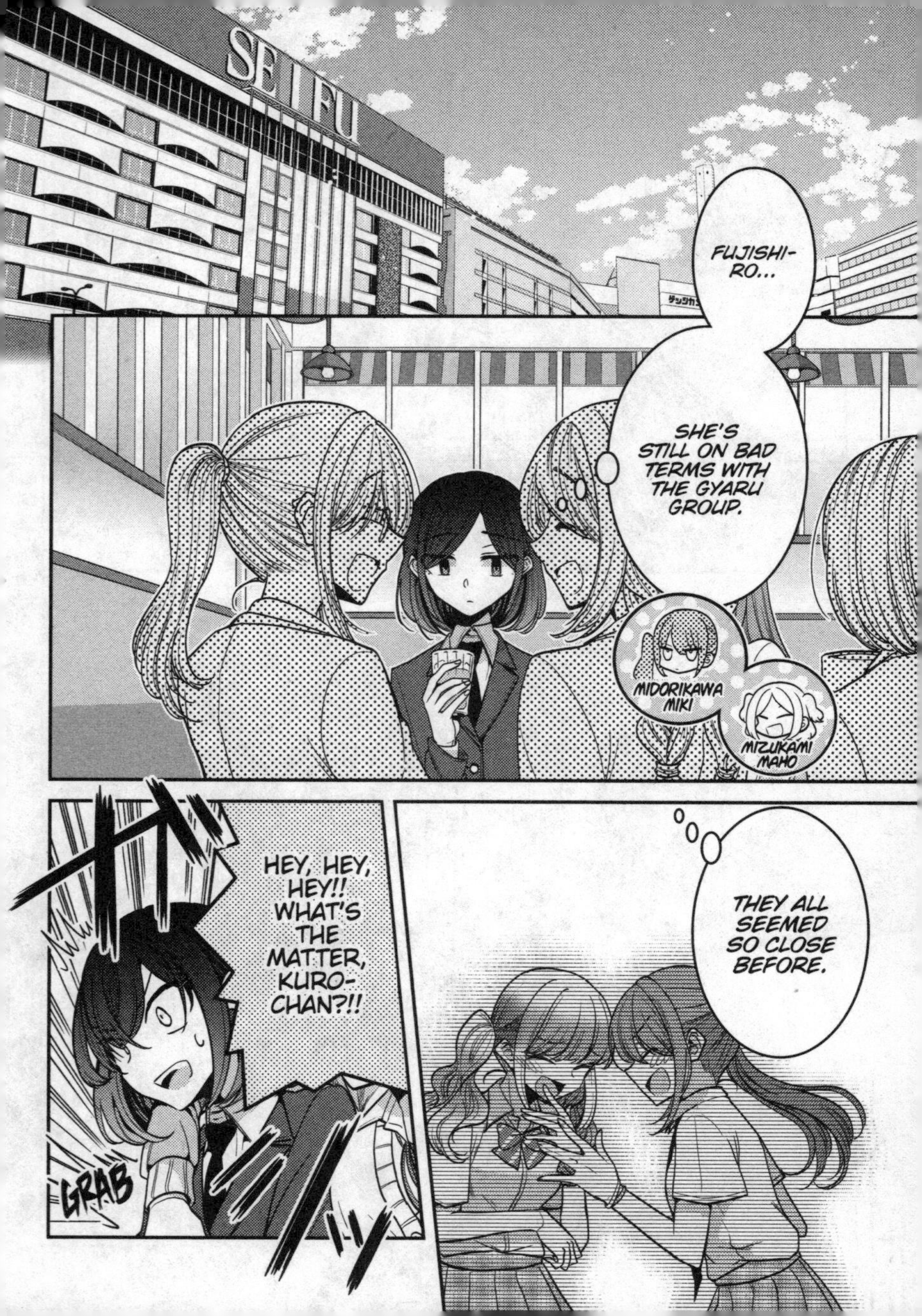
SEIFU
FUJISHIRO...
SHE'S STILL ON BAD TERMS WITH THE GYARU GROUP.
MIDORIKAWA MIKI
MIZUKAMI MAHO
THEY ALL SEEMED SO CLOSE BEFORE.
HEY, HEY, HEY!! WHAT'S THE MATTER, KURO-CHAN?!!
GRAB

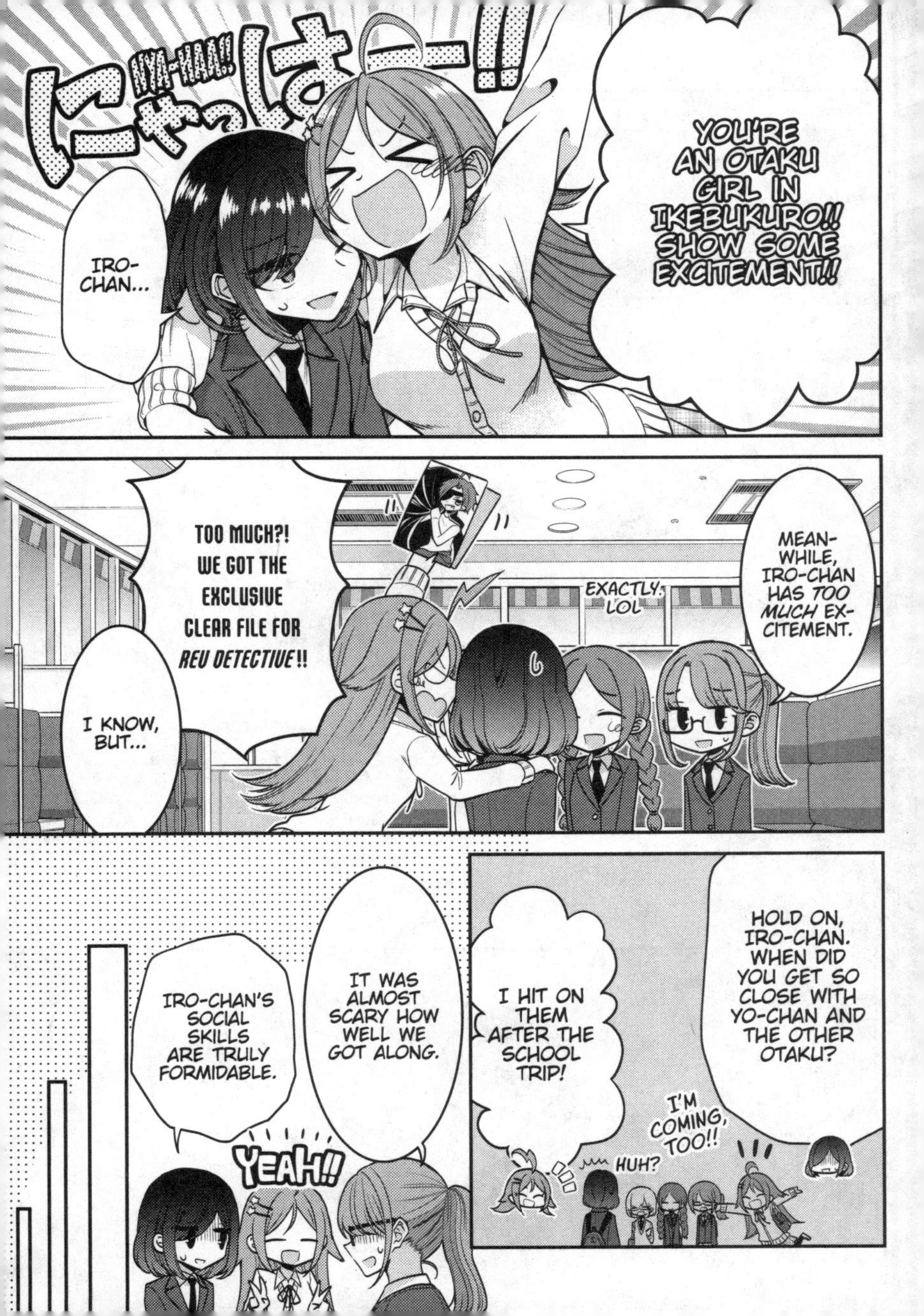
にゃっはーー!!
NYA-HAA!!
YOU'RE AN OTAKU GIRL IN IKEBUKURO!! SHOW SOME EXCITEMENT!!
IRO-CHAN...
MEAN-WHILE, IRO-CHAN HAS TOO MUCH EX-CITEMENT.
EXACTLY. LOL
TOO MUCH?! WE GOT THE EXCLUSIVE CLEAR FILE FOR REV DETECTIVE!!
I KNOW, BUT...
HOLD ON, IRO-CHAN. WHEN DID YOU GET SO CLOSE WITH YO-CHAN AND THE OTHER OTAKU?
I HIT ON THEM AFTER THE SCHOOL TRIP!
I'M COMING, TOO!!
HUH?
IT WAS ALMOST SCARY HOW WELL WE GOT ALONG.
IRO-CHAN'S SOCIAL SKILLS ARE TRULY FORMIDABLE.
YEAH!!

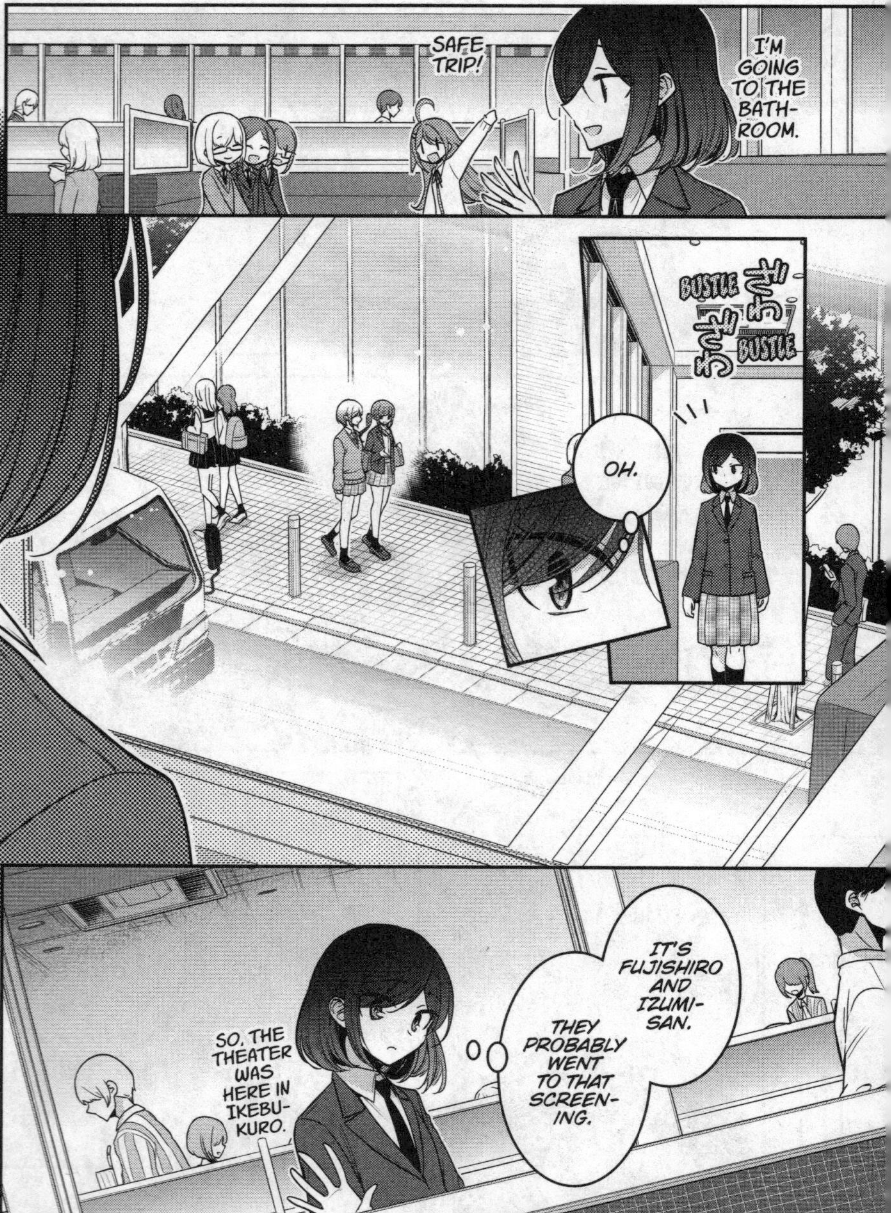
I'M GOING TO THE BATH-ROOM.
SAFE TRIP!
ざわ BUSTLE
ざわ BUSTLE
OH.
IT'S FUJISHIRO AND IZUMI-SAN.
THEY PROBABLY WENT TO THAT SCREEN-ING.
SO, THE THEATER WAS HERE IN IKEBU-KURO.

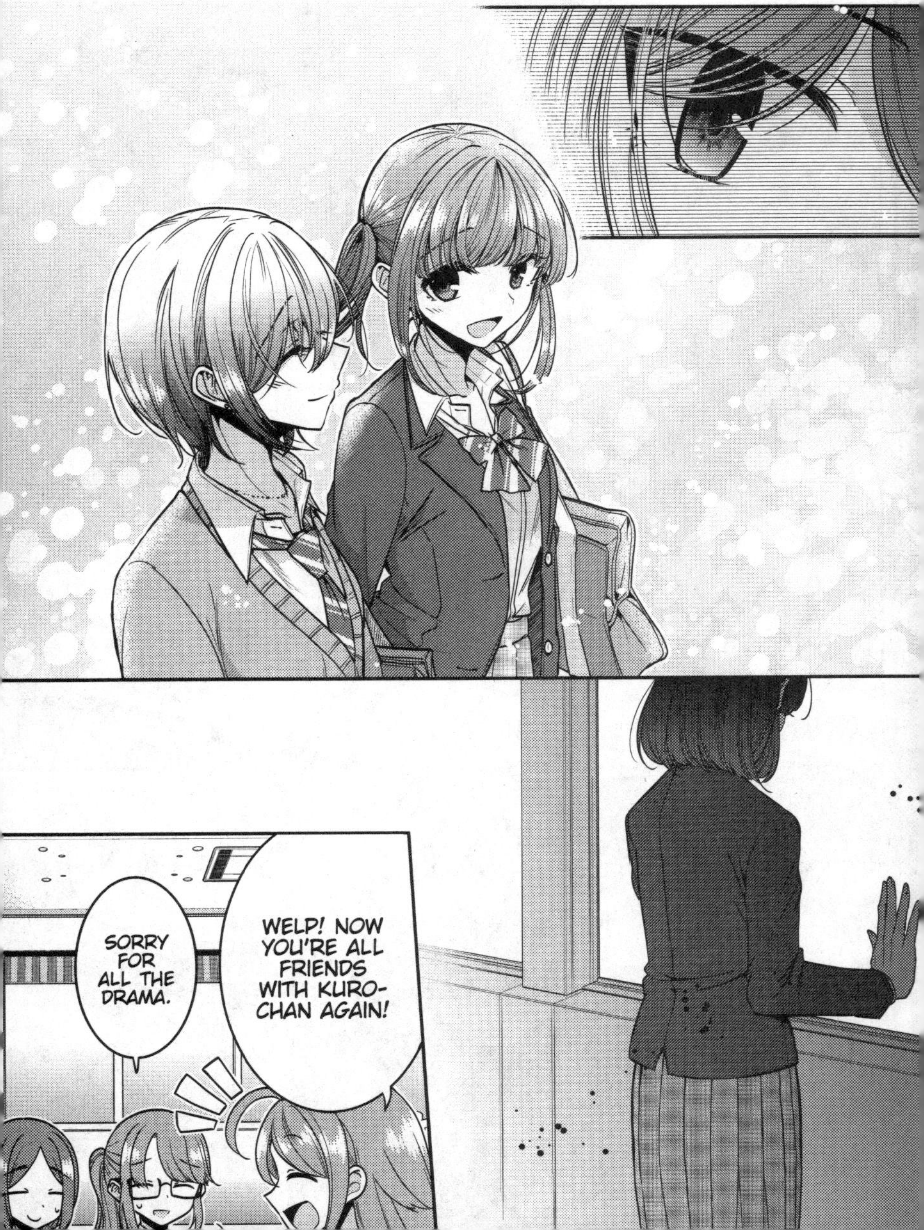
WELP! NOW YOU'RE ALL FRIENDS WITH KURO-CHAN AGAIN!
SORRY FOR ALL THE DRAMA.

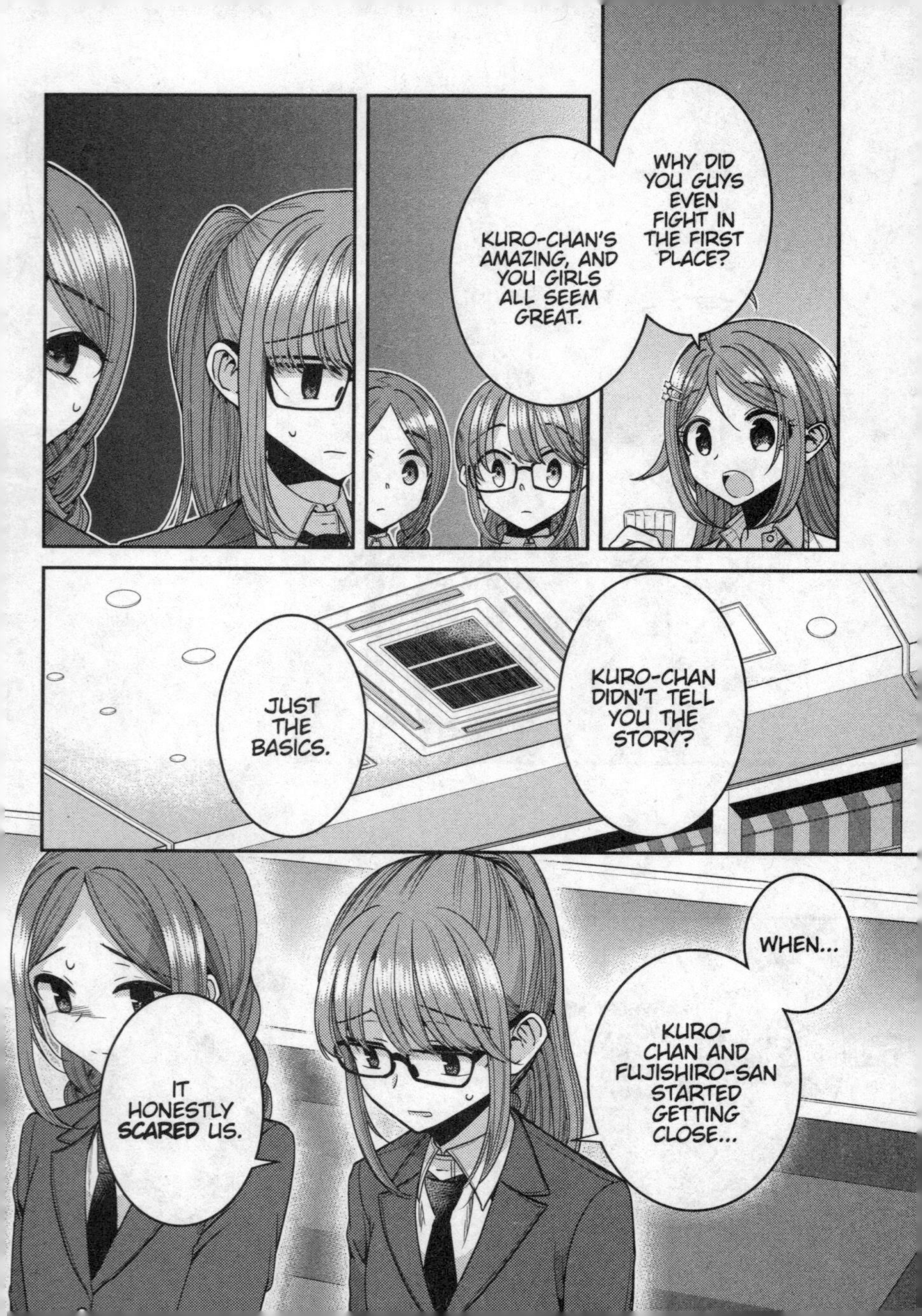
WHY DID YOU GUYS EVEN FIGHT IN THE FIRST PLACE?
KURO-CHAN'S AMAZING, AND YOU GIRLS ALL SEEM GREAT.
KURO-CHAN DIDN'T TELL YOU THE STORY?
JUST THE BASICS.
WHEN...
KURO-CHAN AND FUJISHIRO-SAN STARTED GETTING CLOSE...
IT HONESTLY SCARED US.

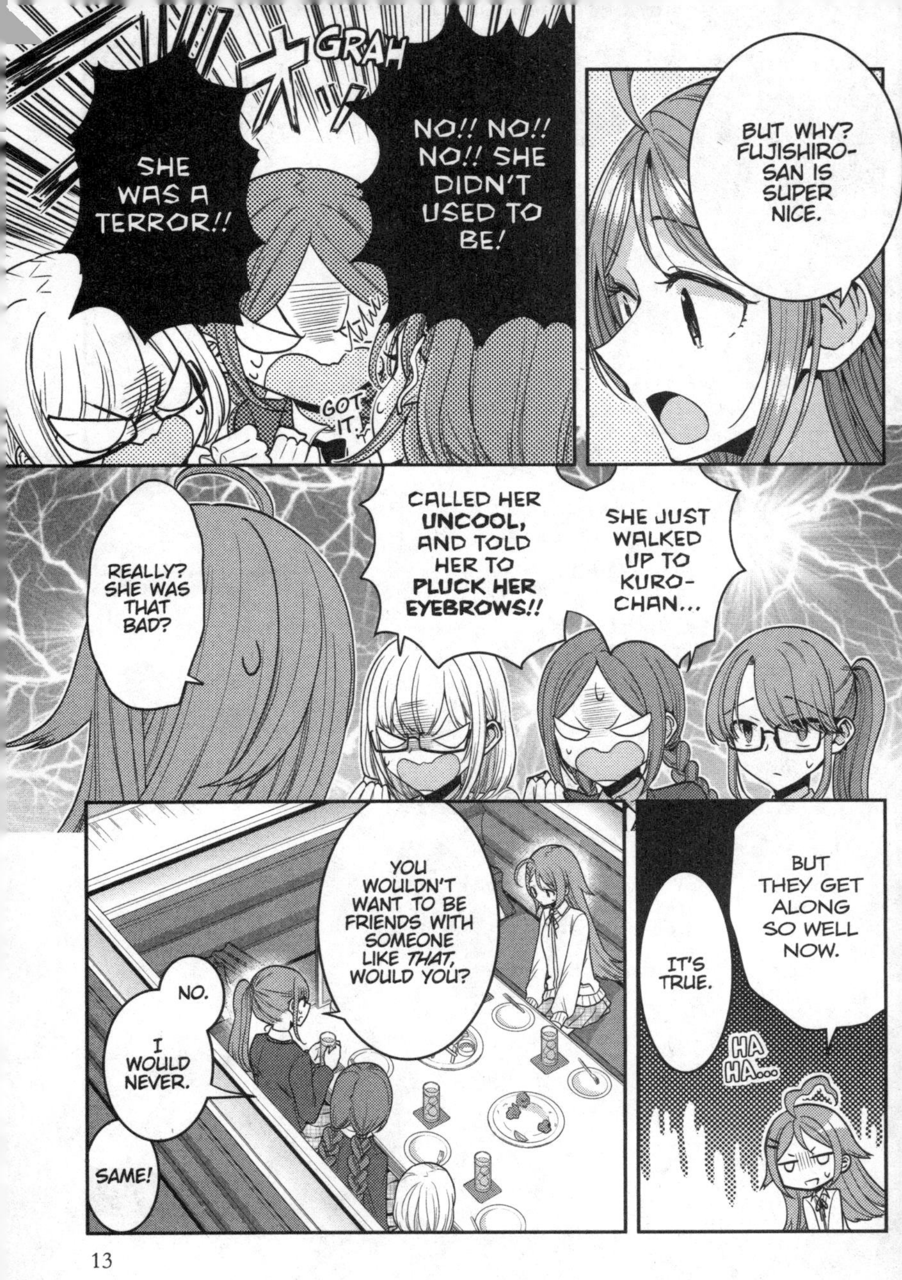
BUT WHY? FUJISHIRO-SAN IS SUPER NICE.
GRAH
NO!! NO!! NO!! SHE DIDN'T USED TO BE!
SHE WAS A TERROR!!
GOT IT.
SHE JUST WALKED UP TO KURO-CHAN...
CALLED HER UNCOOL, AND TOLD HER TO PLUCK HER EYEBROWS!!
REALLY? SHE WAS THAT BAD?
BUT THEY GET ALONG SO WELL NOW.
IT'S TRUE.
HA HA...
YOU WOULDN'T WANT TO BE FRIENDS WITH SOMEONE LIKE THAT, WOULD YOU?
NO.
I WOULD NEVER.
SAME!

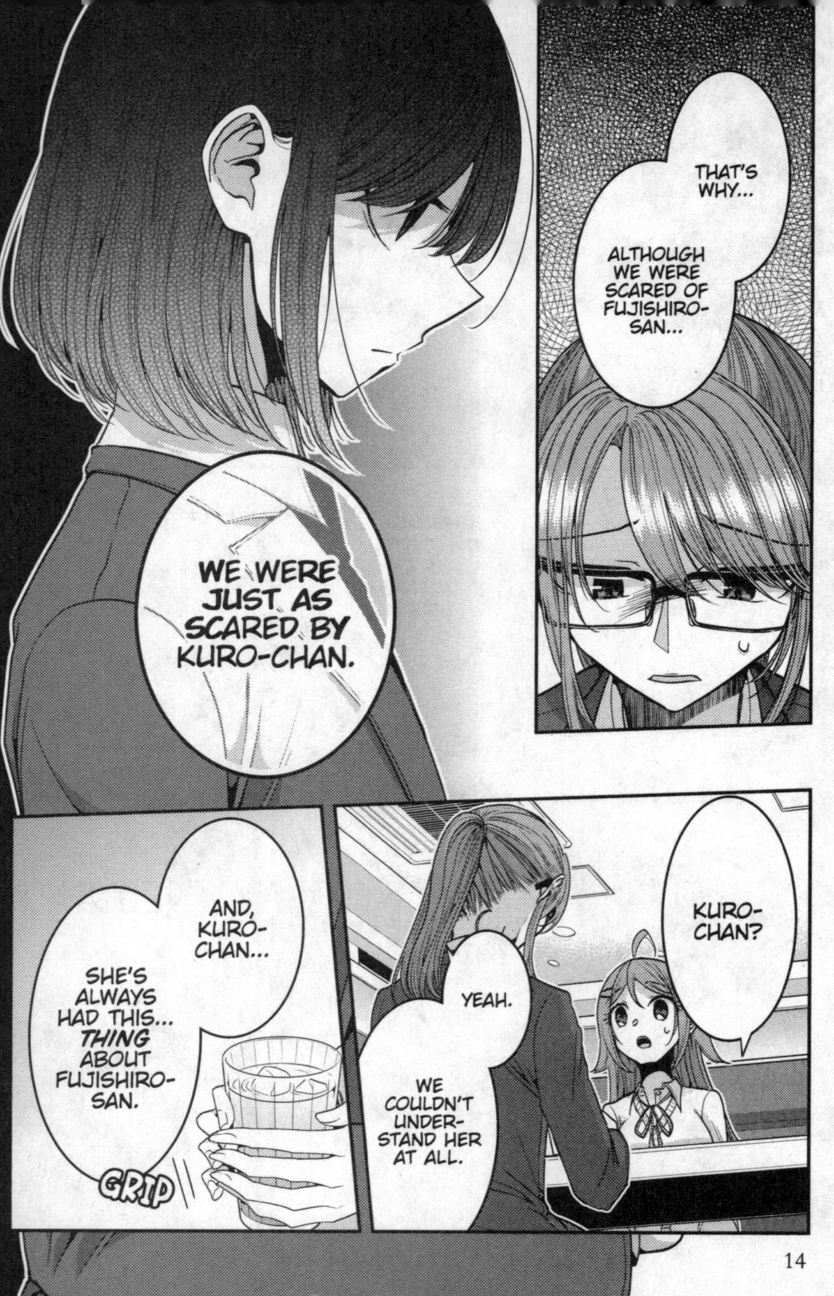
THAT'S WHY...
ALTHOUGH WE WERE SCARED OF FUJISHIRO-SAN...
WE WERE JUST AS SCARED BY KURO-CHAN.
KURO-CHAN?
YEAH.
WE COULDN'T UNDER-STAND HER AT ALL.
AND, KURO-CHAN...
SHE'S ALWAYS HAD THIS... *THING* ABOUT FUJISHIRO-SAN.
GRIP

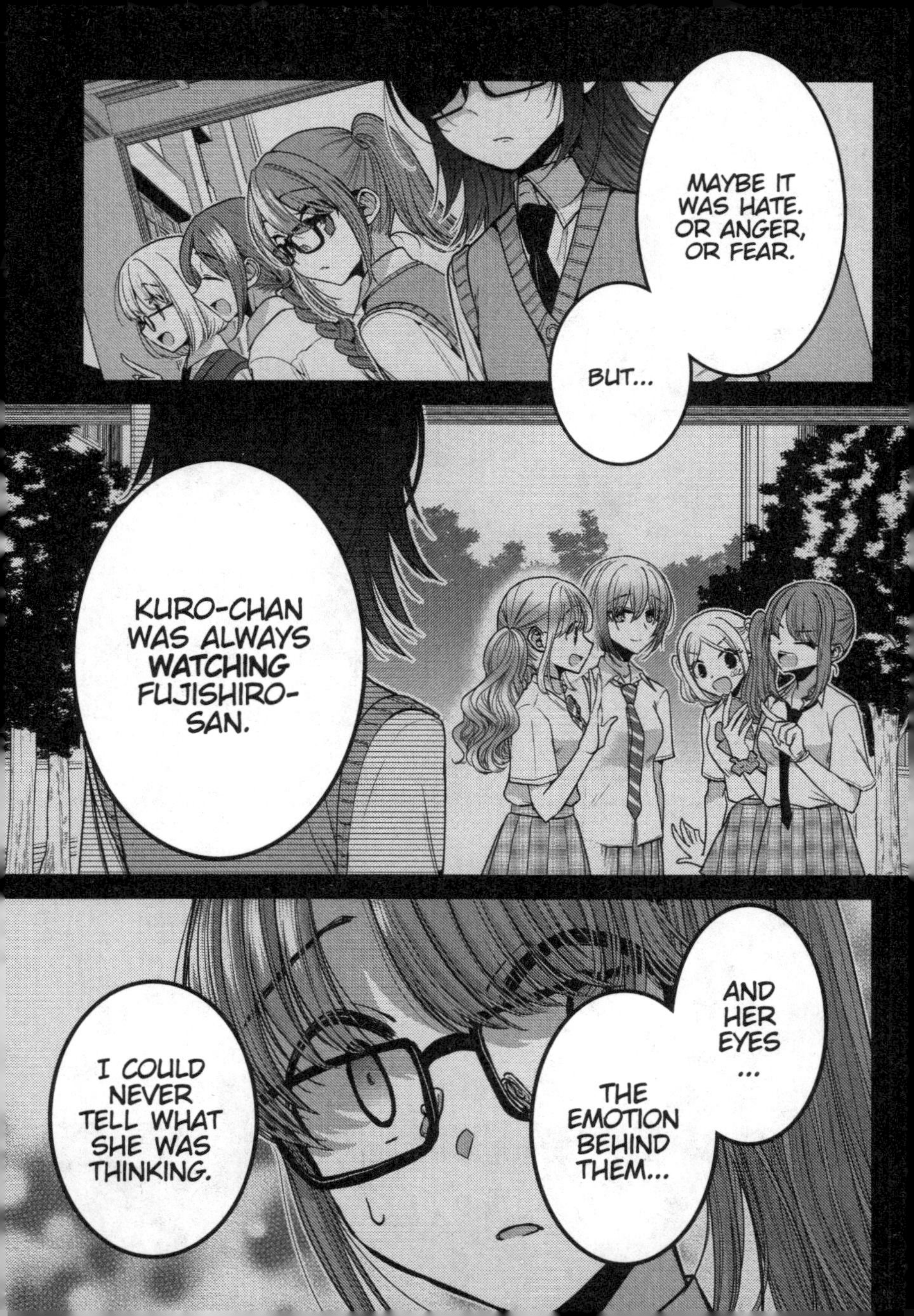
MAYBE IT WAS HATE. OR ANGER, OR FEAR.
BUT...
KURO-CHAN WAS ALWAYS WATCHING FUJISHIRO-SAN.
AND HER EYES...
THE EMOTION BEHIND THEM...
I COULD NEVER TELL WHAT SHE WAS THINKING.

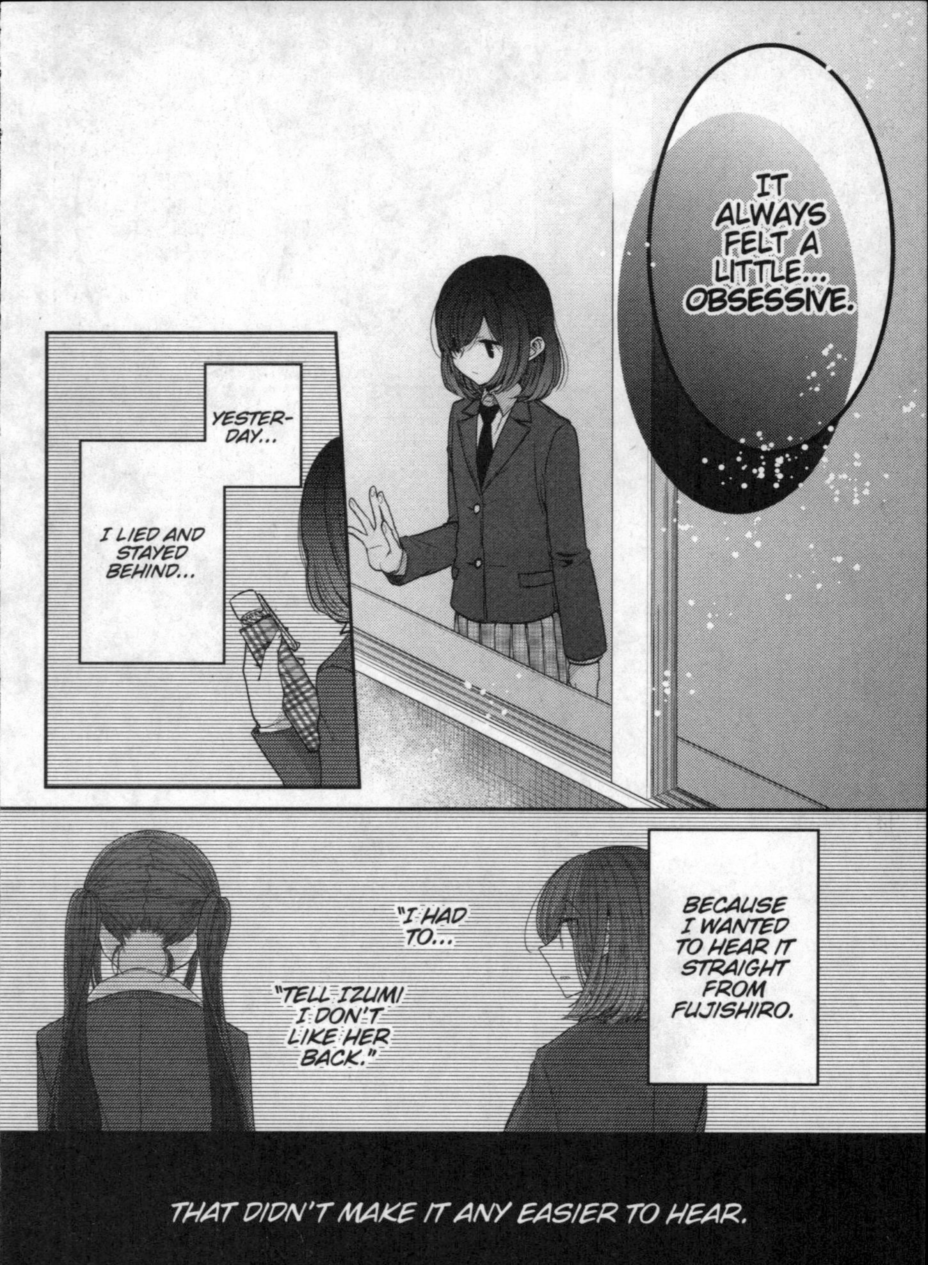
IT ALWAYS FELT A LITTLE... OBSESSIVE.
YESTER-DAY...
I LIED AND STAYED BEHIND...
BECAUSE I WANTED TO HEAR IT STRAIGHT FROM FUJISHIRO.
"I HAD TO...
"TELL IZUMI I DON'T LIKE HER BACK."
THAT DIDN'T MAKE IT ANY EASIER TO HEAR.

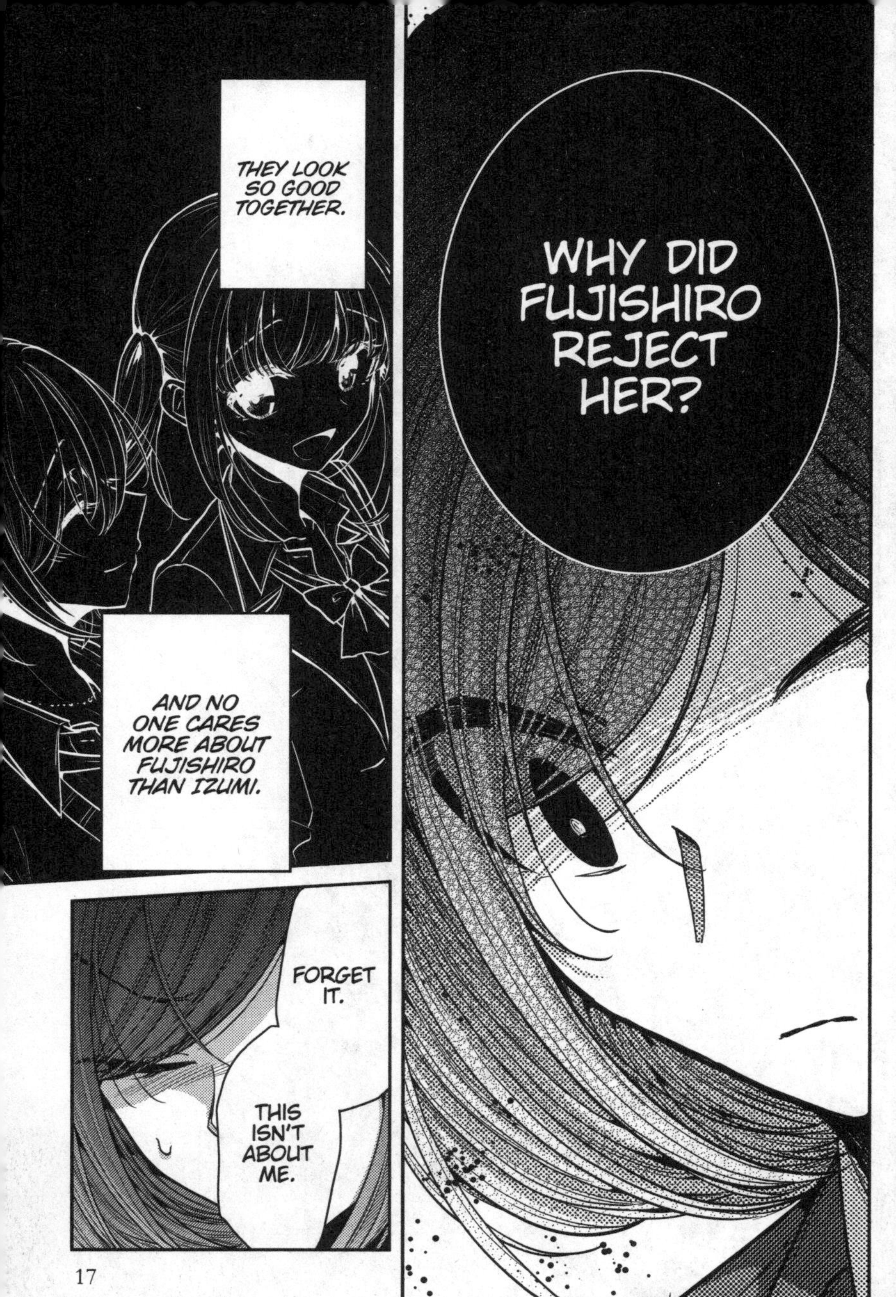
WHY DID FUJISHIRO REJECT HER?
THEY LOOK SO GOOD TOGETHER.
AND NO ONE CARES MORE ABOUT FUJISHIRO THAN IZUMI.
FORGET IT.
THIS ISN'T ABOUT ME.

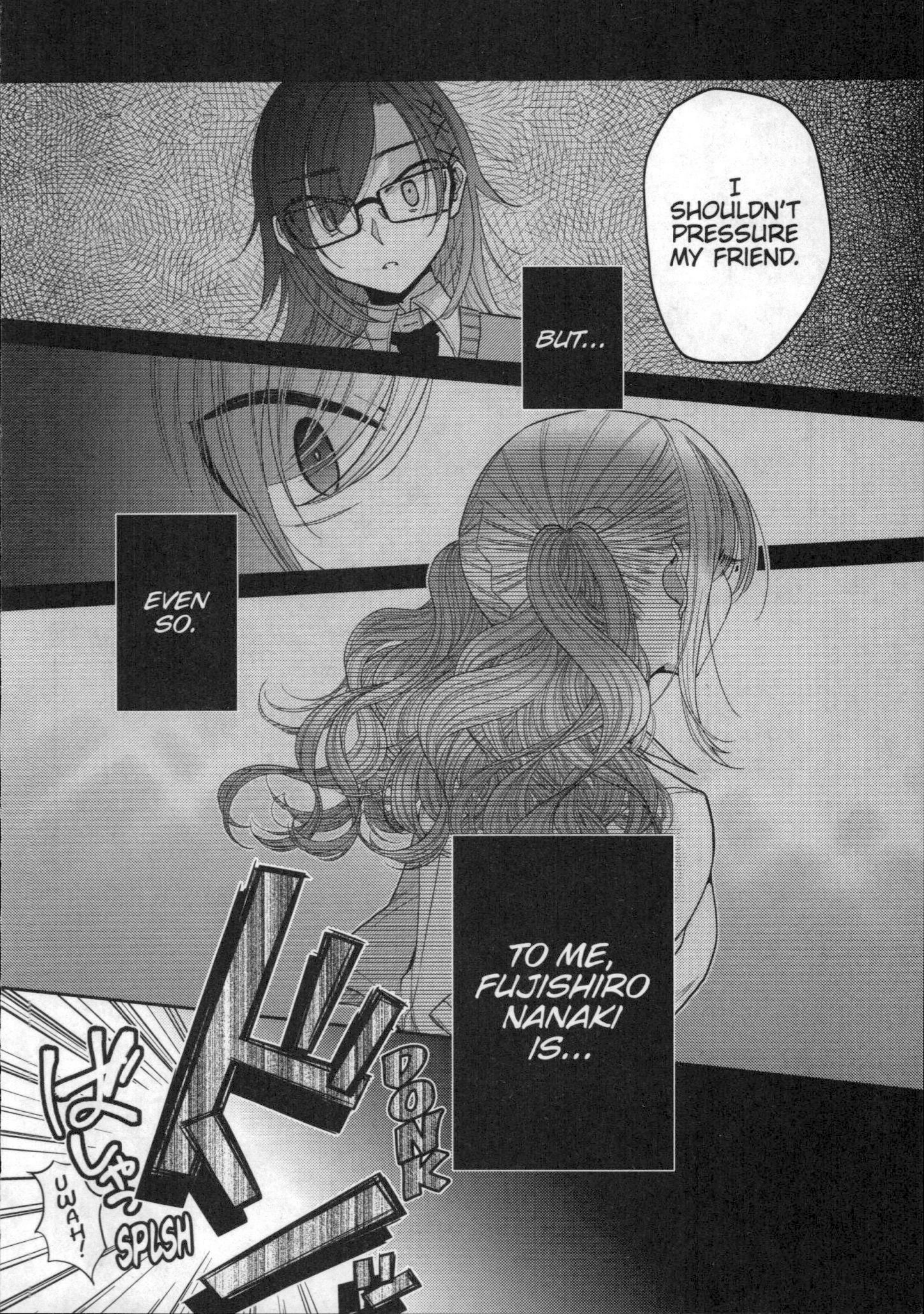
I SHOULDN'T PRESSURE MY FRIEND.
BUT...
EVEN SO.
TO ME, FUJISHIRO NANAKI IS...
DONK
UWAH!
SPLSH

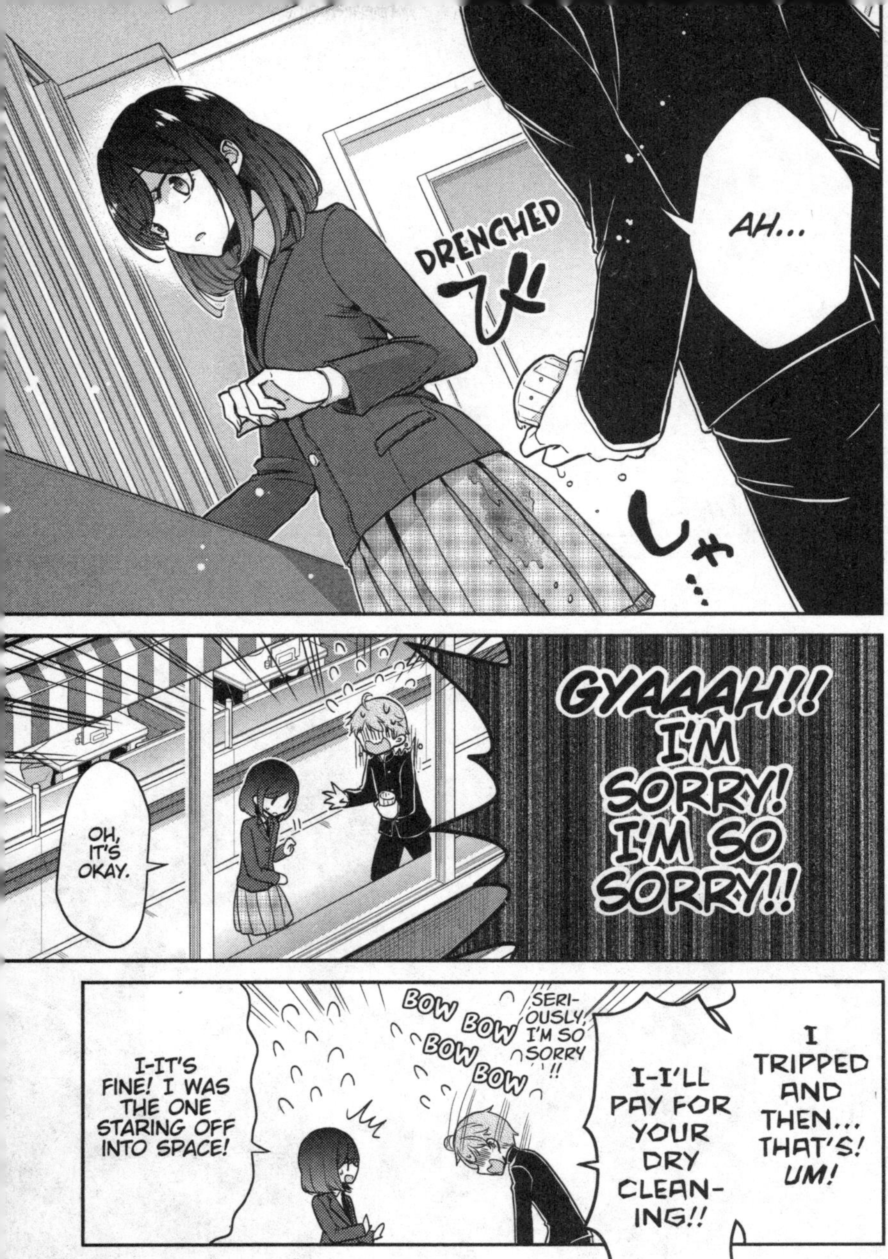

AH...
DRENCHED
び
しゃ...
GYAAAH!! I'M SORRY! I'M SO SORRY!!
OH, IT'S OKAY.
I TRIPPED AND THEN... THAT'S! UM!
I-I'LL PAY FOR YOUR DRY CLEANING!!
SERIOUSLY, I'M SO SORRY!!
BOW BOW BOW BOW
I-IT'S FINE! I WAS THE ONE STARING OFF INTO SPACE!

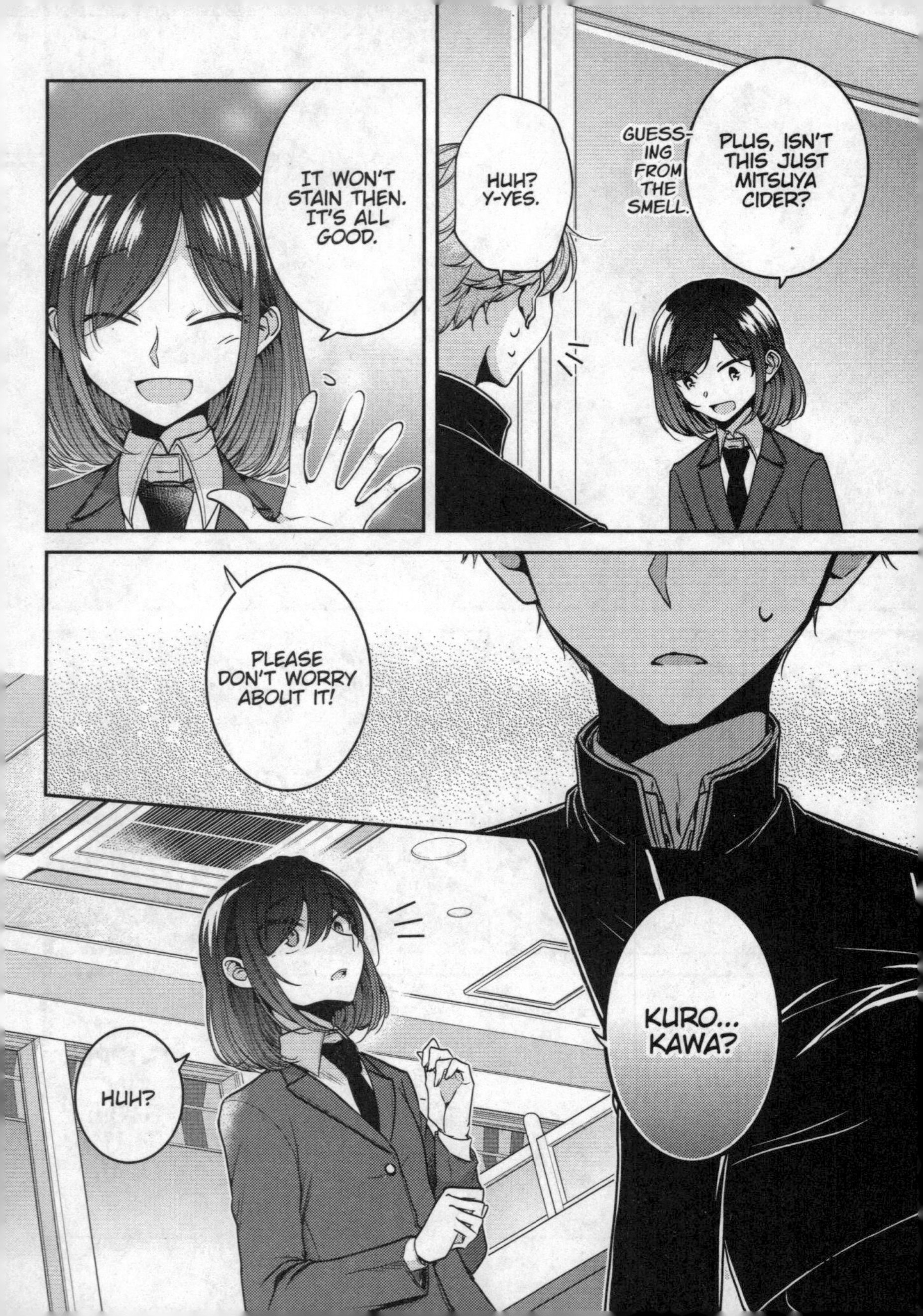
PLUS, ISN'T THIS JUST MITSUYA CIDER?
GUESSING FROM THE SMELL.
HUH? Y-YES.
IT WON'T STAIN THEN. IT'S ALL GOOD.
PLEASE DON'T WORRY ABOUT IT!
KURO... KAWA?
HUH?

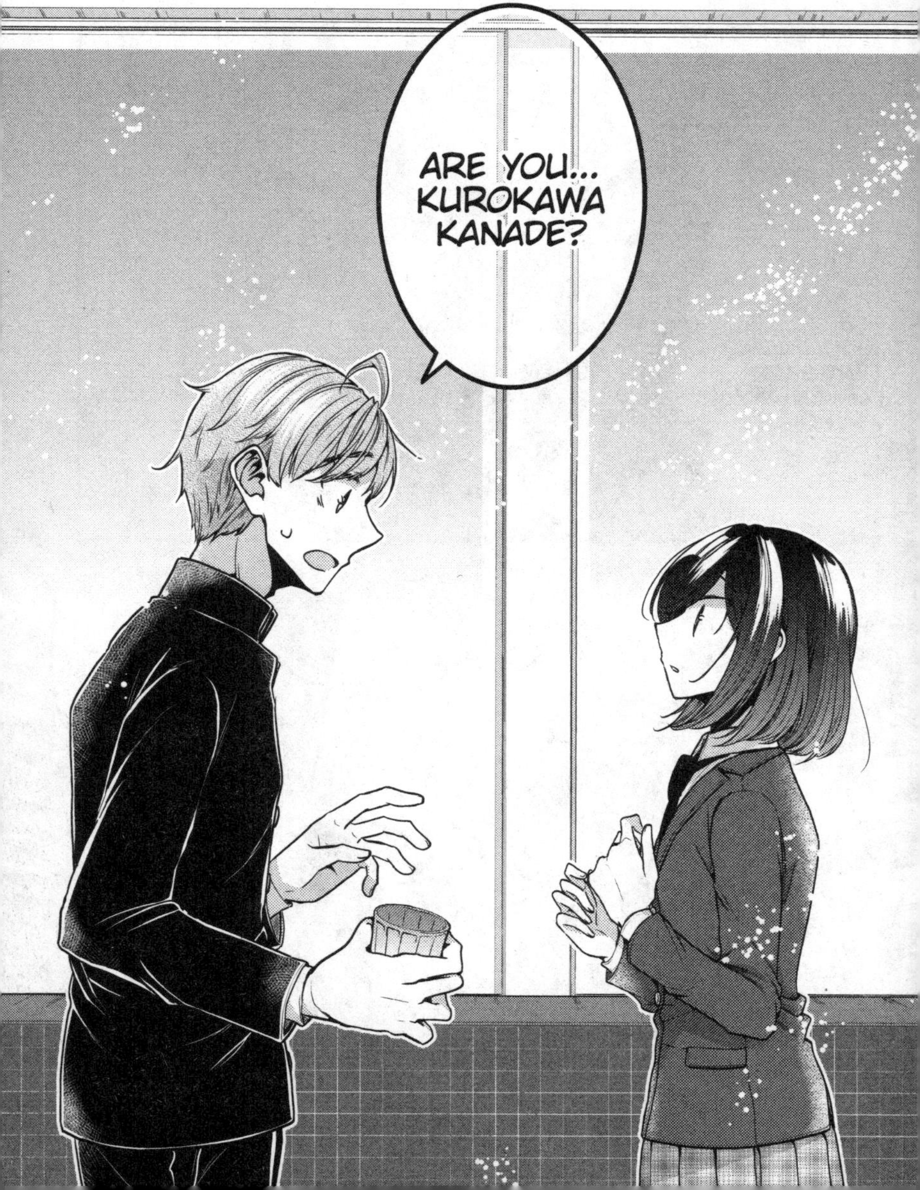
ARE YOU... KUROKAWA KANADE?

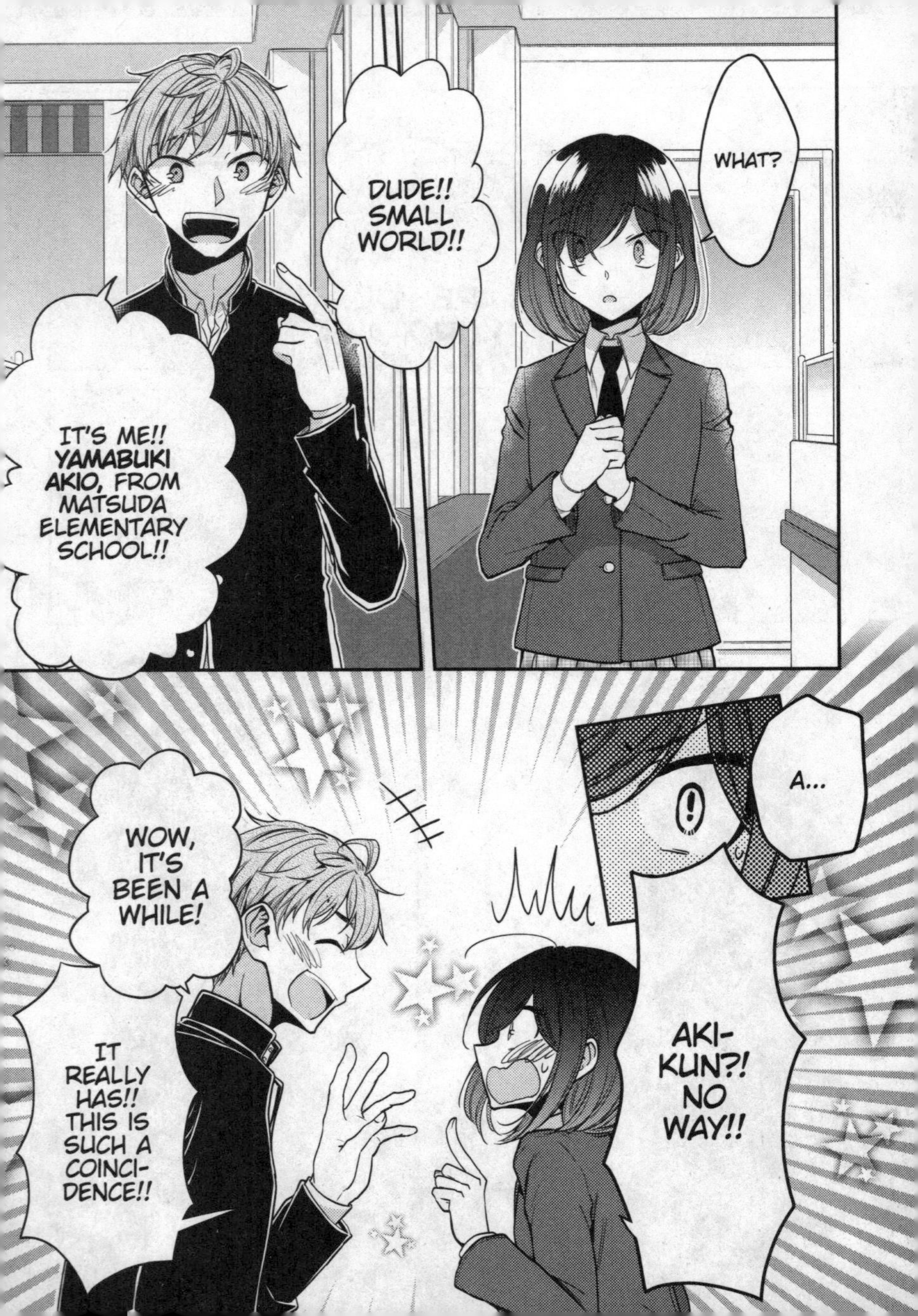
WHAT?
DUDE!! SMALL WORLD!!
IT'S ME!! YAMABUKI AKIO, FROM MATSUDA ELEMENTARY SCHOOL!!
A...
AKI-KUN?! NO WAY!!
WOW, IT'S BEEN A WHILE!
IT REALLY HAS!! THIS IS SUCH A COINCIDENCE!!

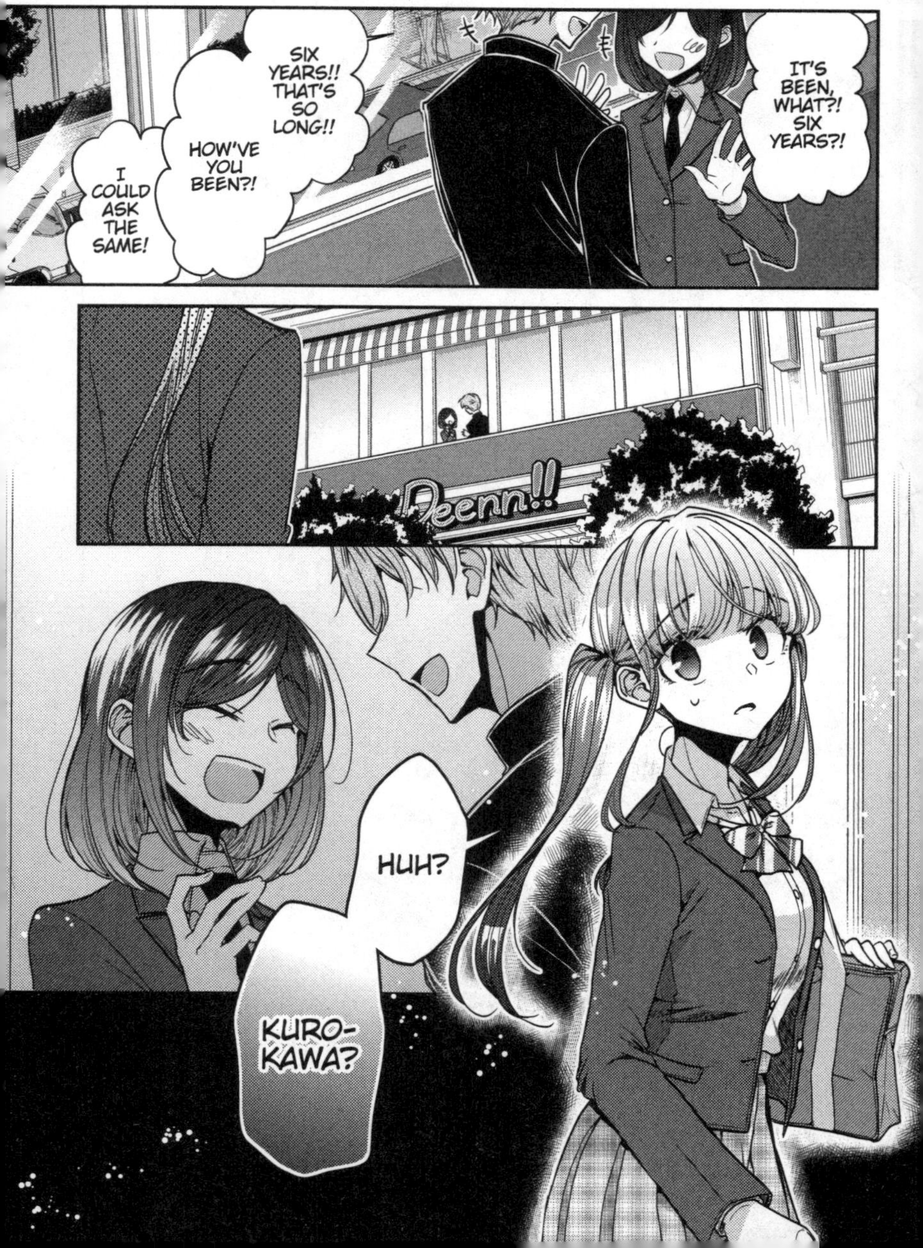
IT'S BEEN, WHAT?! SIX YEARS?!
SIX YEARS!! THAT'S SO LONG!!
HOW'VE YOU BEEN?!
I COULD ASK THE SAME!
Deenn!!
HUH?
KURO-KAWA?

Failed Princesses

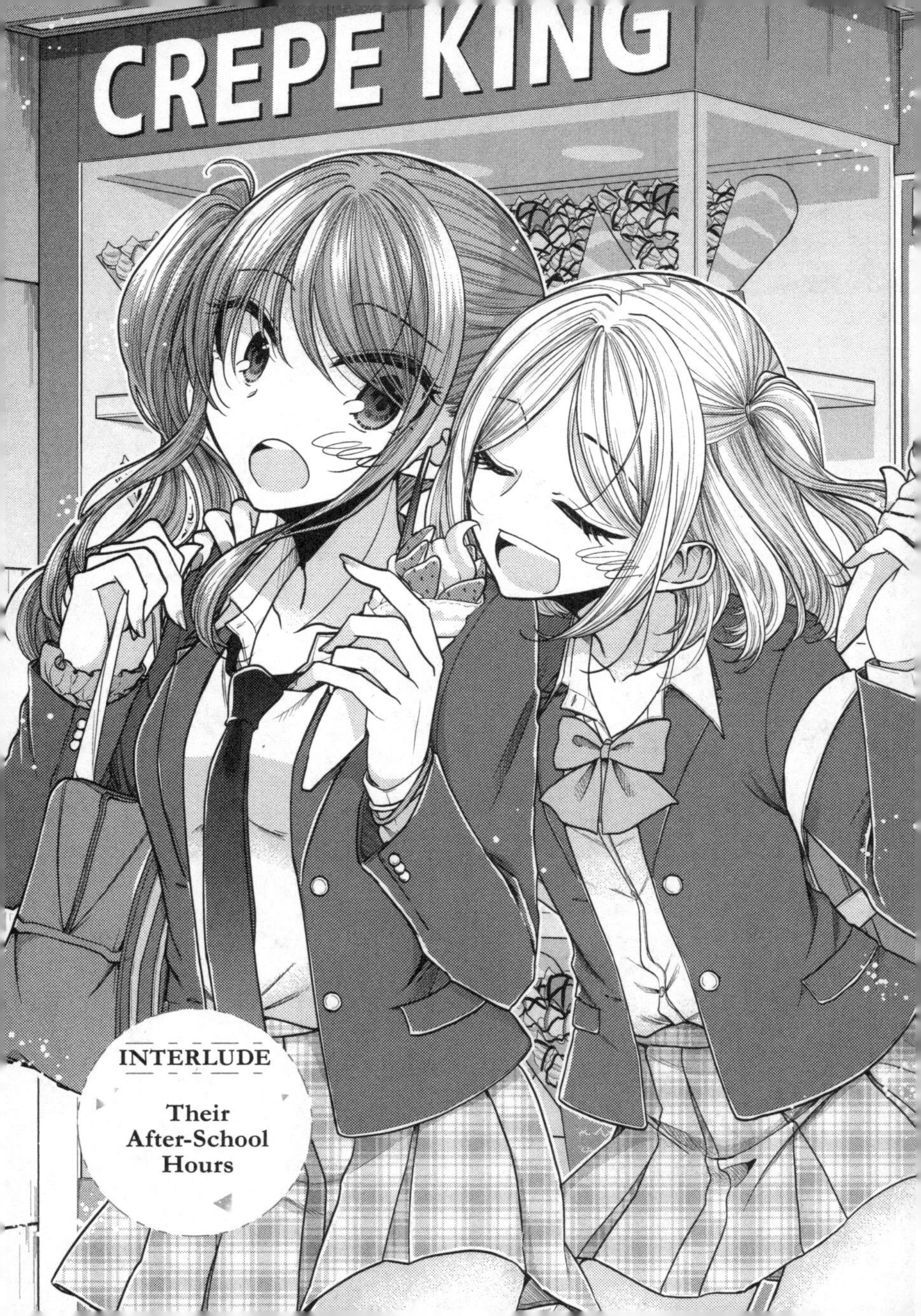
CREPE KING
INTERLUDE
Their After-School Hours

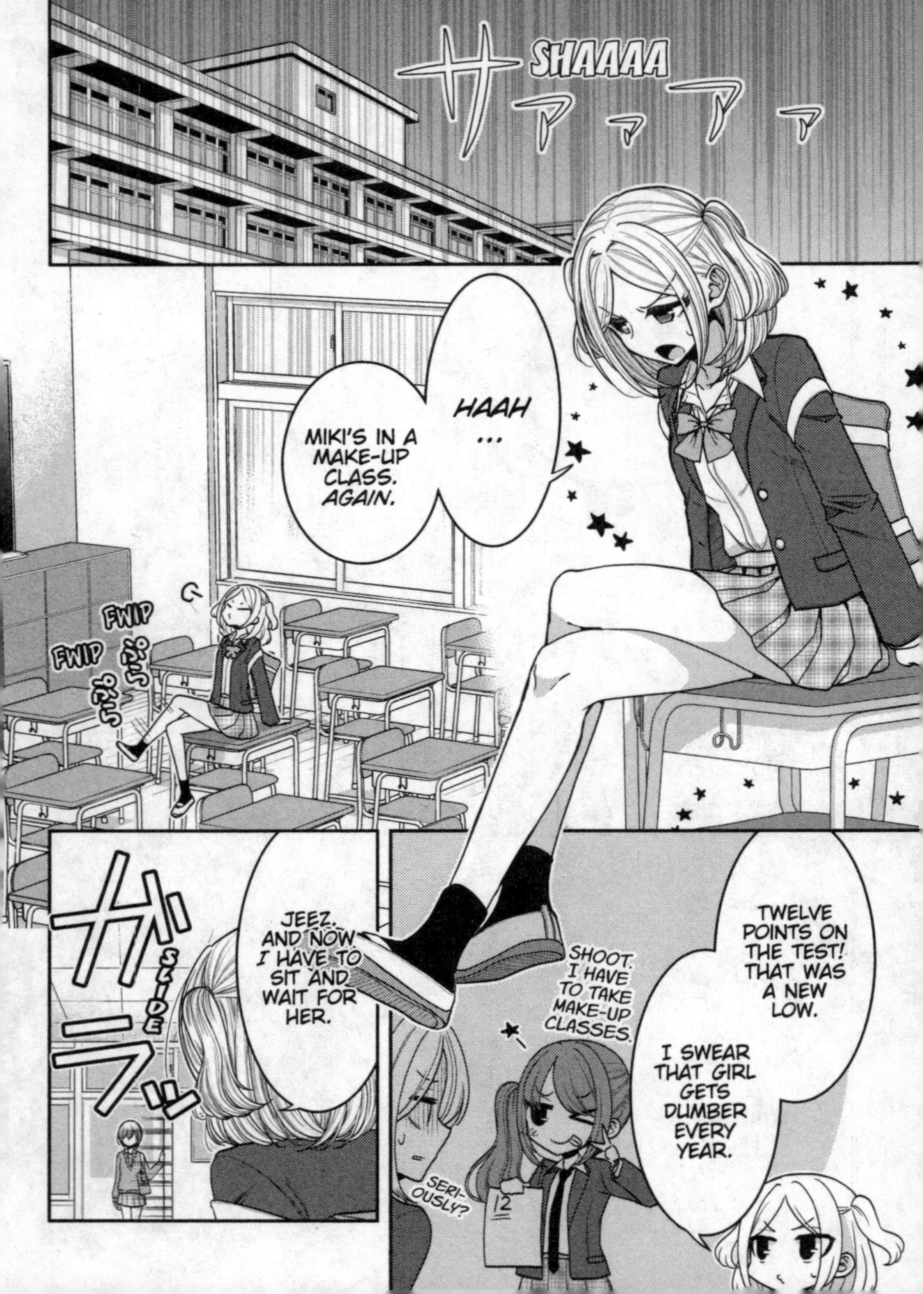
SHAAAA
HAAH ...
MIKI'S IN A MAKE-UP CLASS. AGAIN.
FWIP
FWIP
TWELVE POINTS ON THE TEST! THAT WAS A NEW LOW.
I SWEAR THAT GIRL GETS DUMBER EVERY YEAR.
SHOOT. I HAVE TO TAKE MAKE-UP CLASSES.
SERI-OUSLY?
12
JEEZ. AND NOW I HAVE TO SIT AND WAIT FOR HER.
SLIDE

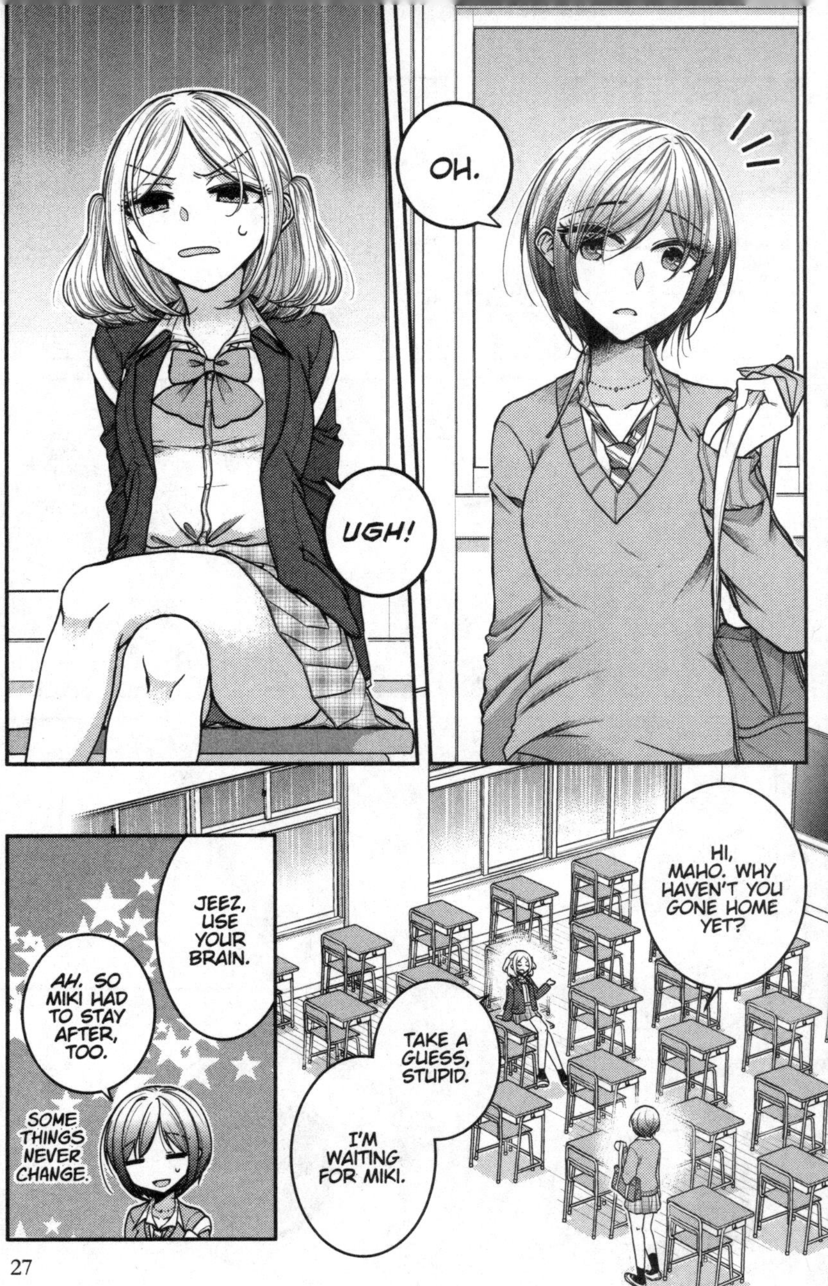
OH.
UGH!
HI, MAHO. WHY HAVEN'T YOU GONE HOME YET?
TAKE A GUESS, STUPID.
I'M WAITING FOR MIKI.
JEEZ, USE YOUR BRAIN.
AH. SO MIKI HAD TO STAY AFTER, TOO.
SOME THINGS NEVER CHANGE.

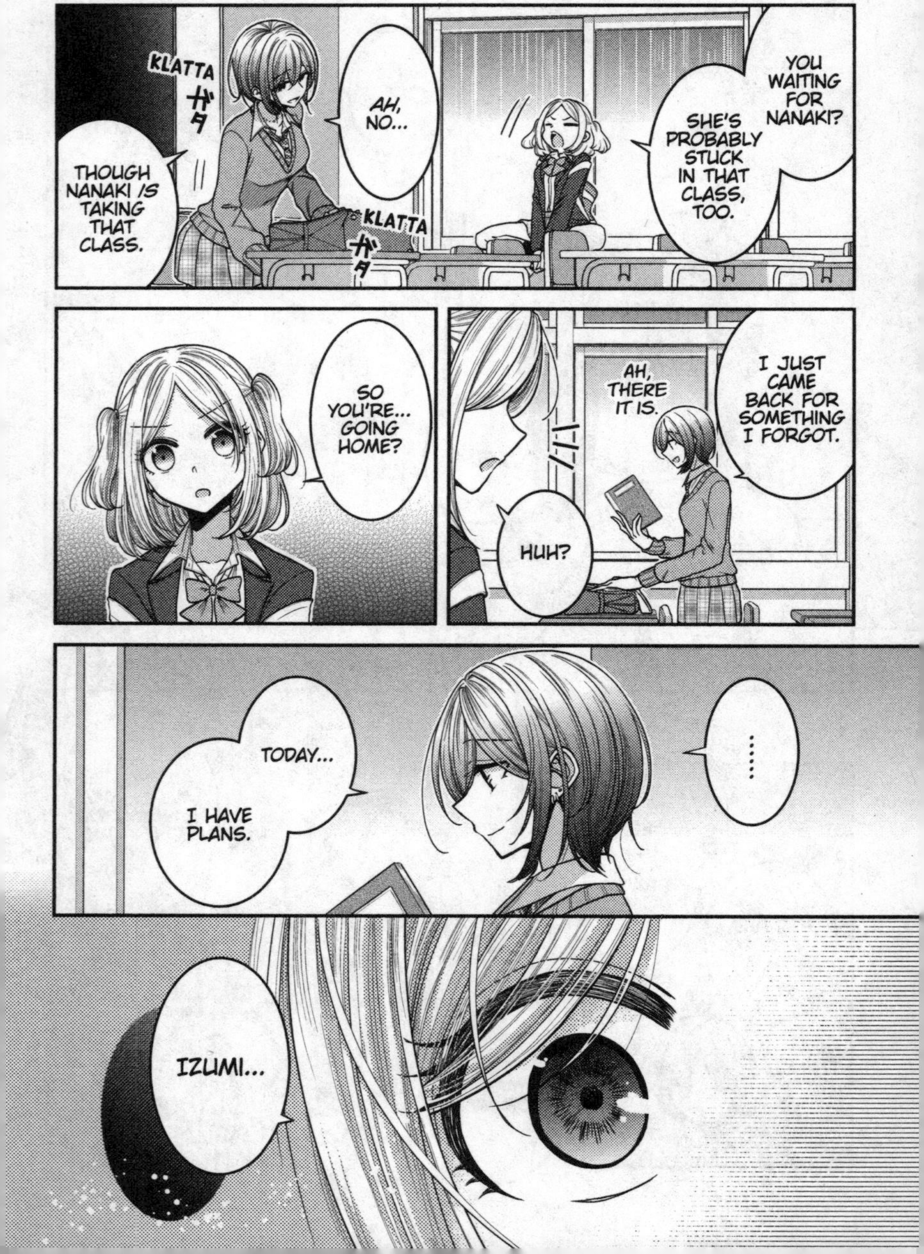
YOU WAITING FOR NANAKI?
SHE'S PROBABLY STUCK IN THAT CLASS, TOO.
AH, NO...
KLATTA ガタ
THOUGH NANAKI IS TAKING THAT CLASS.
KLATTA ガタ
I JUST CAME BACK FOR SOMETHING I FORGOT.
AH, THERE IT IS.
HUH?
SO YOU'RE... GOING HOME?
......
TODAY... I HAVE PLANS.
IZUMI...

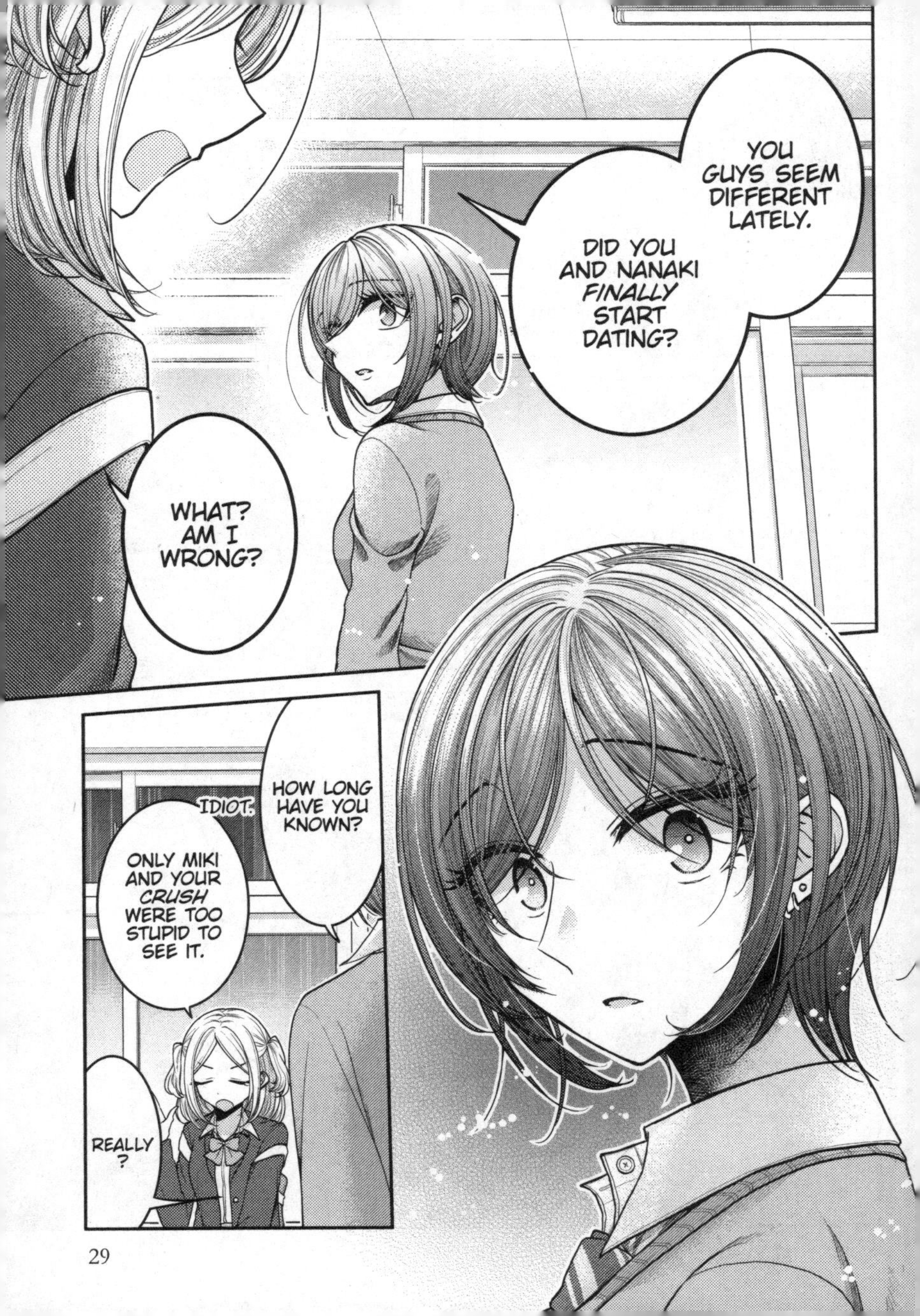

YOU GUYS SEEM DIFFERENT LATELY.
DID YOU AND NANAKI *FINALLY* START DATING?
WHAT? AM I WRONG?
HOW LONG HAVE YOU KNOWN?
IDIOT.
ONLY MIKI AND YOUR *CRUSH* WERE TOO STUPID TO SEE IT.
REALLY?

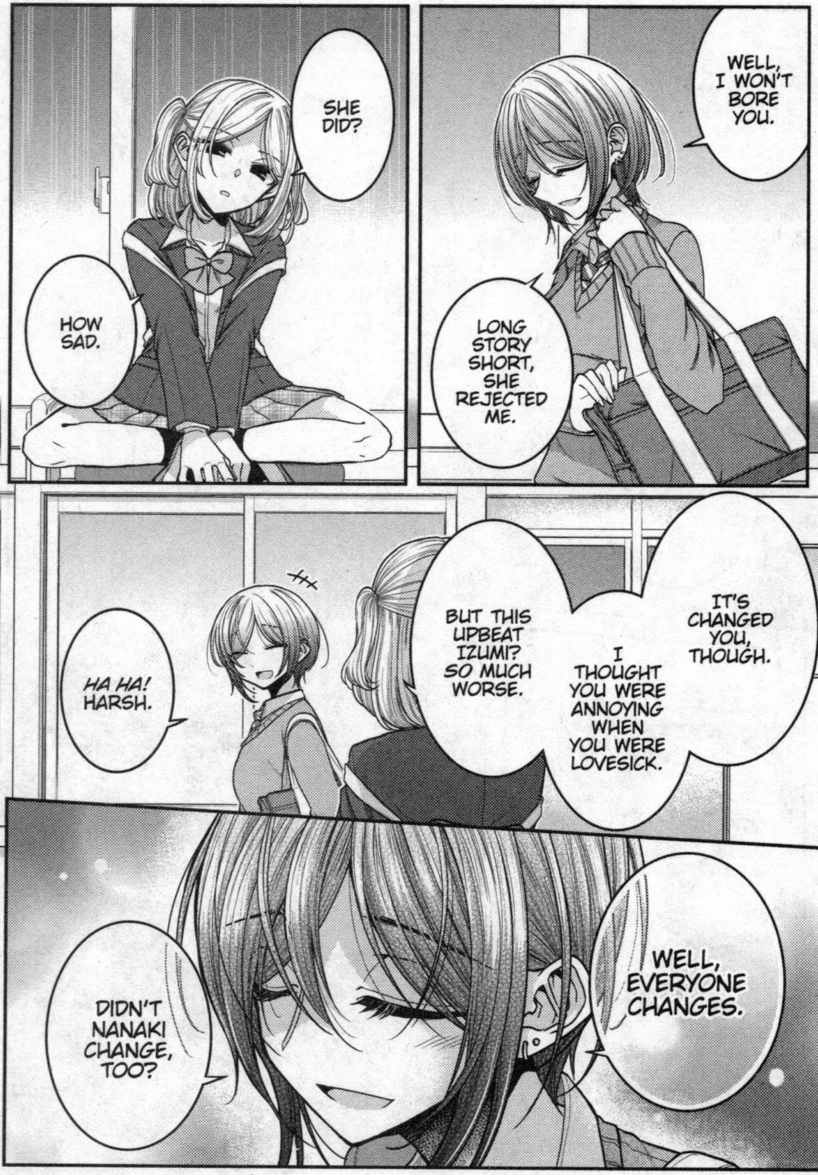
WELL, I WON'T BORE YOU.
LONG STORY SHORT, SHE REJECTED ME.
SHE DID?
HOW SAD.
IT'S CHANGED YOU, THOUGH.
I THOUGHT YOU WERE ANNOYING WHEN YOU WERE LOVESICK.
BUT THIS UPBEAT IZUMI? SO MUCH WORSE.
HA HA! HARSH.
WELL, EVERYONE CHANGES.
DIDN'T NANAKI CHANGE, TOO?

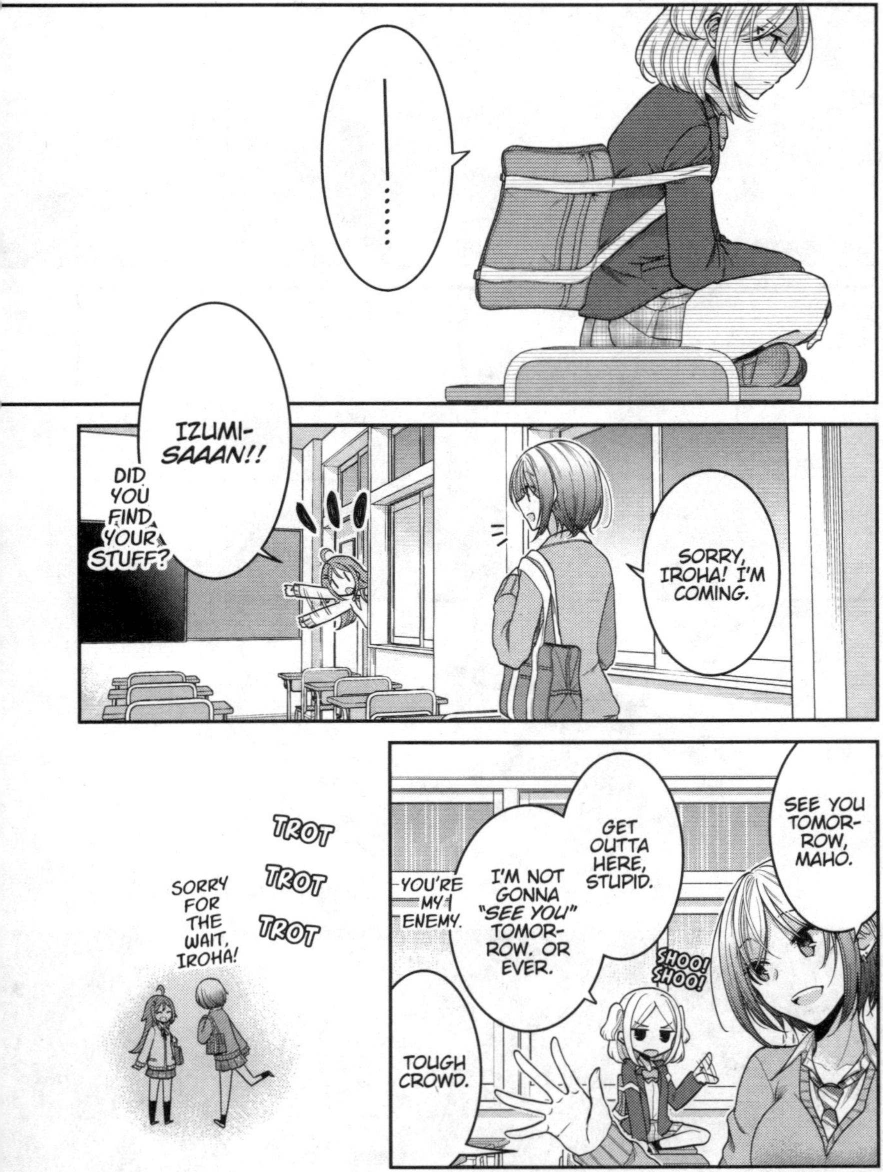
……!
SORRY, IROHA! I'M COMING.
IZUMI-SAAAN!!
DID YOU FIND YOUR STUFF?
SEE YOU TOMORROW, MAHO.
GET OUTTA HERE, STUPID.
I'M NOT GONNA "SEE YOU" TOMORROW. OR EVER.
YOU'RE MY ENEMY.
SHOO! SHOO!
TOUGH CROWD.
TROT
TROT
TROT
SORRY FOR THE WAIT, IROHA!

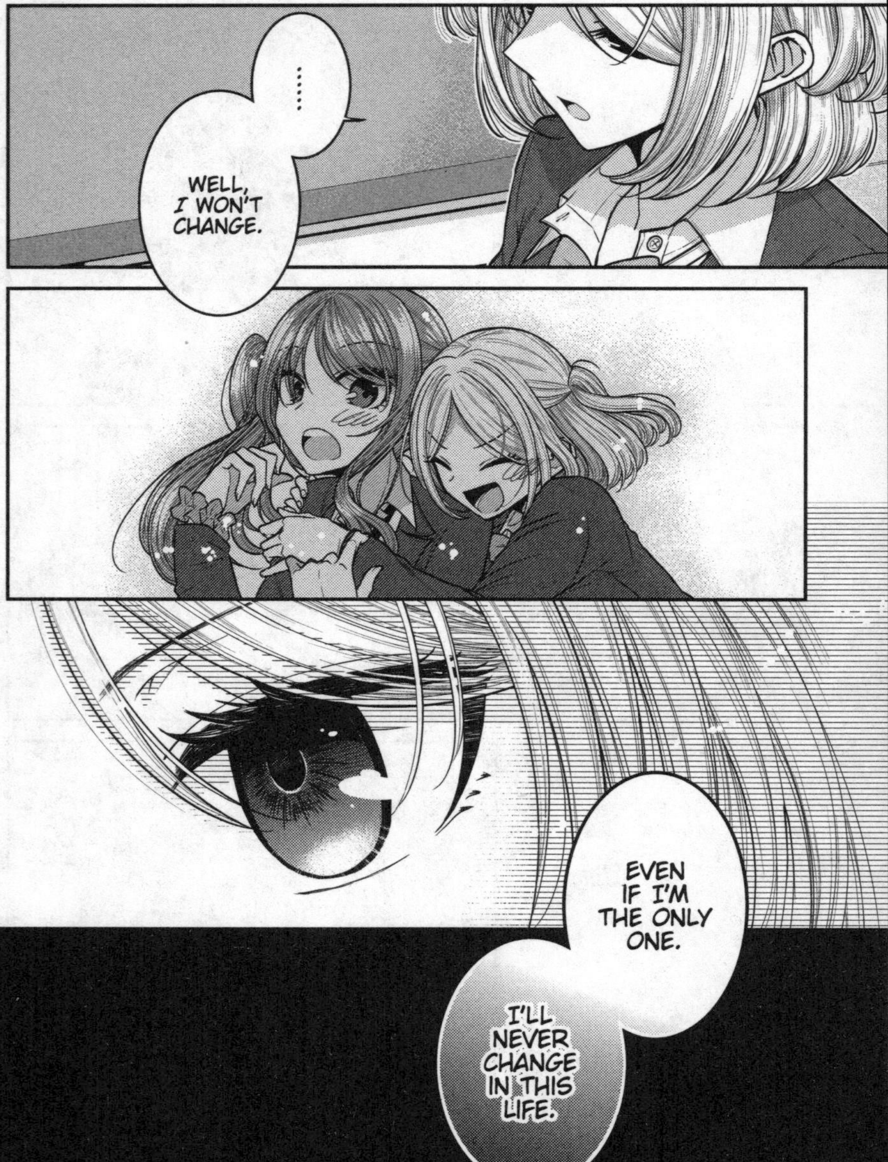
......
WELL, I WON'T CHANGE.
EVEN IF I'M THE ONLY ONE.
I'LL NEVER CHANGE IN THIS LIFE.

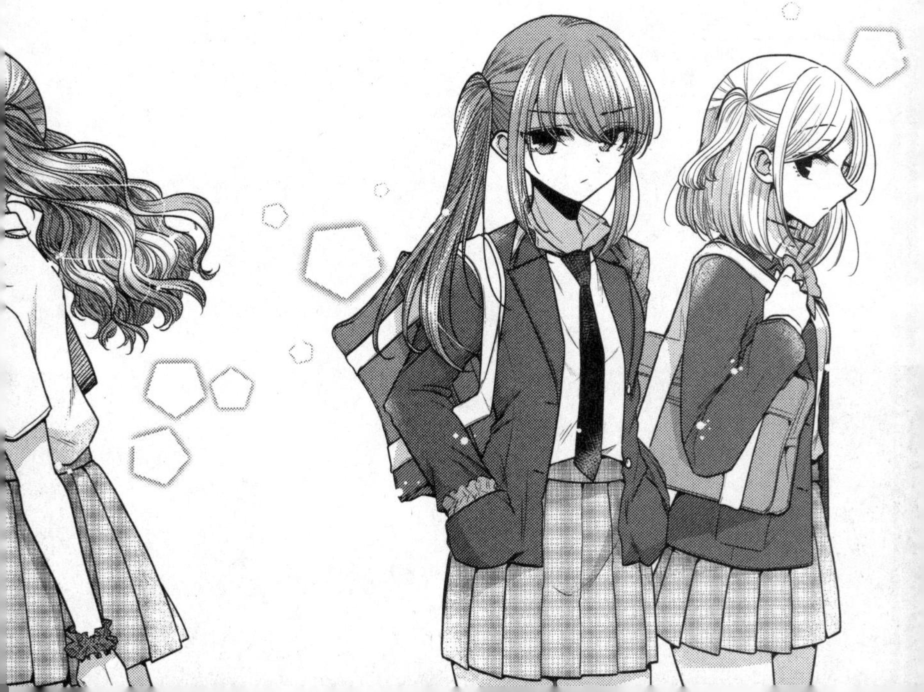

Failed Princesses

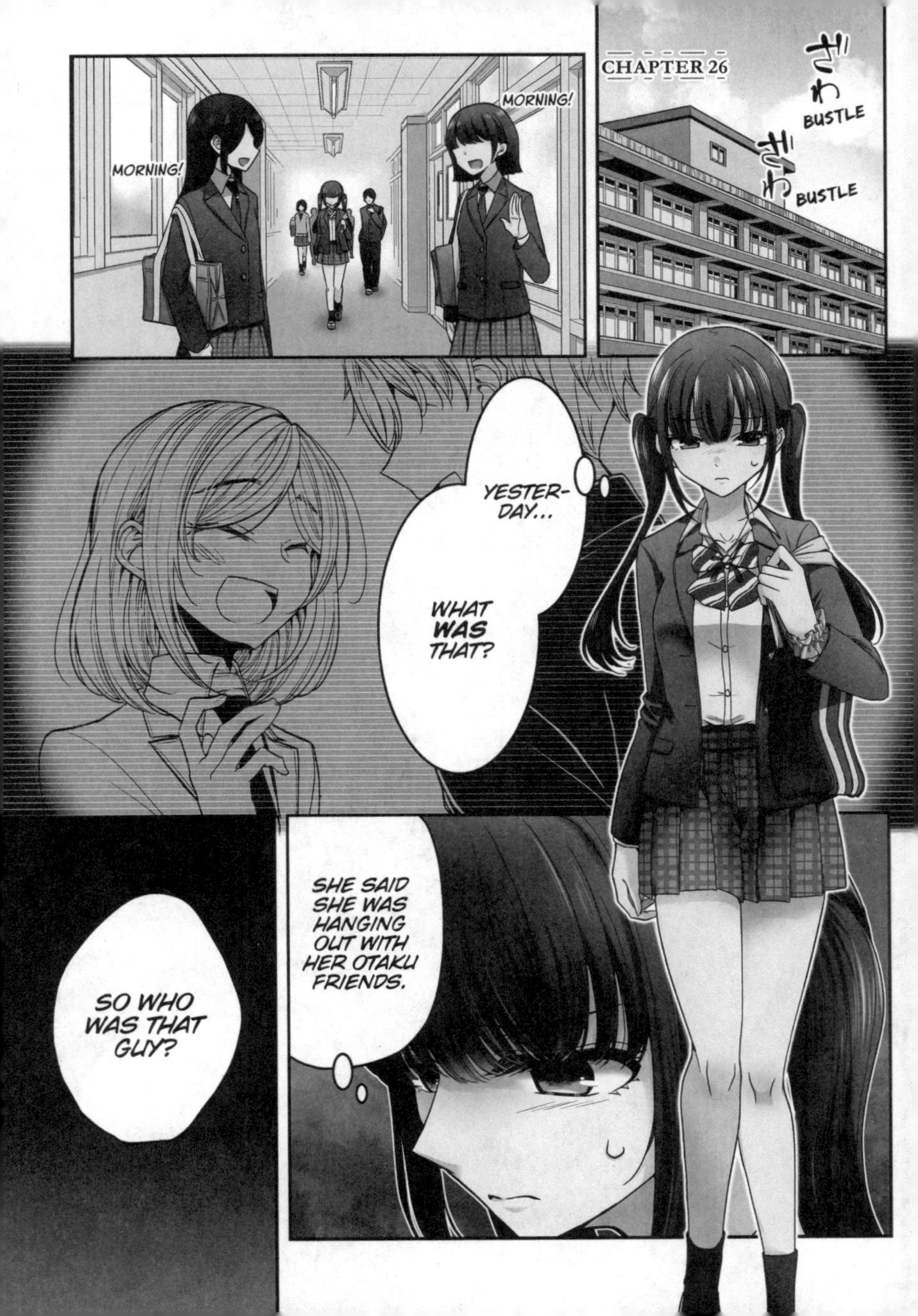
CHAPTER 26
ざわ
BUSTLE
ざわ
BUSTLE
MORNING!
MORNING!
YESTER-DAY...
WHAT WAS THAT?
SHE SAID SHE WAS HANGING OUT WITH HER OTAKU FRIENDS.
SO WHO WAS THAT GUY?

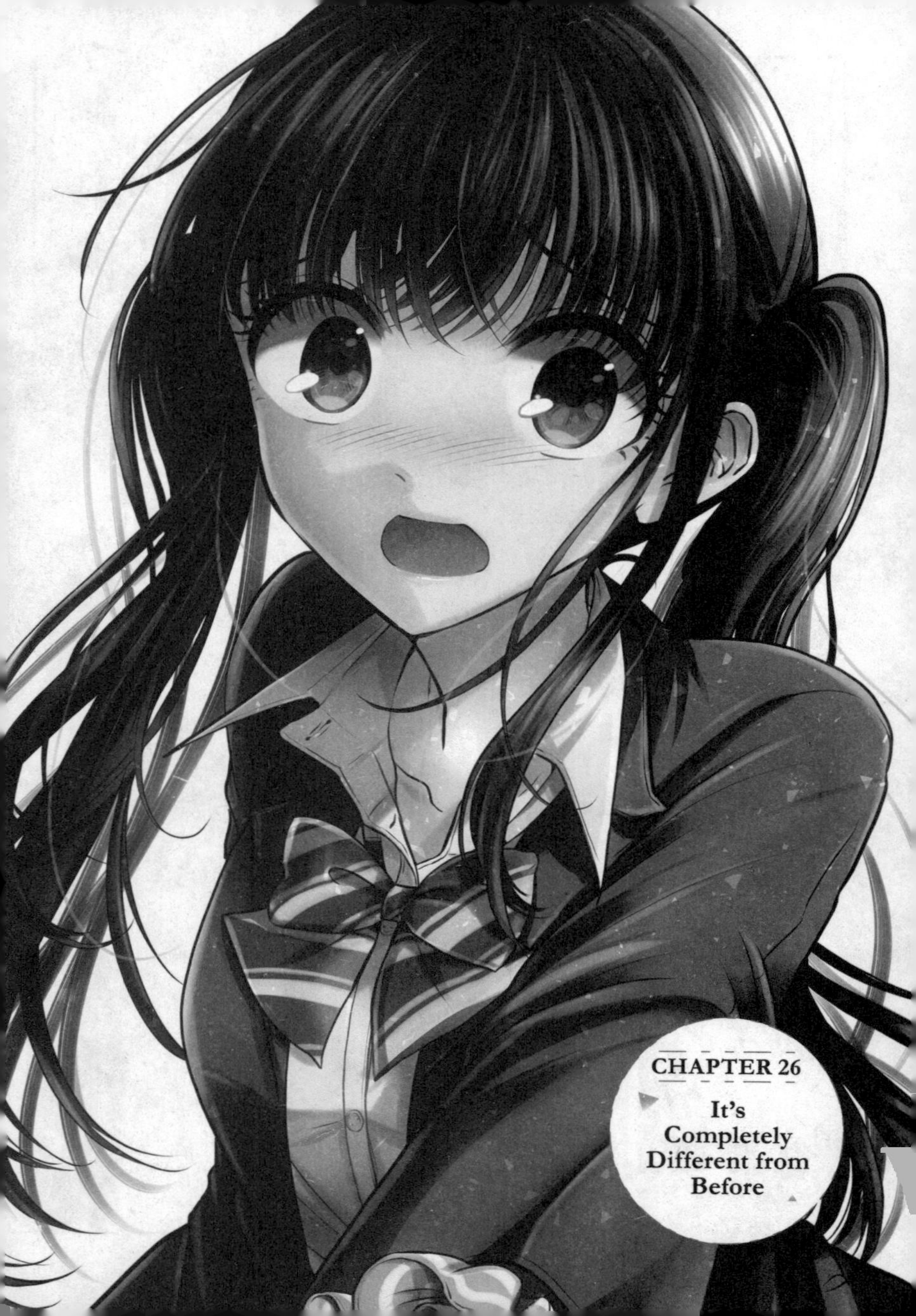
CHAPTER 26
It's Completely Different from Before

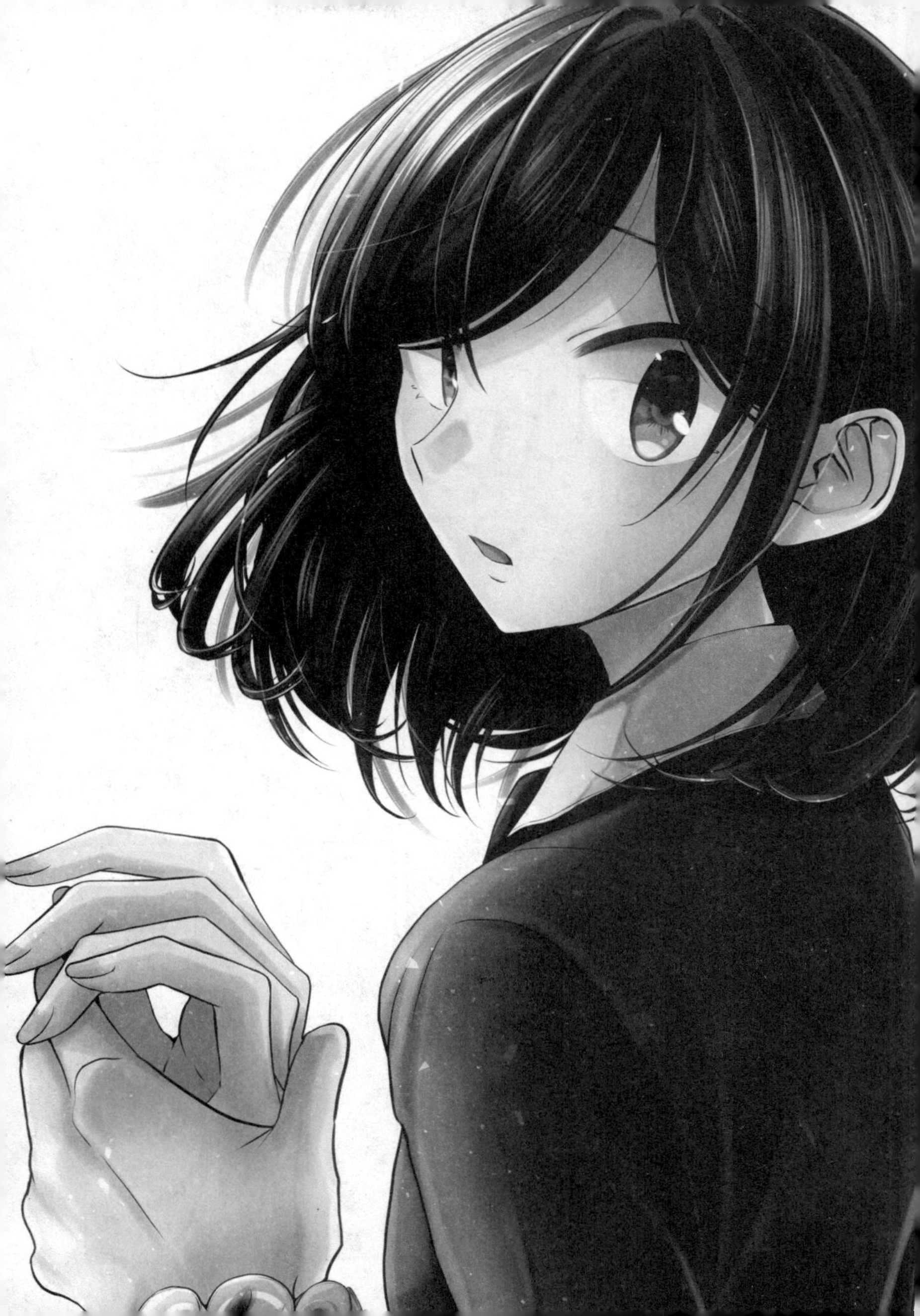

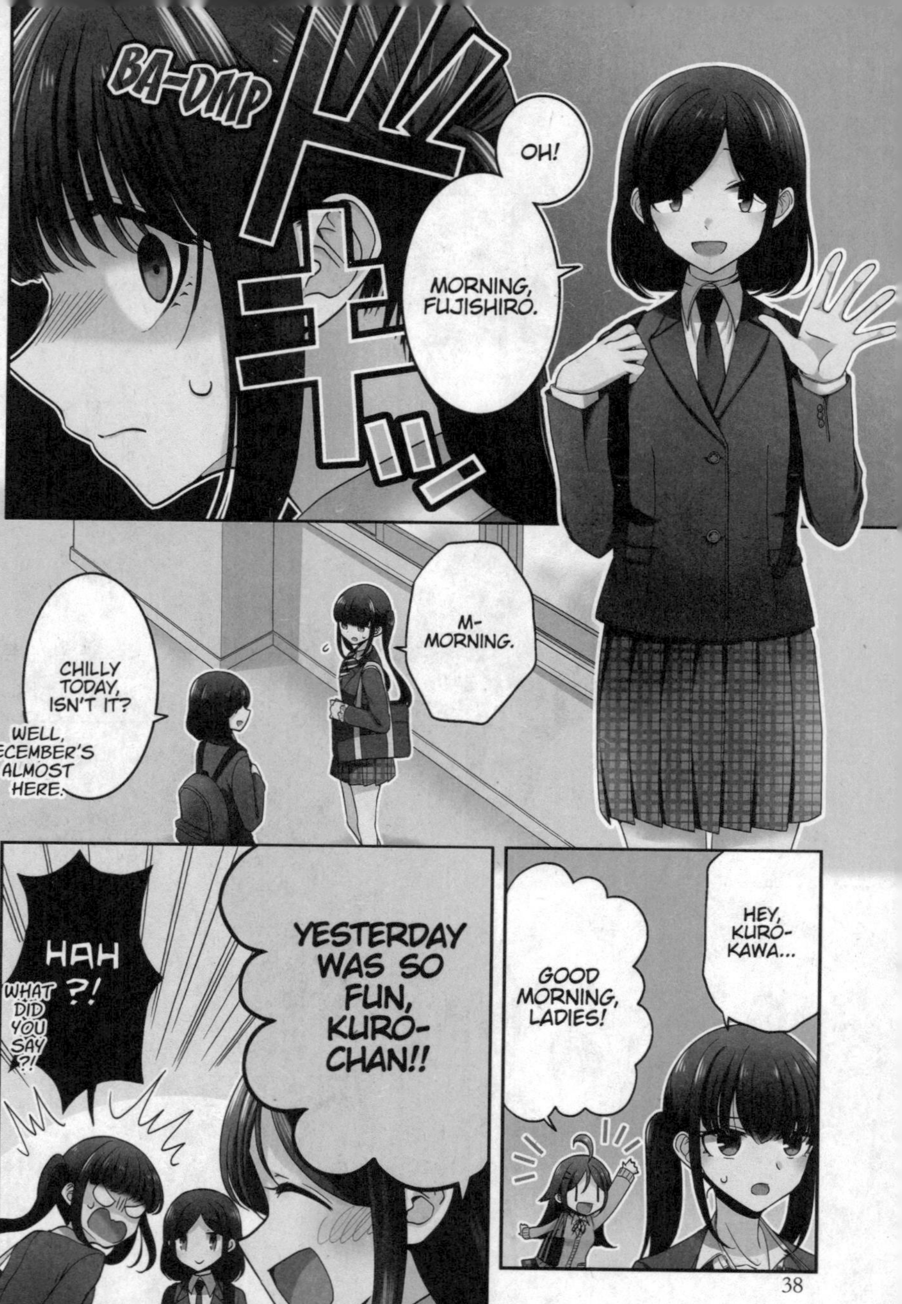

OH!
MORNING, FUJISHIRO.
BA-DMP
M- MORNING.
CHILLY TODAY, ISN'T IT?
WELL, DECEMBER'S ALMOST HERE.
HEY, KURO-KAWA...
GOOD MORNING, LADIES!
YESTERDAY WAS SO FUN, KURO-CHAN!!
HAH ?!
WHAT DID YOU SAY ?!

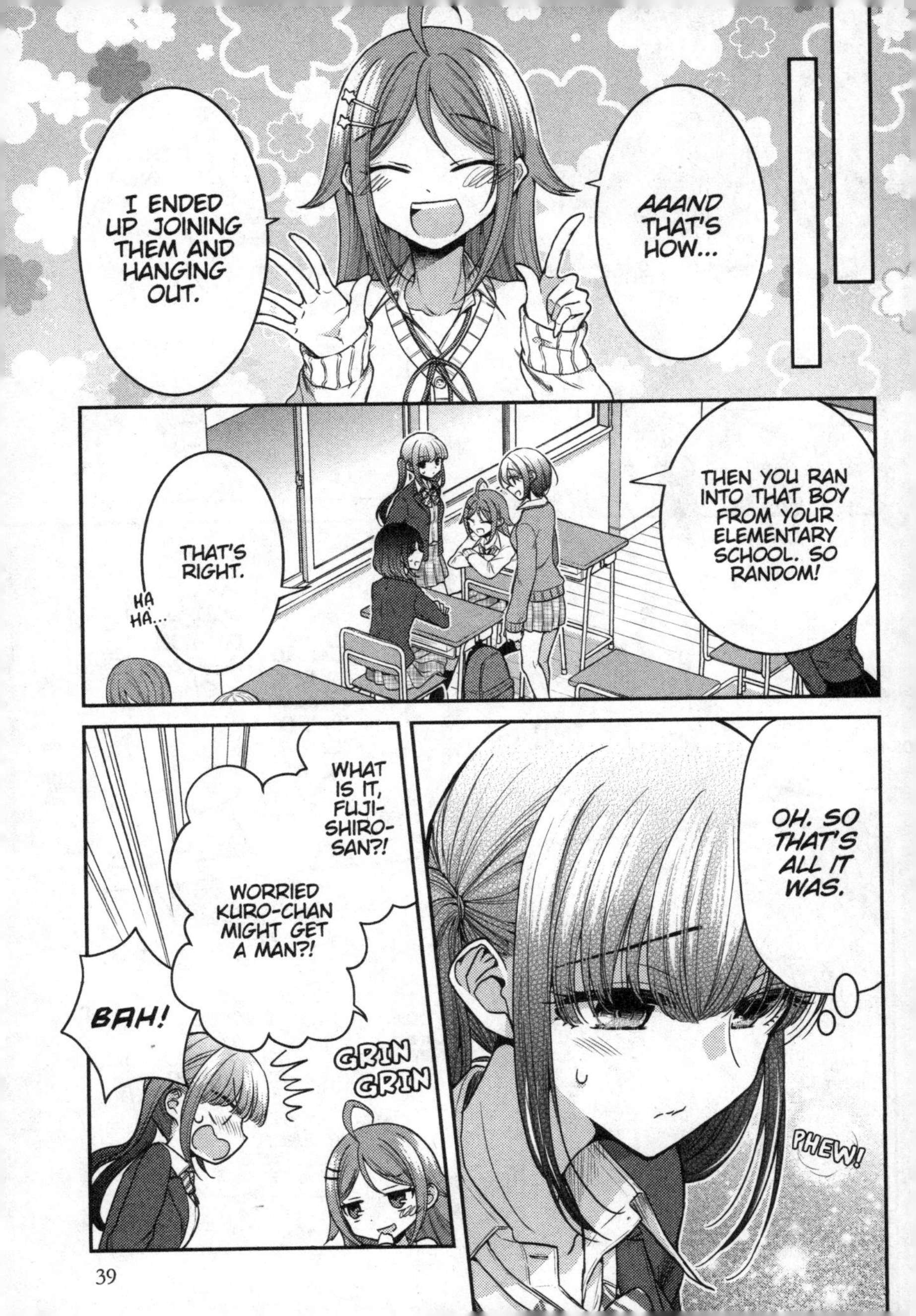
AAAND THAT'S HOW...
I ENDED UP JOINING THEM AND HANGING OUT.
THEN YOU RAN INTO THAT BOY FROM YOUR ELEMENTARY SCHOOL. SO RANDOM!
THAT'S RIGHT.
HA HA...
OH. SO THAT'S ALL IT WAS.
PHEW!
WHAT IS IT, FUJI-SHIRO-SAN?!
WORRIED KURO-CHAN MIGHT GET A MAN?!
GRIN GRIN
BAH!

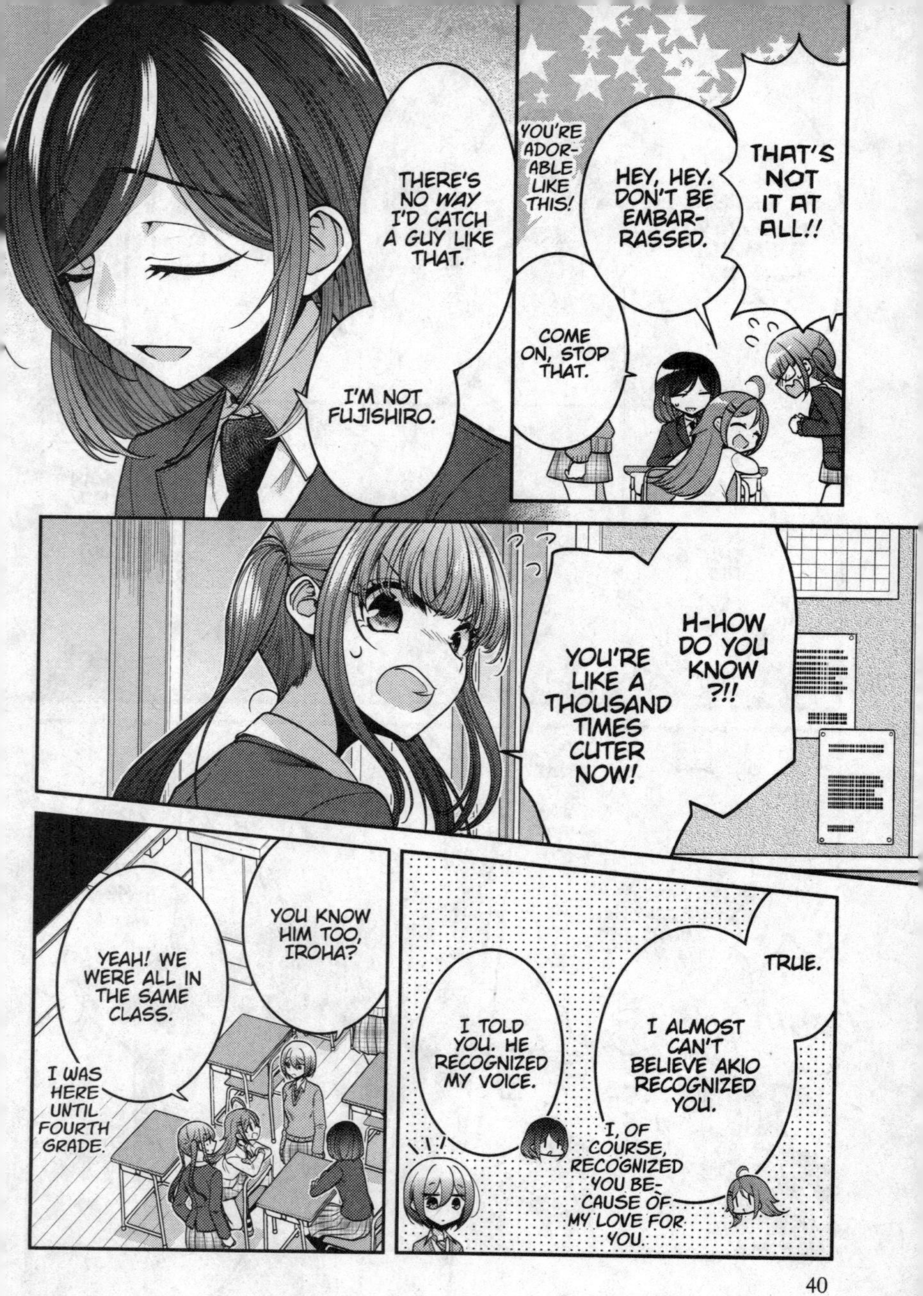
THAT'S NOT IT AT ALL!!
HEY, HEY. DON'T BE EMBARRASSED.
YOU'RE ADORABLE LIKE THIS!
COME ON, STOP THAT.
THERE'S NO *WAY* I'D CATCH A GUY LIKE THAT.
I'M NOT FUJISHIRO.
H-HOW DO YOU KNOW ?!!
YOU'RE LIKE A THOUSAND TIMES CUTER NOW!
TRUE.
I ALMOST CAN'T BELIEVE AKIO RECOGNIZED YOU.
I TOLD YOU. HE RECOGNIZED MY VOICE.
I, OF COURSE, RECOGNIZED YOU BECAUSE OF MY LOVE FOR YOU.
YOU KNOW HIM TOO, IROHA?
YEAH! WE WERE ALL IN THE SAME CLASS.
I WAS HERE UNTIL FOURTH GRADE.

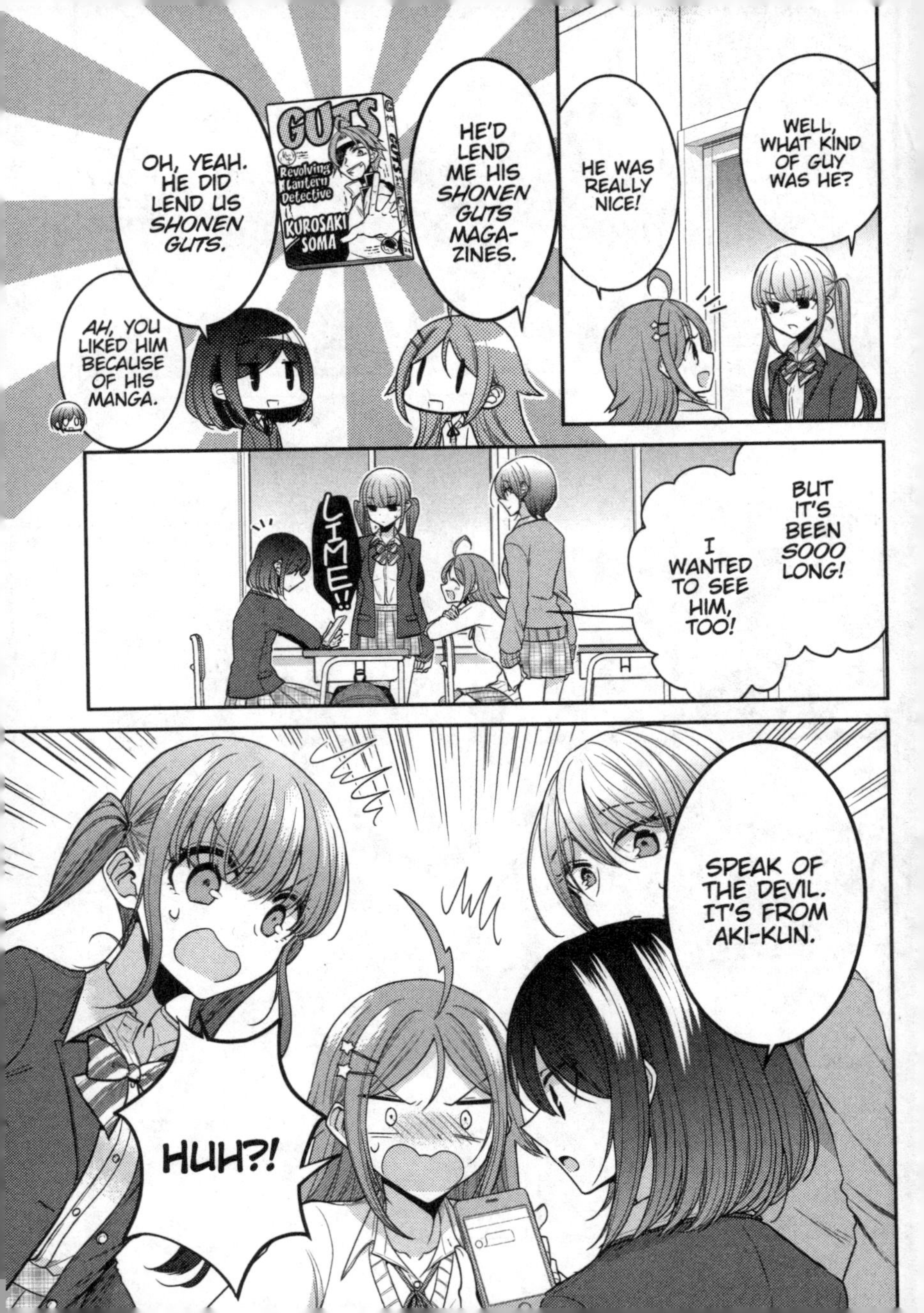
WELL, WHAT KIND OF GUY WAS HE?
HE WAS REALLY NICE!
HE'D LEND ME HIS SHONEN GUTS MAGAZINES.
GUTS
Revolving Lantern Detective
KUROSAKI SOMA
OH, YEAH. HE DID LEND US SHONEN GUTS.
AH, YOU LIKED HIM BECAUSE OF HIS MANGA.
BUT IT'S BEEN SOOO LONG!
I WANTED TO SEE HIM, TOO!
LIME!!
SPEAK OF THE DEVIL. IT'S FROM AKI-KUN.
HUH?!

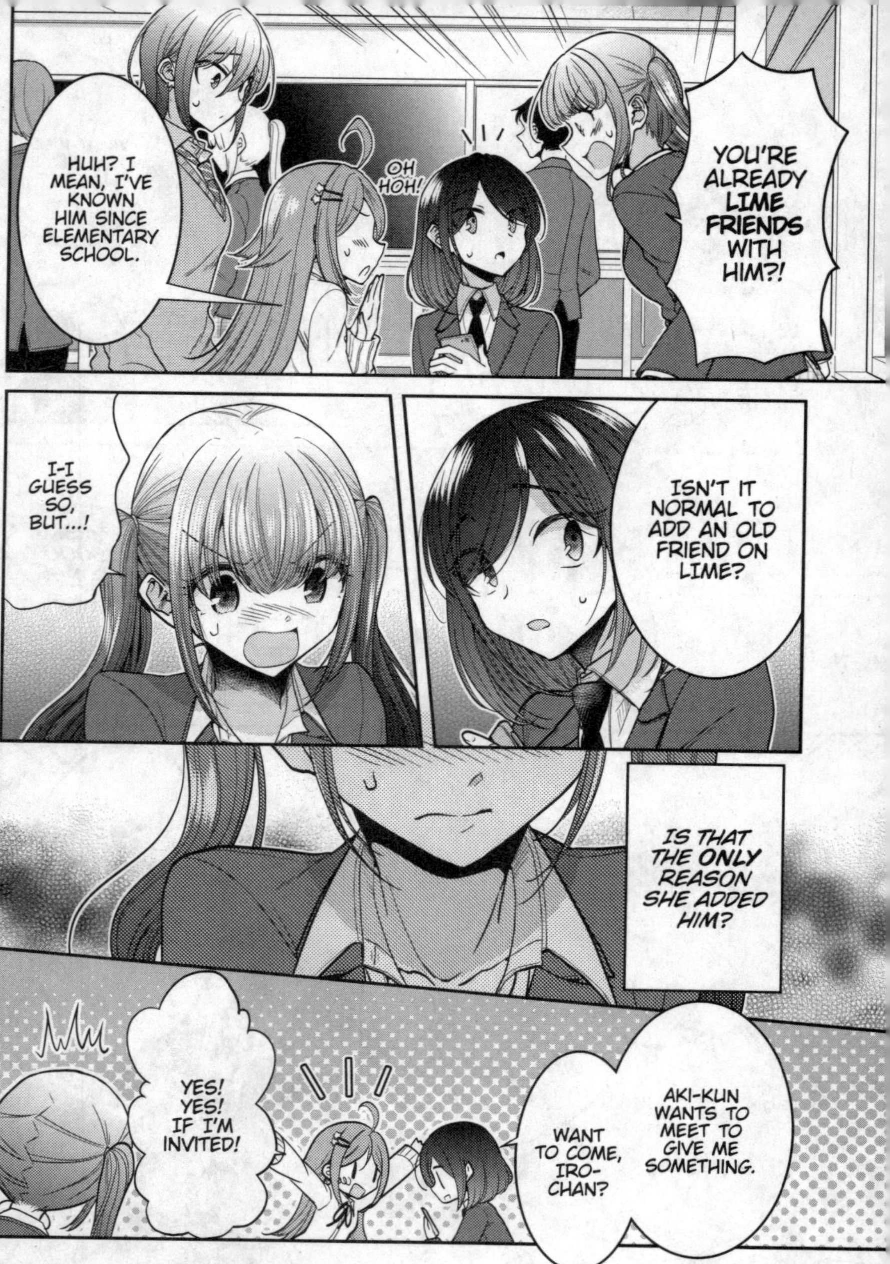
YOU'RE ALREADY LIME FRIENDS WITH HIM?!
OH HOH!
HUH? I MEAN, I'VE KNOWN HIM SINCE ELEMENTARY SCHOOL.
ISN'T IT NORMAL TO ADD AN OLD FRIEND ON LIME?
I-I GUESS SO, BUT...!
IS THAT THE ONLY REASON SHE ADDED HIM?
AKI-KUN WANTS TO MEET TO GIVE ME SOMETHING.
WANT TO COME, IRO-CHAN?
YES! YES! IF I'M INVITED!

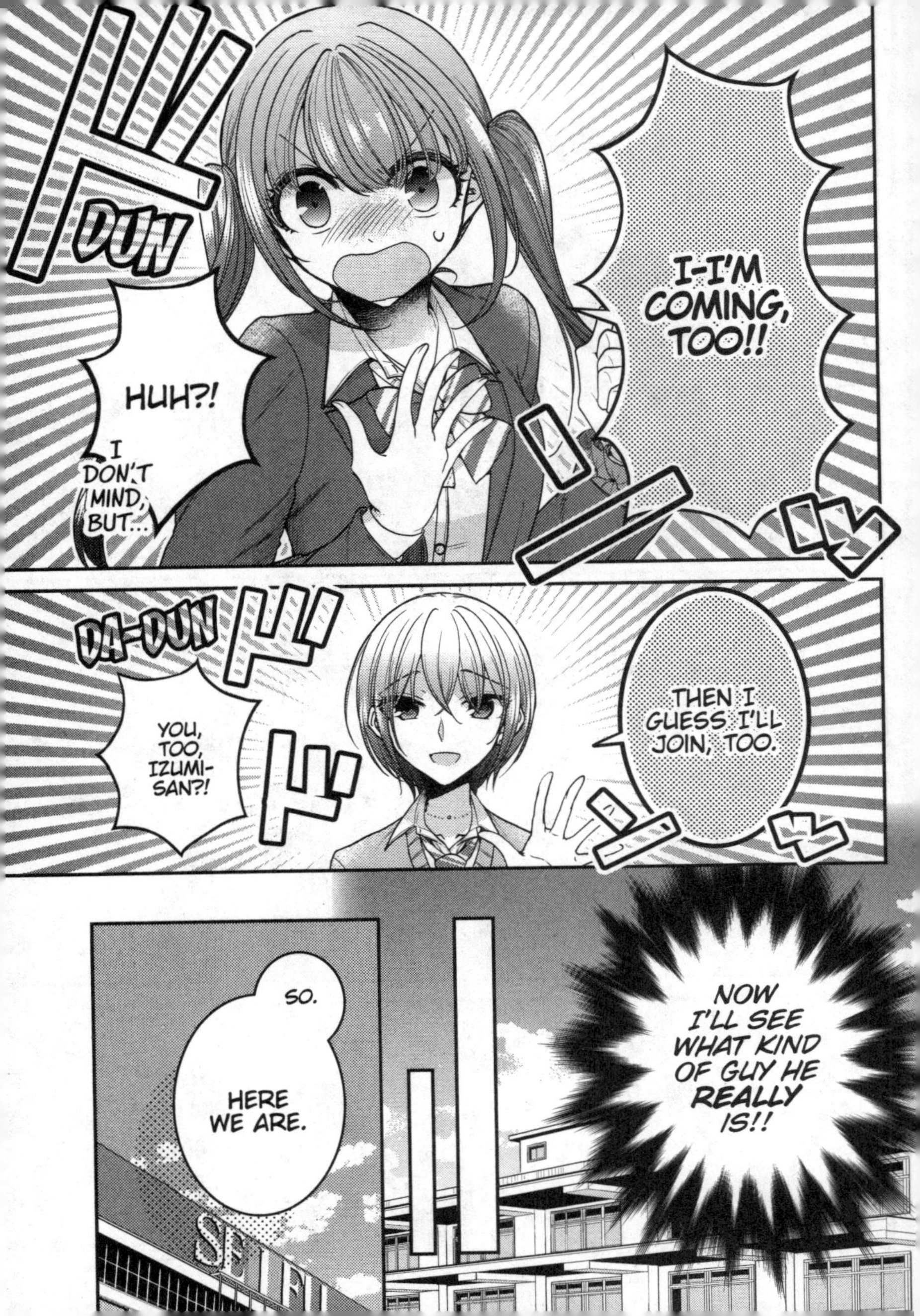
I-I'M COMING, TOO!!
DUN
HUH?!
I DON'T MIND, BUT...
THEN I GUESS I'LL JOIN, TOO.
DA-DUN
YOU, TOO, IZUMI-SAN?!
NOW I'LL SEE WHAT KIND OF GUY HE REALLY IS!!
SO.
HERE WE ARE.

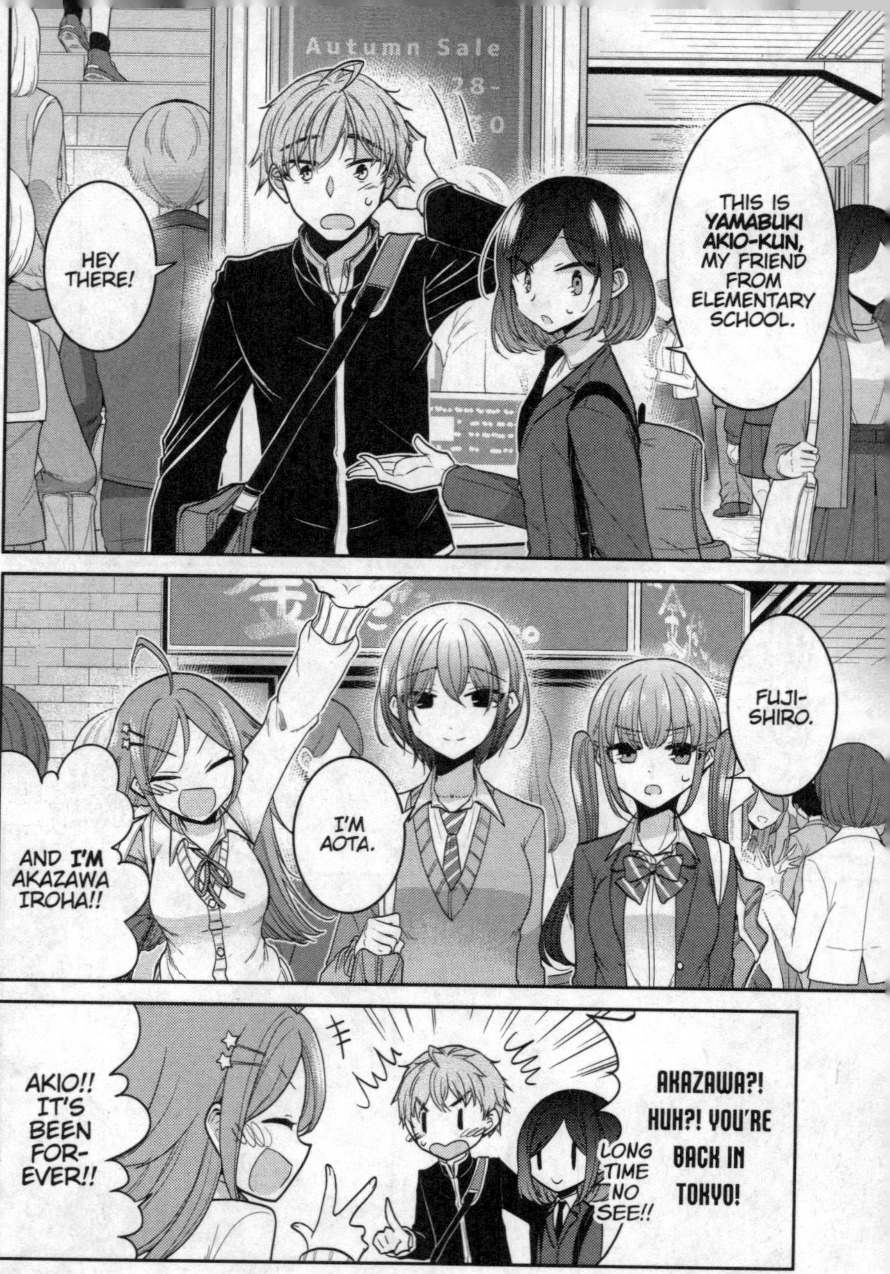
Autumn Sale
THIS IS YAMABUKI AKIO-KUN, MY FRIEND FROM ELEMENTARY SCHOOL.
HEY THERE!
FUJI-SHIRO.
I'M AOTA.
AND I'M AKAZAWA IROHA!!
AKAZAWA?! HUH?! YOU'RE BACK IN TOKYO!
LONG TIME NO SEE!!
AKIO!! IT'S BEEN FOR-EVER!!

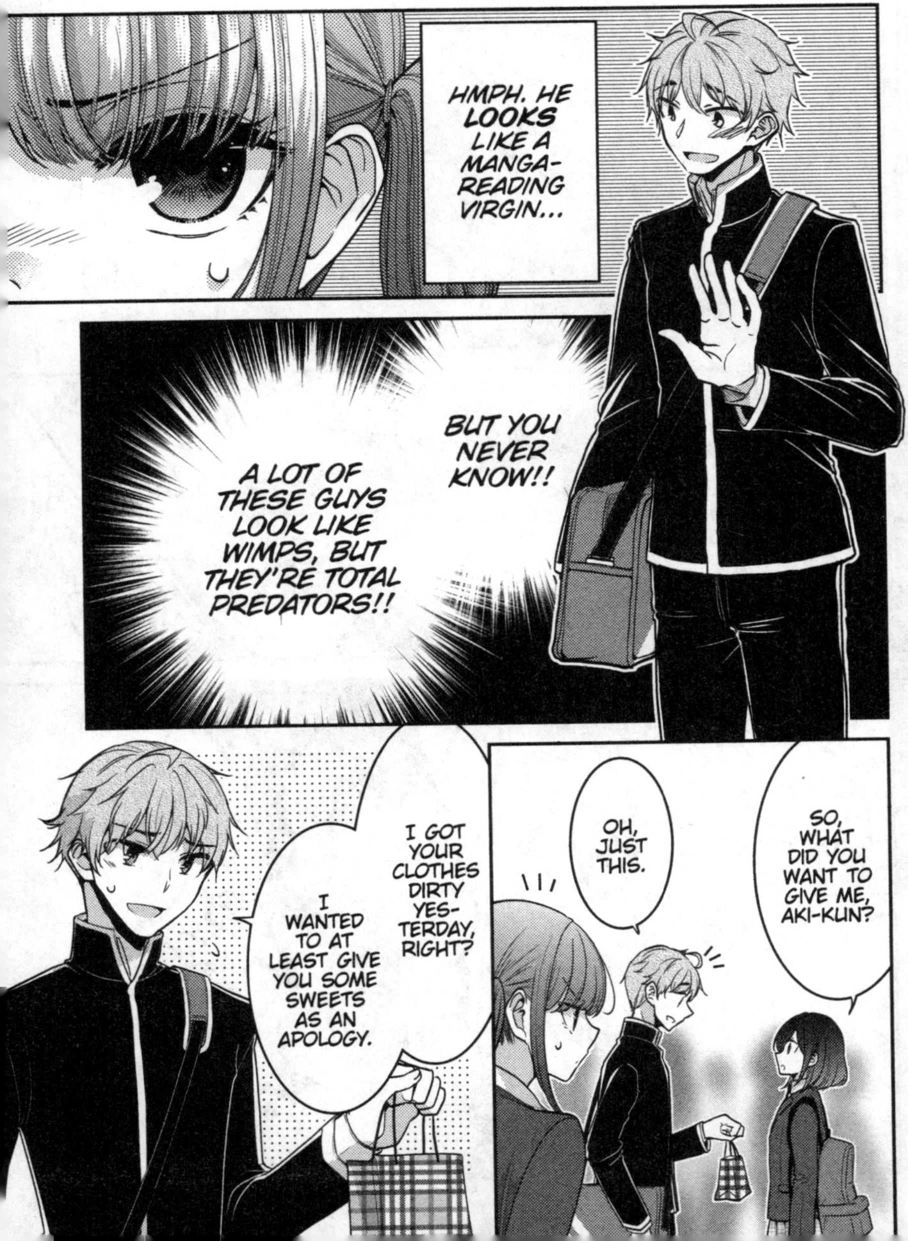
HMPH. HE LOOKS LIKE A MANGA-READING VIRGIN...
BUT YOU NEVER KNOW!!
A LOT OF THESE GUYS LOOK LIKE WIMPS, BUT THEY'RE TOTAL PREDATORS!!
SO, WHAT DID YOU WANT TO GIVE ME, AKI-KUN?
OH, JUST THIS.
I GOT YOUR CLOTHES DIRTY YES-TERDAY, RIGHT?
I WANTED TO AT LEAST GIVE YOU SOME SWEETS AS AN APOLOGY.

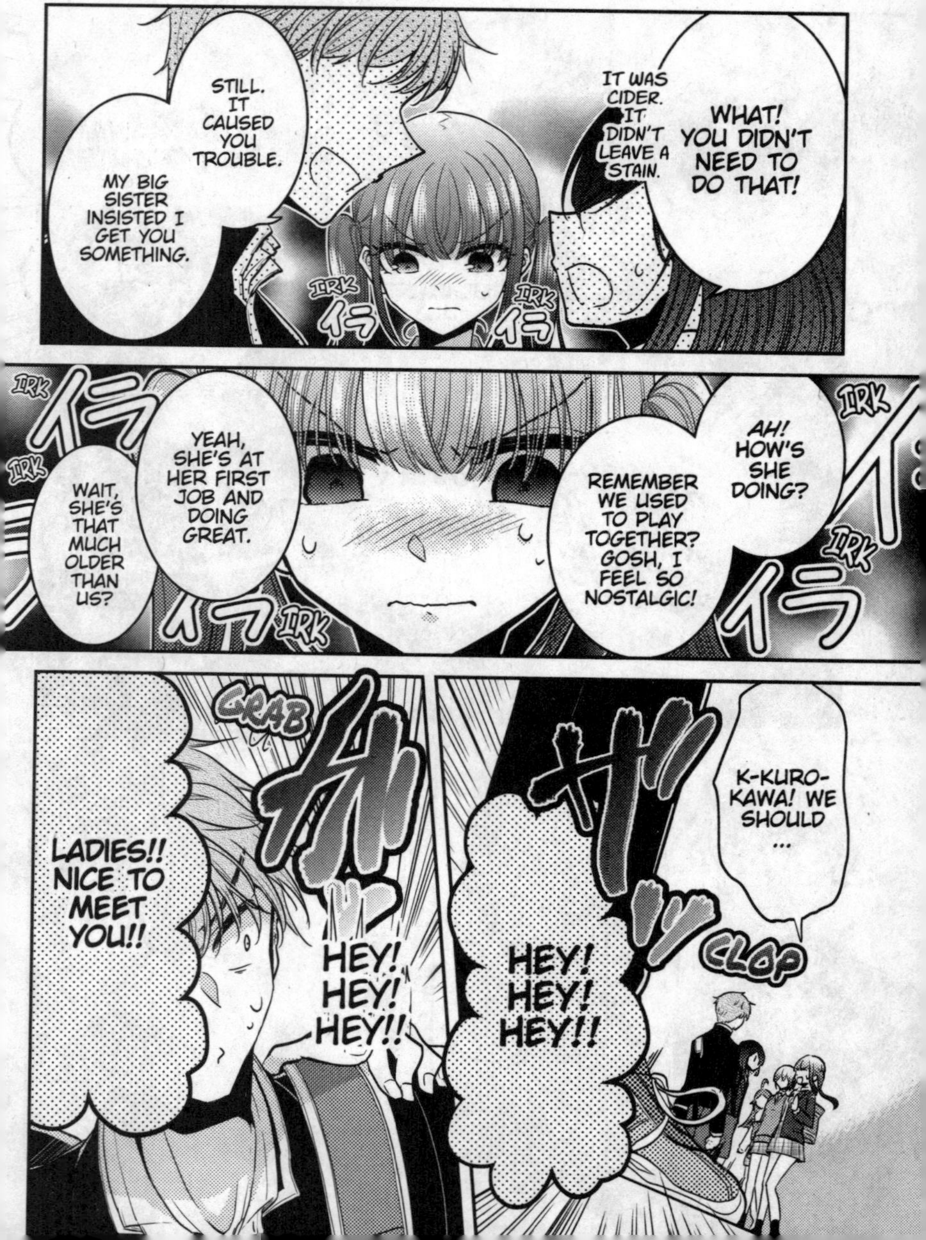
WHAT! YOU DIDN'T NEED TO DO THAT!
IT WAS CIDER. IT DIDN'T LEAVE A STAIN.
STILL. IT CAUSED YOU TROUBLE.
MY BIG SISTER INSISTED I GET YOU SOMETHING.
IRK イラ
IRK イラ
IRK イラ
AH! HOW'S SHE DOING?
REMEMBER WE USED TO PLAY TOGETHER? GOSH, I FEEL SO NOSTALGIC!
YEAH, SHE'S AT HER FIRST JOB AND DOING GREAT.
WAIT, SHE'S THAT MUCH OLDER THAN US?
IRK イラ
IRK
IRK
K-KURO-KAWA! WE SHOULD ...
CLOP
HEY! HEY! HEY!!
GRAB
HEY! HEY! HEY!!
LADIES!! NICE TO MEET YOU!!

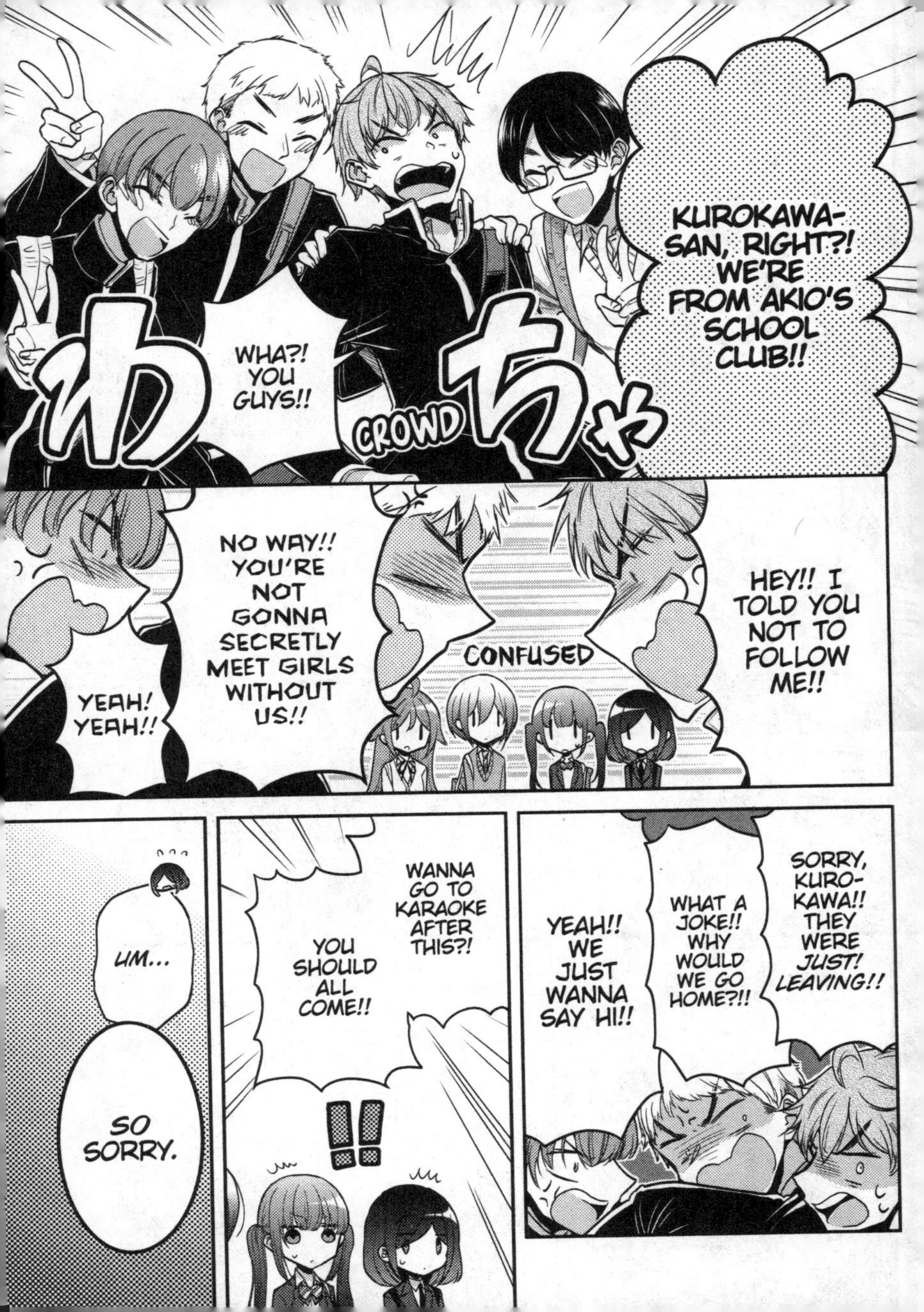
KUROKAWA-SAN, RIGHT?! WE'RE FROM AKIO'S SCHOOL CLUB!!
ちゃ
CROWD
WHA?! YOU GUYS!!
わ
HEY!! I TOLD YOU NOT TO FOLLOW ME!!
CONFUSED
NO WAY!! YOU'RE NOT GONNA SECRETLY MEET GIRLS WITHOUT US!!
YEAH! YEAH!!
SORRY, KURO-KAWA!! THEY WERE JUST! LEAVING!!
WHAT A JOKE!! WHY WOULD WE GO HOME?!!
YEAH!! WE JUST WANNA SAY HI!!
WANNA GO TO KARAOKE AFTER THIS?!
YOU SHOULD ALL COME!!
!!
UM...
SO SORRY.

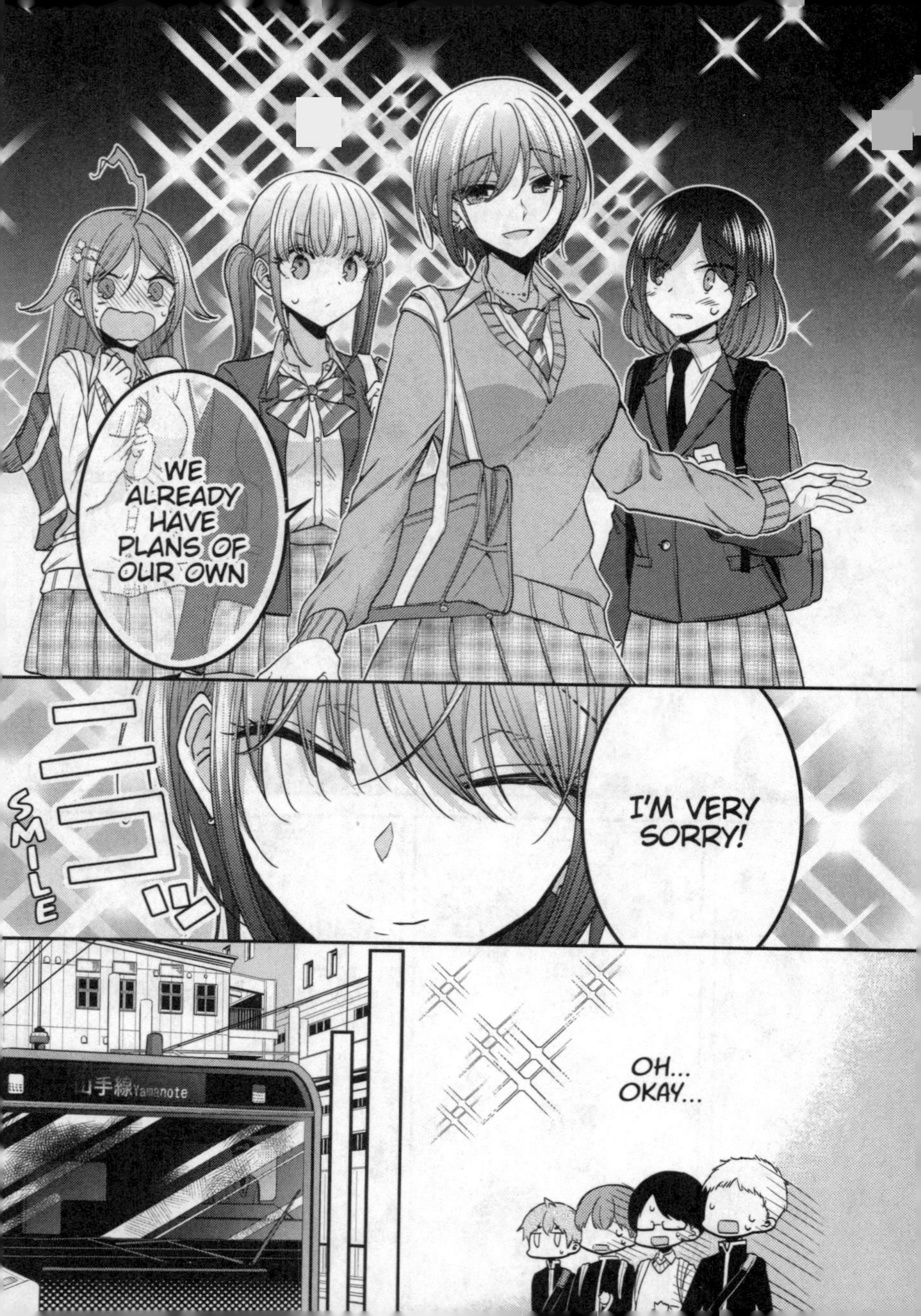
WE ALREADY HAVE PLANS OF OUR OWN
I'M VERY SORRY!
SMILE
山手線Yamanote
OH... OKAY...

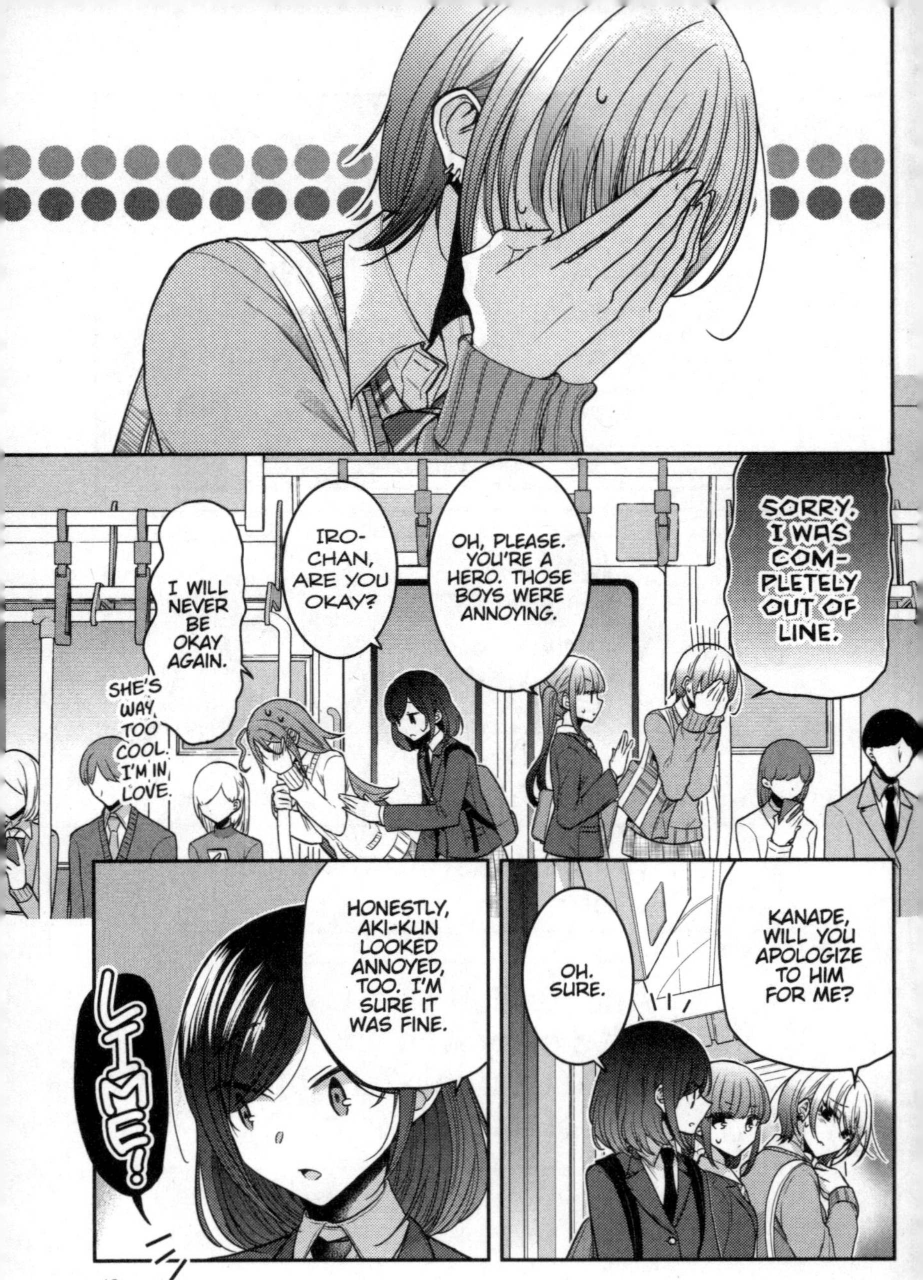

SORRY. I WAS COM-PLETELY OUT OF LINE.
OH, PLEASE. YOU'RE A HERO. THOSE BOYS WERE ANNOYING.
IRO-CHAN, ARE YOU OKAY?
I WILL NEVER BE OKAY AGAIN.
SHE'S WAY TOO COOL. I'M IN LOVE.
KANADE, WILL YOU APOLOGIZE TO HIM FOR ME?
OH. SURE.
HONESTLY, AKI-KUN LOOKED ANNOYED, TOO. I'M SURE IT WAS FINE.
LIME!

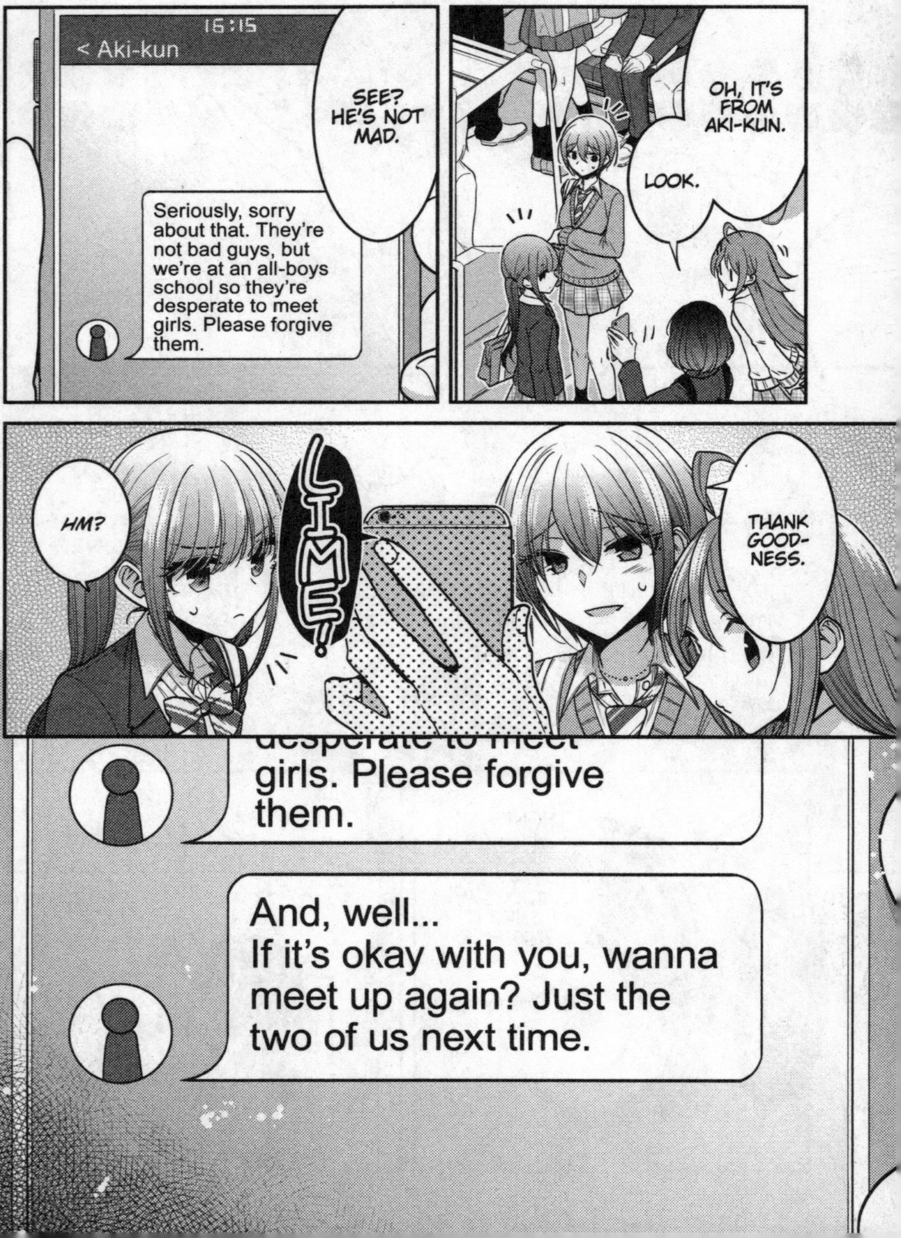
OH, IT'S FROM AKI-KUN.
LOOK.
16:15
< Aki-kun
SEE? HE'S NOT MAD.
Seriously, sorry about that. They're not bad guys, but we're at an all-boys school so they're desperate to meet girls. Please forgive them.
THANK GOODNESS.
LIME!
HM?
girls. Please forgive them.
And, well...
If it's okay with you, wanna meet up again? Just the two of us next time.

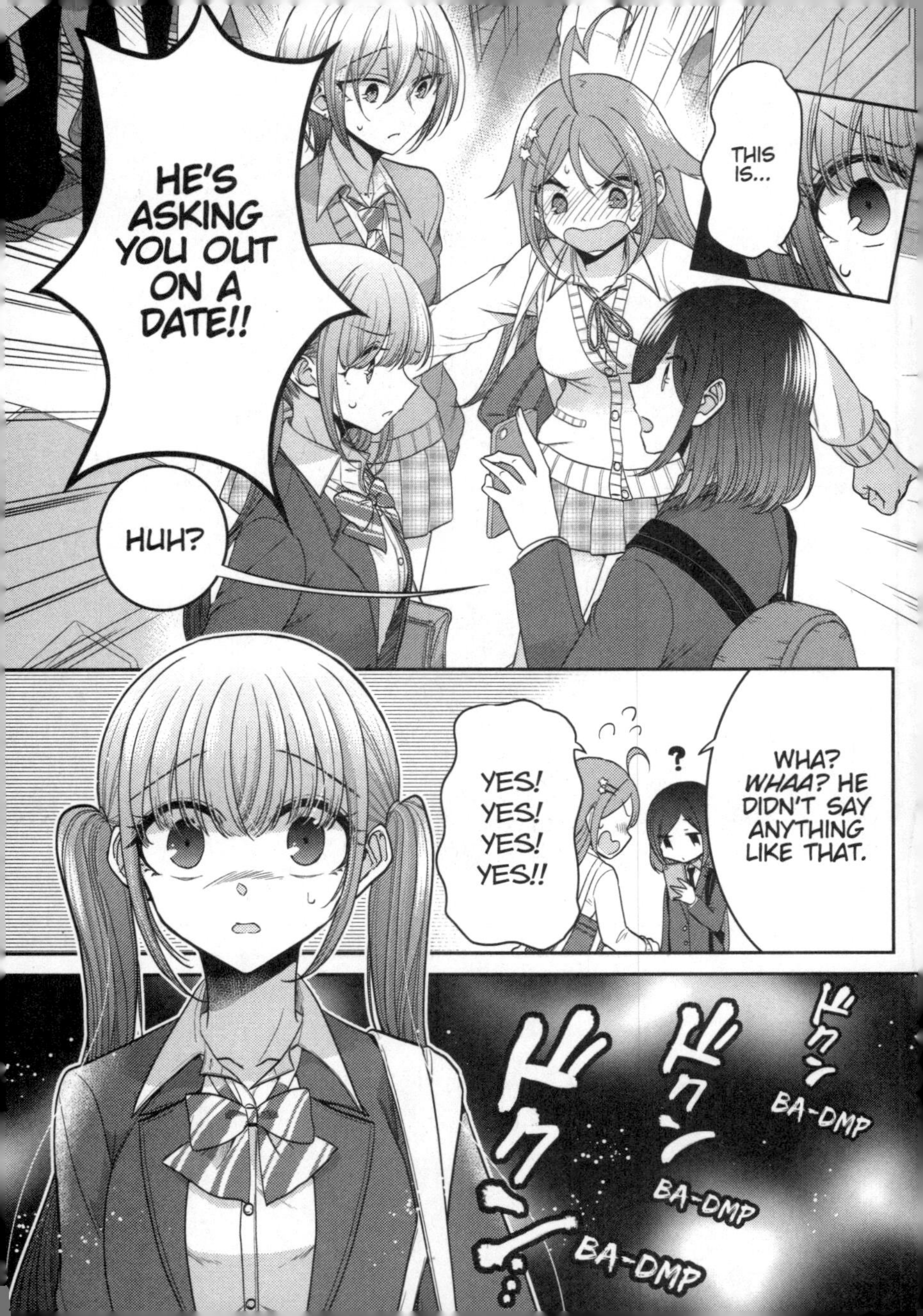
THIS IS...
HE'S ASKING YOU OUT ON A DATE!!
HUH?
WHA? *WHAA?* HE DIDN'T SAY ANYTHING LIKE THAT.
?
YES! YES! YES! YES!!
BA-DMP
BA-DMP
BA-DMP

Failed Princesses

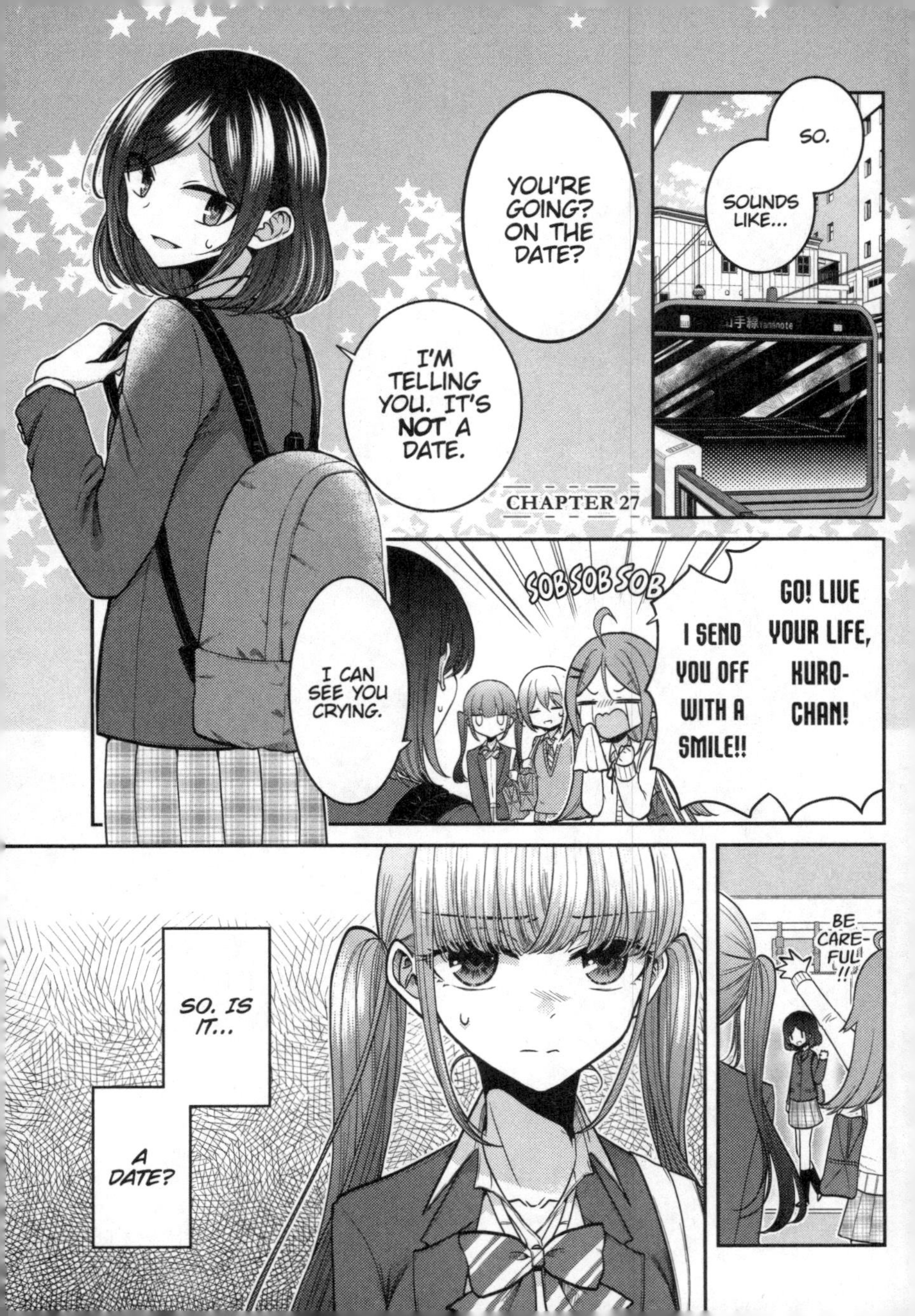
SO.
SOUNDS LIKE...
YOU'RE GOING? ON THE DATE?
I'M TELLING YOU. IT'S NOT A DATE.
CHAPTER 27
GO! LIVE YOUR LIFE, KURO-CHAN!
I SEND YOU OFF WITH A SMILE!!
SOB SOB SOB
I CAN SEE YOU CRYING.
BE CAREFUL!!
SO. IS IT...
A DATE?

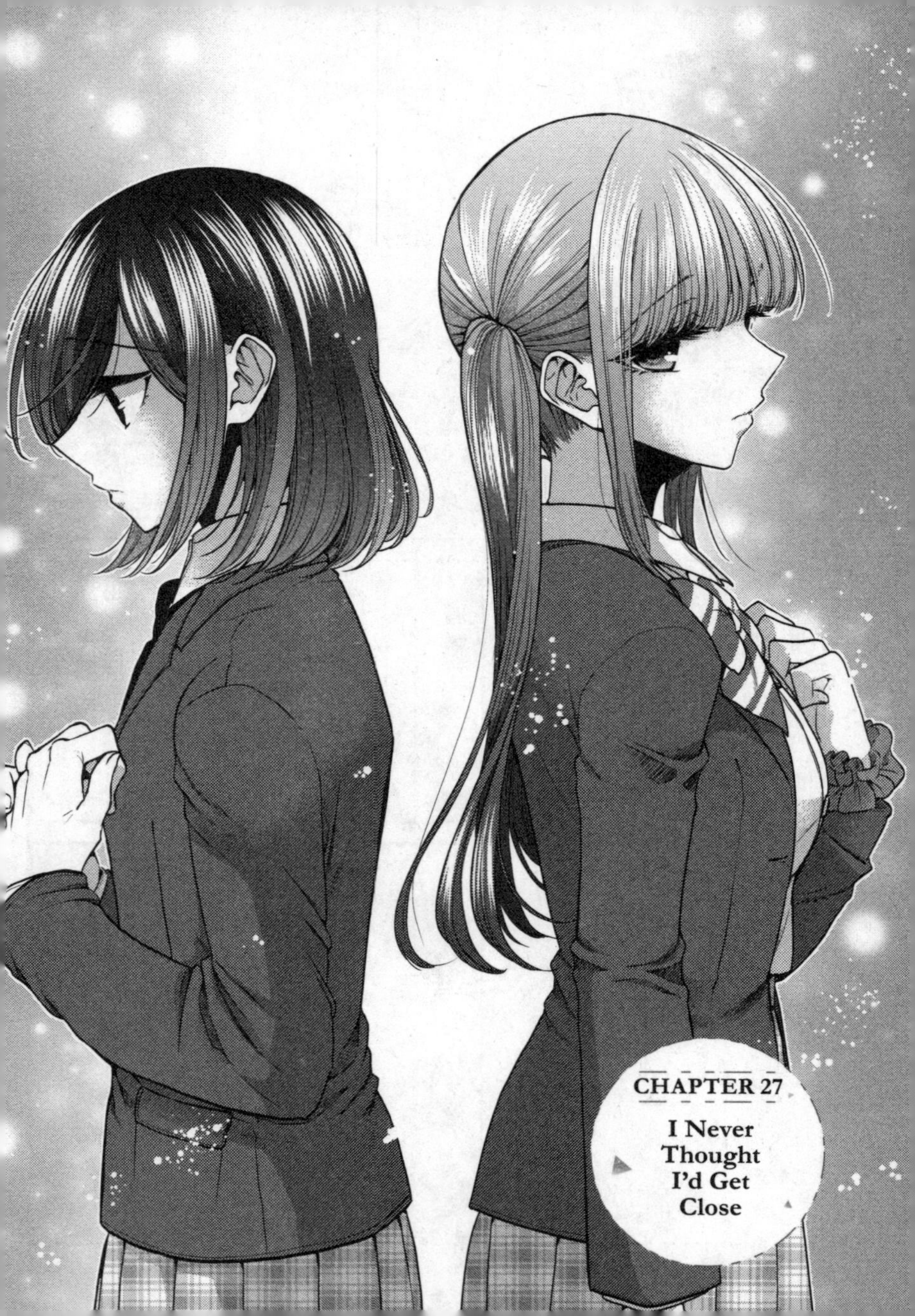
CHAPTER 27
I Never Thought I'd Get Close

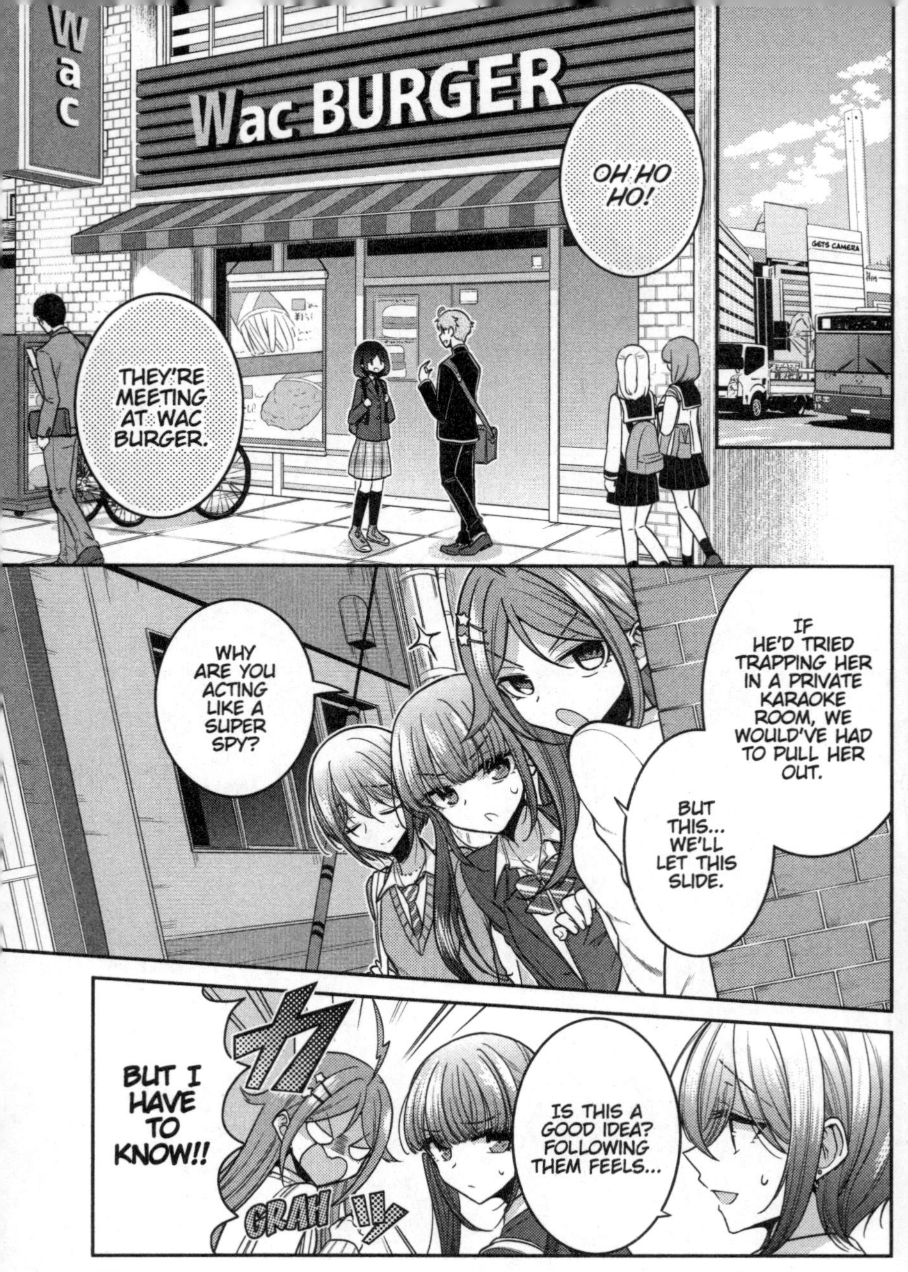
Wac BURGER
Wac
GETS CAMERA
OH HO HO!
THEY'RE MEETING AT WAC BURGER.
IF HE'D TRIED TRAPPING HER IN A PRIVATE KARAOKE ROOM, WE WOULD'VE HAD TO PULL HER OUT.
BUT THIS... WE'LL LET THIS SLIDE.
WHY ARE YOU ACTING LIKE A SUPER SPY?
IS THIS A GOOD IDEA? FOLLOWING THEM FEELS...
BUT I HAVE TO KNOW!!
GRAH

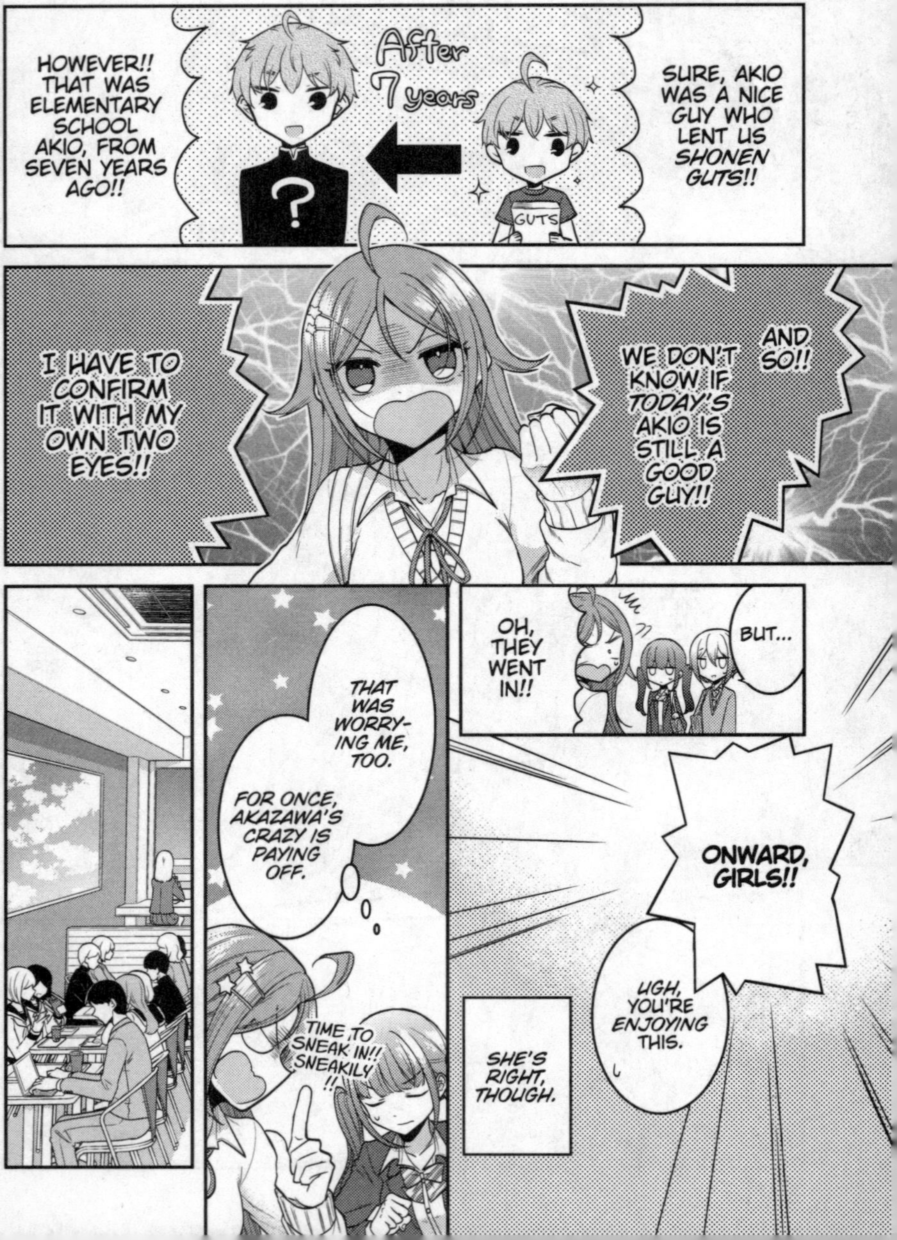
SURE, AKIO WAS A NICE GUY WHO LENT US SHONEN GUTS!!
GUTS
After 7 years
HOWEVER!! THAT WAS ELEMENTARY SCHOOL AKIO, FROM SEVEN YEARS AGO!!
AND SO!!
WE DON'T KNOW IF TODAY'S AKIO IS STILL A GOOD GUY!!
I HAVE TO CONFIRM IT WITH MY OWN TWO EYES!!
BUT...
OH, THEY WENT IN!!
ONWARD, GIRLS!!
UGH, YOU'RE ENJOYING THIS.
SHE'S RIGHT, THOUGH.
THAT WAS WORRYING ME, TOO.
FOR ONCE, AKAZAWA'S CRAZY IS PAYING OFF.
TIME TO SNEAK IN!! SNEAKILY!!

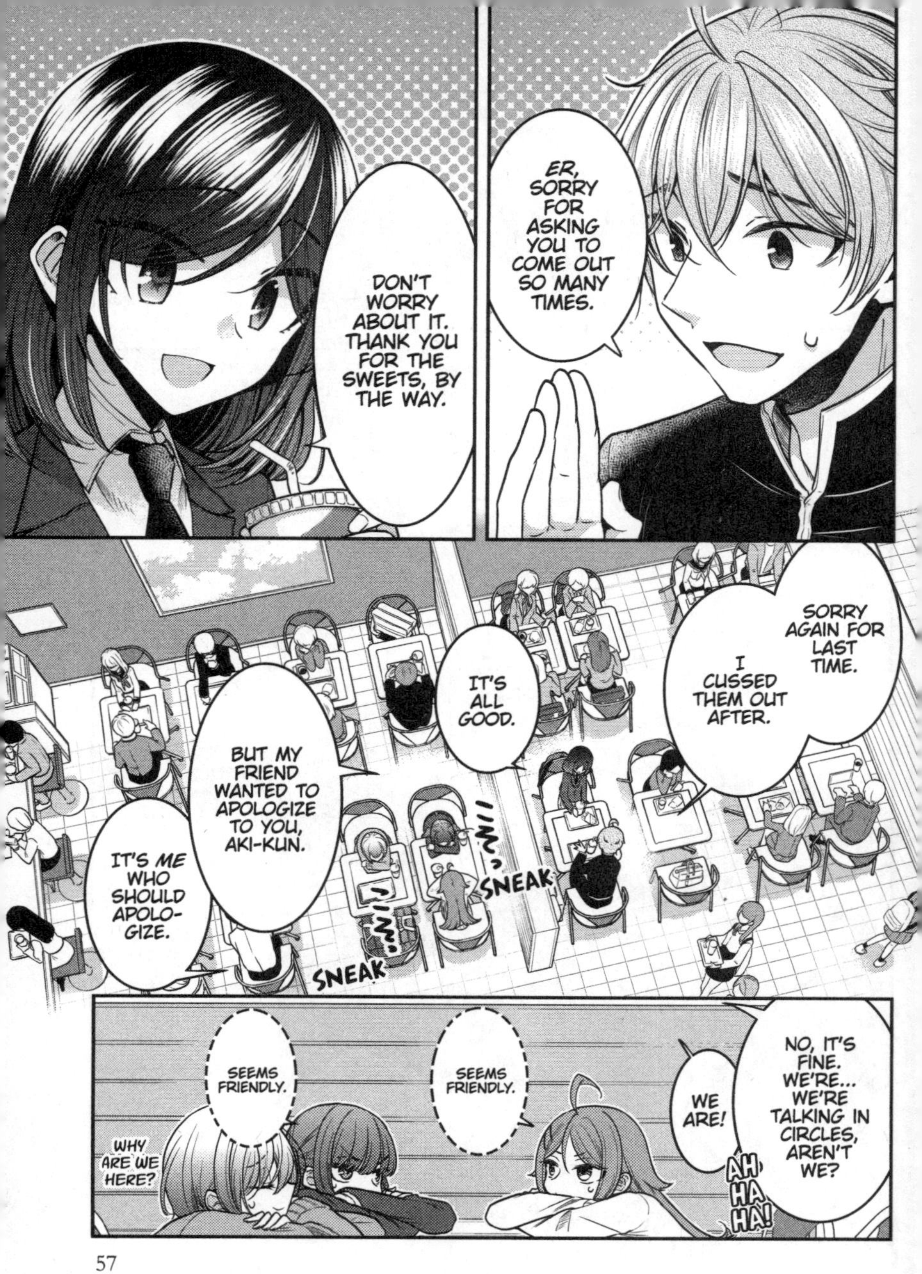
ER, SORRY FOR ASKING YOU TO COME OUT SO MANY TIMES.
DON'T WORRY ABOUT IT. THANK YOU FOR THE SWEETS, BY THE WAY.
SORRY AGAIN FOR LAST TIME.
I CUSSED THEM OUT AFTER.
IT'S ALL GOOD.
BUT MY FRIEND WANTED TO APOLOGIZE TO YOU, AKI-KUN.
IT'S *ME* WHO SHOULD APOLOGIZE.
SNEAK
SNEAK
NO, IT'S FINE. WE'RE... WE'RE TALKING IN CIRCLES, AREN'T WE?
WE ARE!
AH HA HA HA!
SEEMS FRIENDLY.
SEEMS FRIENDLY.
WHY ARE WE HERE?

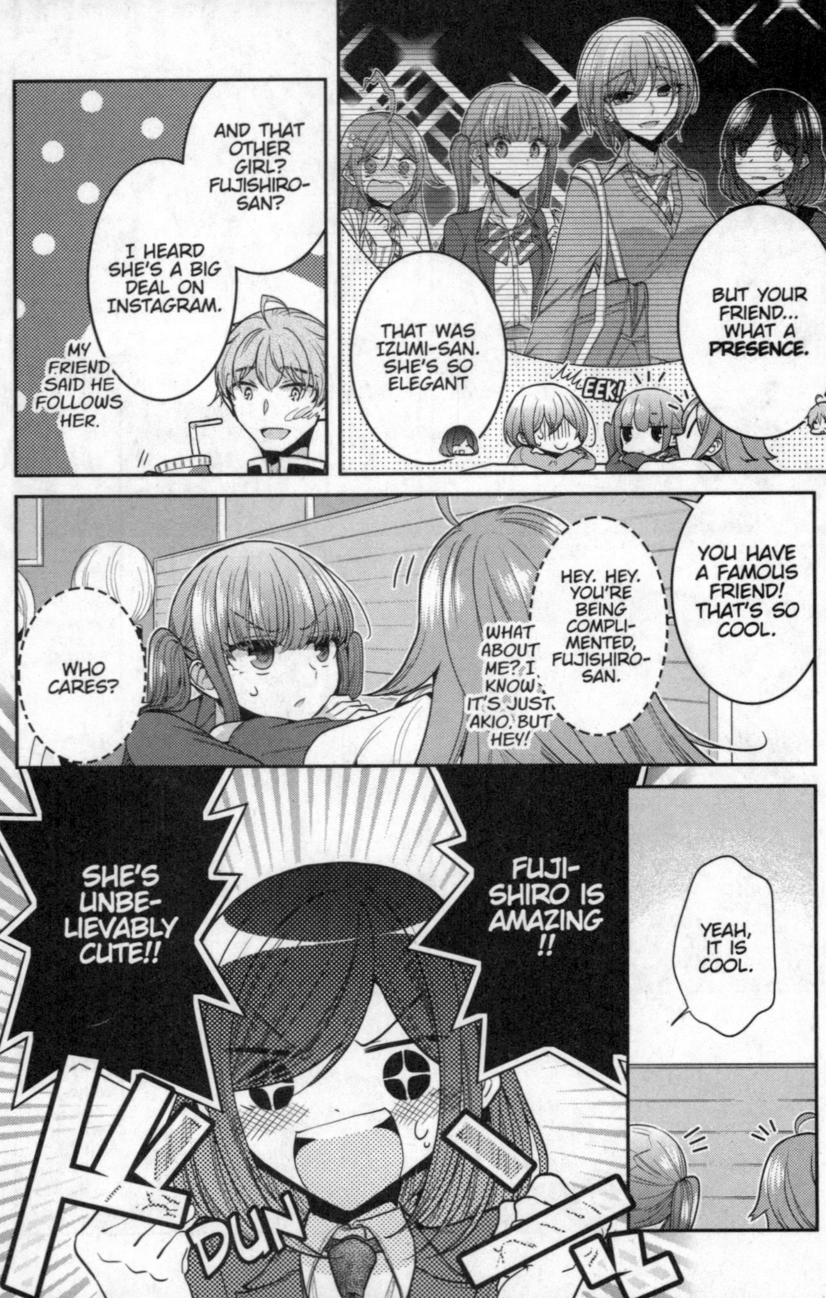

BUT YOUR FRIEND... WHAT A PRESENCE.
EEK!
THAT WAS IZUMI-SAN. SHE'S SO ELEGANT
AND THAT OTHER GIRL? FUJISHIRO-SAN?
I HEARD SHE'S A BIG DEAL ON INSTAGRAM.
MY FRIEND SAID HE FOLLOWS HER.
YOU HAVE A FAMOUS FRIEND! THAT'S SO COOL.
HEY. HEY. YOU'RE BEING COMPLIMENTED, FUJISHIRO-SAN.
WHAT ABOUT ME? I KNOW IT'S JUST AKIO, BUT HEY!
WHO CARES?
YEAH, IT IS COOL.
FUJI-SHIRO IS AMAZING!!
SHE'S UNBE-LIEVABLY CUTE!!
DUN

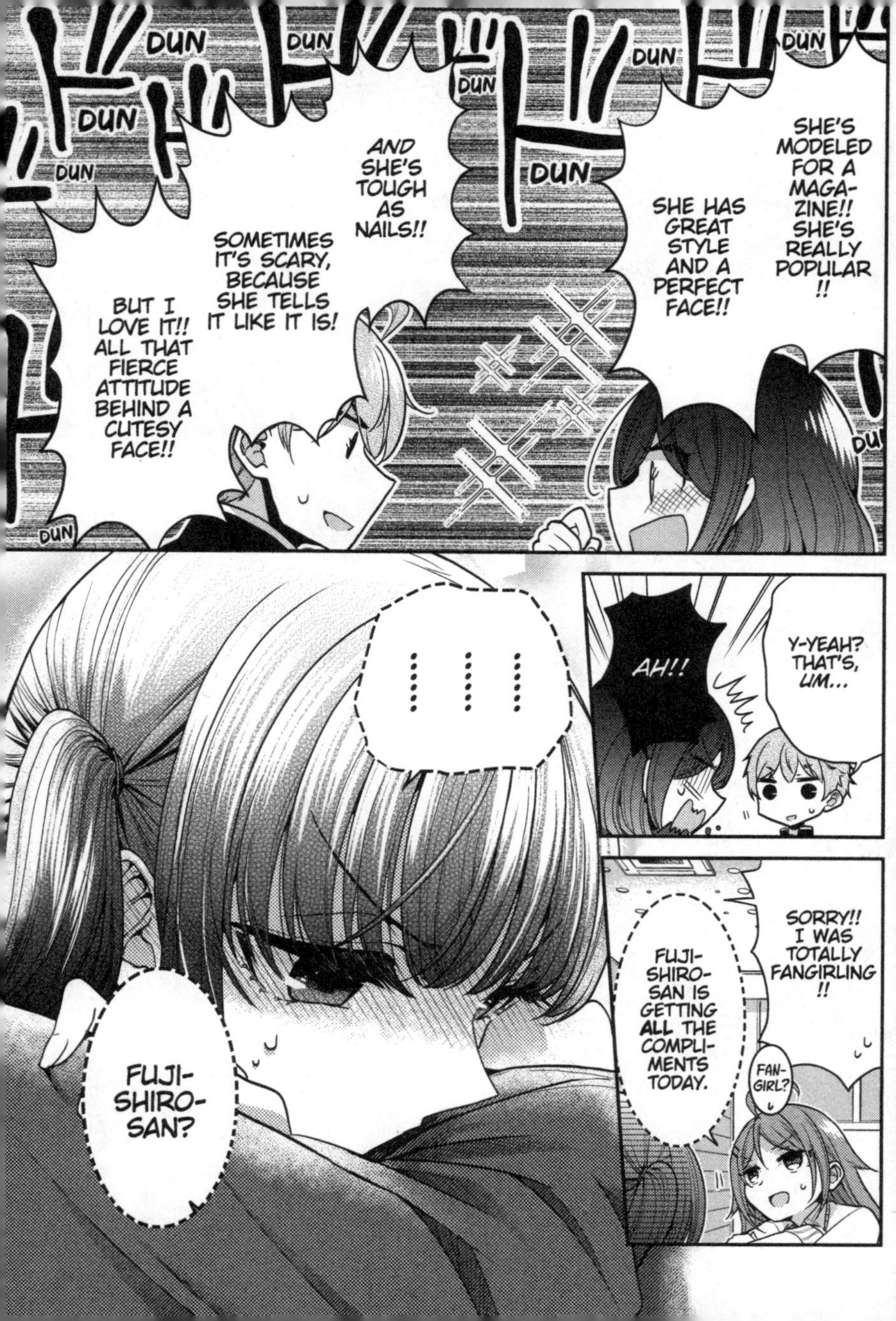
DUN
DUN
DUN
DUN
DUN
DUN
DUN
DUN
DUN
SHE'S MODELED FOR A MAGAZINE!! SHE'S REALLY POPULAR!!
SHE HAS GREAT STYLE AND A PERFECT FACE!!
AND SHE'S TOUGH AS NAILS!!
SOMETIMES IT'S SCARY, BECAUSE SHE TELLS IT LIKE IT IS!
BUT I LOVE IT!! ALL THAT FIERCE ATTITUDE BEHIND A CUTESY FACE!!
DUN
Y-YEAH? THAT'S, UM...
AH!!
SORRY!! I WAS TOTALLY FANGIRLING!!
FAN-GIRL?
FUJI-SHIRO-SAN IS GETTING ALL THE COMPLIMENTS TODAY.
......
FUJI-SHIRO-SAN?

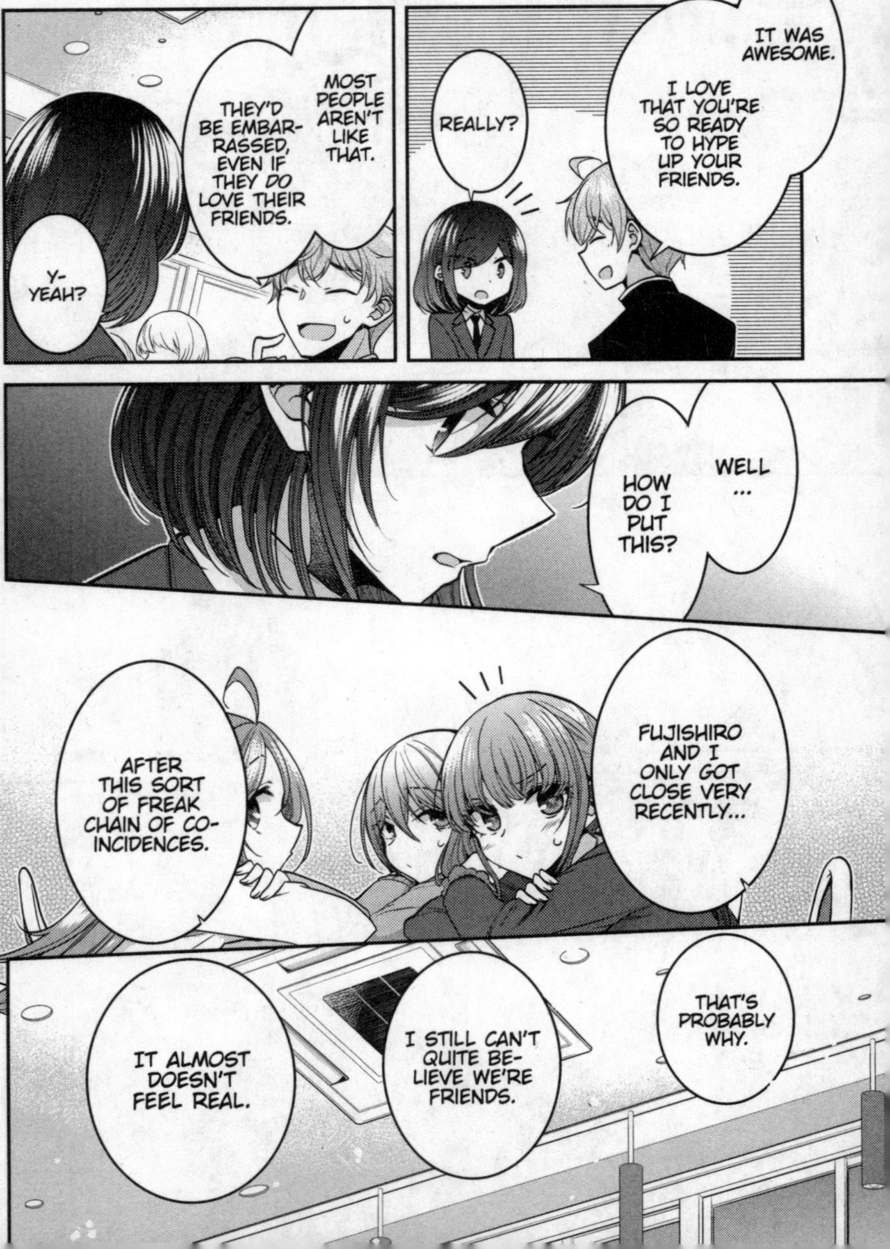
IT WAS AWESOME.
I LOVE THAT YOU'RE SO READY TO HYPE UP YOUR FRIENDS.
REALLY?
MOST PEOPLE AREN'T LIKE THAT.
THEY'D BE EMBARRASSED, EVEN IF THEY *DO* LOVE THEIR FRIENDS.
Y-YEAH?
WELL...
HOW DO I PUT THIS?
FUJISHIRO AND I ONLY GOT CLOSE VERY RECENTLY...
AFTER THIS SORT OF FREAK CHAIN OF COINCIDENCES.
THAT'S PROBABLY WHY.
I STILL CAN'T QUITE BELIEVE WE'RE FRIENDS.
IT ALMOST DOESN'T FEEL REAL.

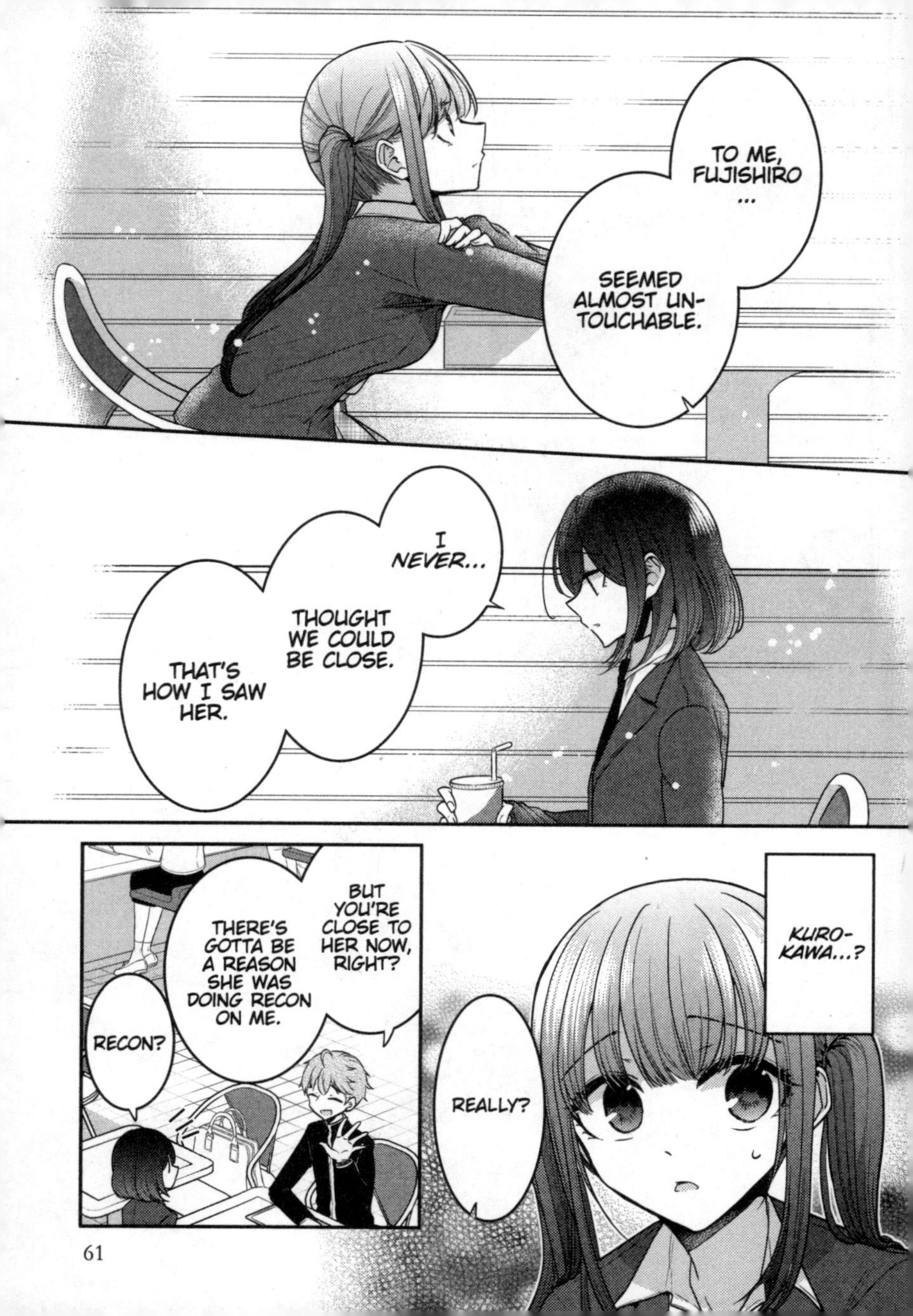
TO ME, FUJISHIRO ...
SEEMED ALMOST UN-TOUCHABLE.
I NEVER...
THOUGHT WE COULD BE CLOSE.
THAT'S HOW I SAW HER.
KURO-KAWA...?
REALLY?
BUT YOU'RE CLOSE TO HER NOW, RIGHT?
THERE'S GOTTA BE A REASON SHE WAS DOING RECON ON ME.
RECON?

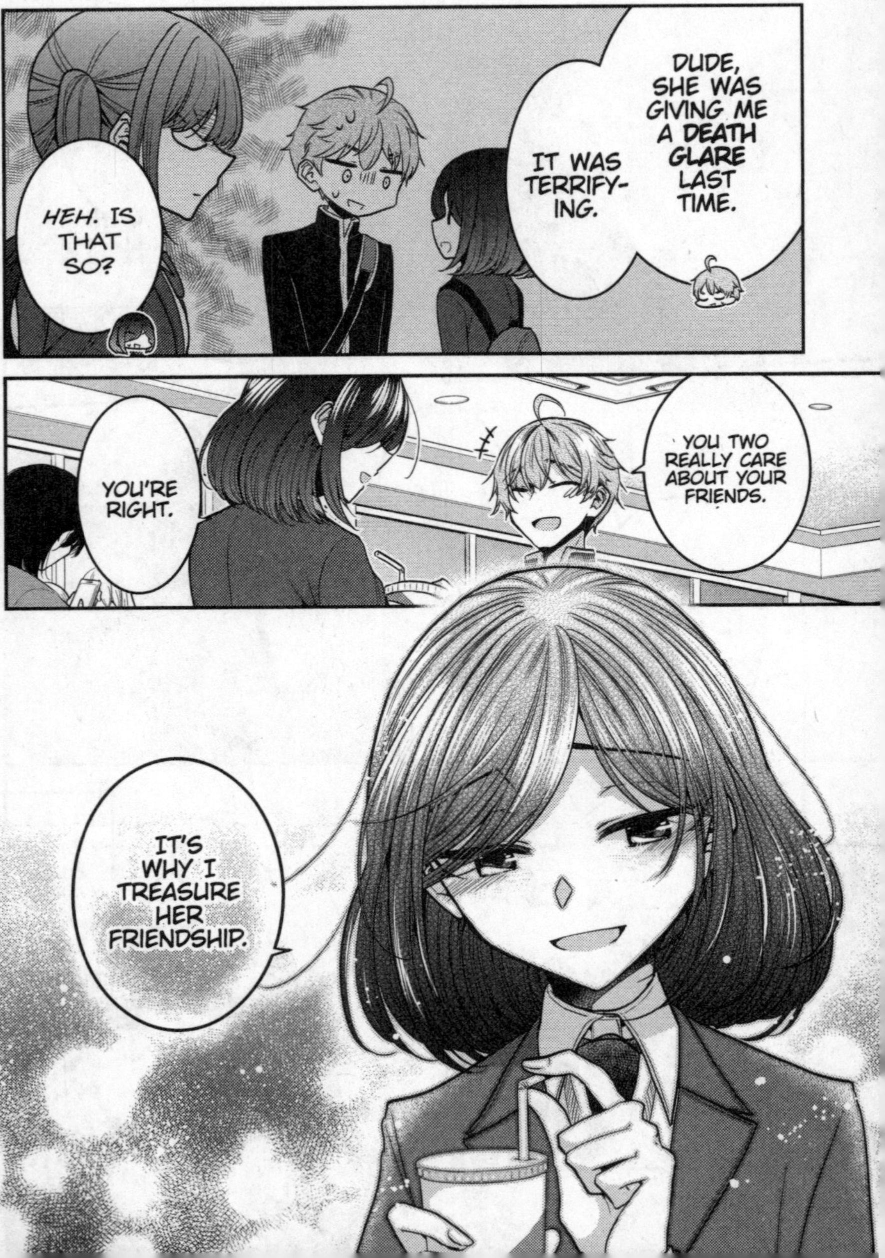
DUDE, SHE WAS GIVING ME A DEATH GLARE LAST TIME.
IT WAS TERRIFY-ING.
HEH. IS THAT SO?
YOU TWO REALLY CARE ABOUT YOUR FRIENDS.
YOU'RE RIGHT.
IT'S WHY I TREASURE HER FRIENDSHIP.

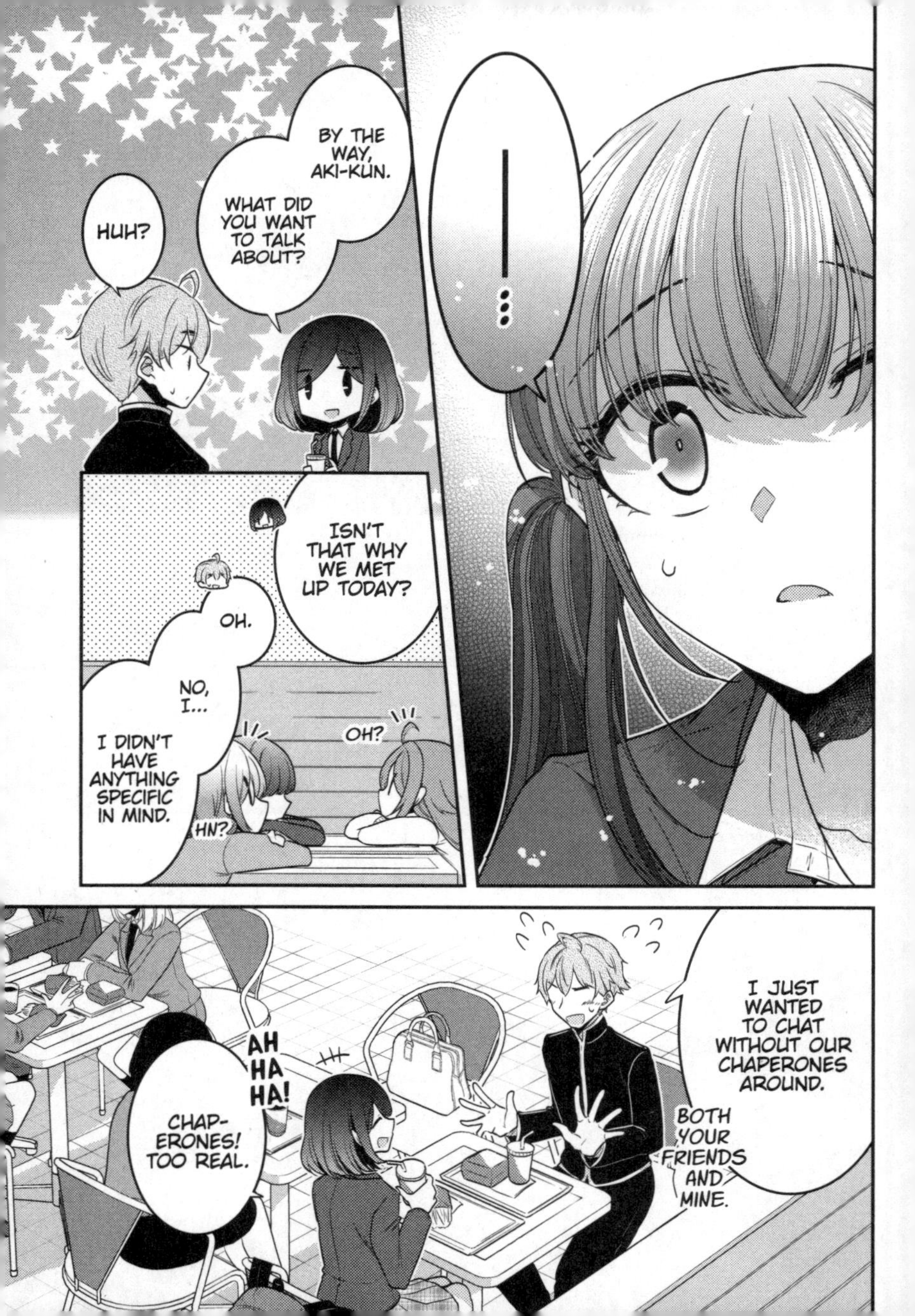
—...
BY THE WAY, AKI-KUN.
WHAT DID YOU WANT TO TALK ABOUT?
HUH?
ISN'T THAT WHY WE MET UP TODAY?
OH.
OH?
NO, I...
I DIDN'T HAVE ANYTHING SPECIFIC IN MIND.
HN?
I JUST WANTED TO CHAT WITHOUT OUR CHAPERONES AROUND.
BOTH YOUR FRIENDS AND MINE.
AH HA HA!
CHAP-ERONES! TOO REAL.

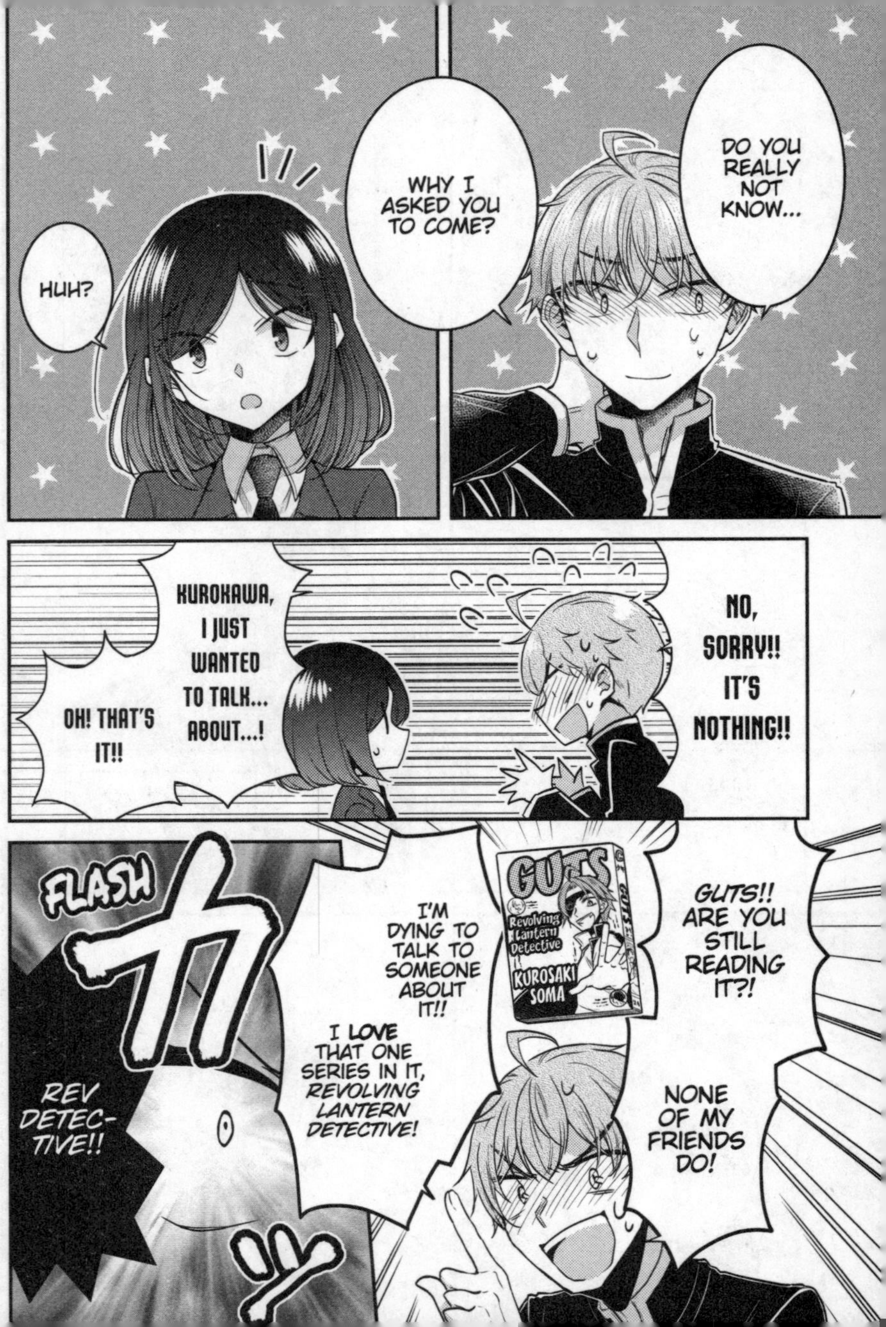
DO YOU REALLY NOT KNOW...
WHY I ASKED YOU TO COME?
HUH?
NO, SORRY!! IT'S NOTHING!!
KUROKAWA, I JUST WANTED TO TALK... ABOUT...!
OH! THAT'S IT!!
GUTS!! ARE YOU STILL READING IT?!
GUTS
Revolving Lantern Detective
KUROSAKI SOMA
I'M DYING TO TALK TO SOMEONE ABOUT IT!!
NONE OF MY FRIENDS DO!
I LOVE THAT ONE SERIES IN IT, REVOLVING LANTERN DETECTIVE!
FLASH
REV DETECTIVE!!

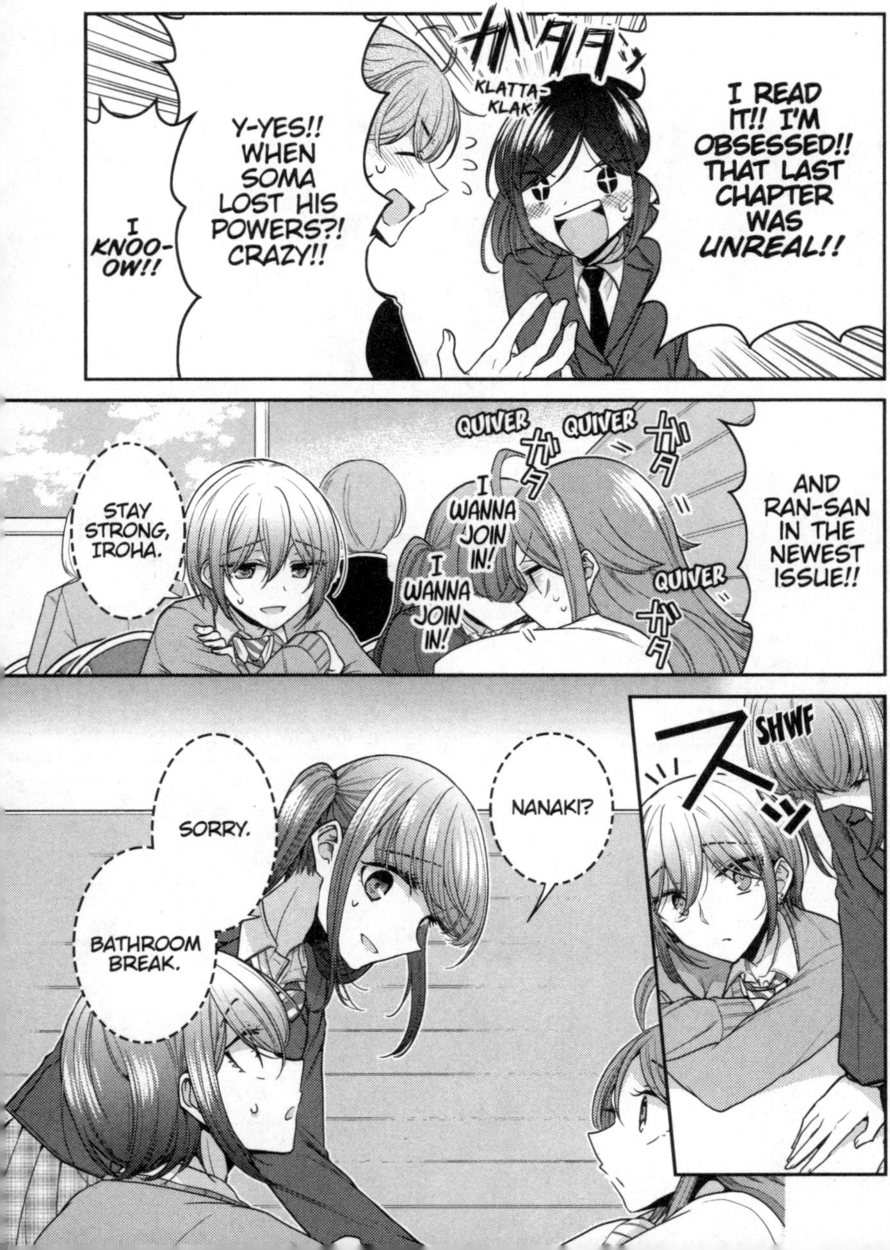
I READ IT!! I'M OBSESSED!! THAT LAST CHAPTER WAS UNREAL!!
カタタッ
KLATTA-KLAK
Y-YES!! WHEN SOMA LOST HIS POWERS?! CRAZY!!
I KNOO-OW!!
AND RAN-SAN IN THE NEWEST ISSUE!!
ガタ
QUIVER
QUIVER
ガタ
QUIVER
ガタ
I WANNA JOIN IN!
I WANNA JOIN IN!
STAY STRONG, IROHA.
スッ
SHWF
NANAKI?
SORRY.
BATHROOM BREAK.

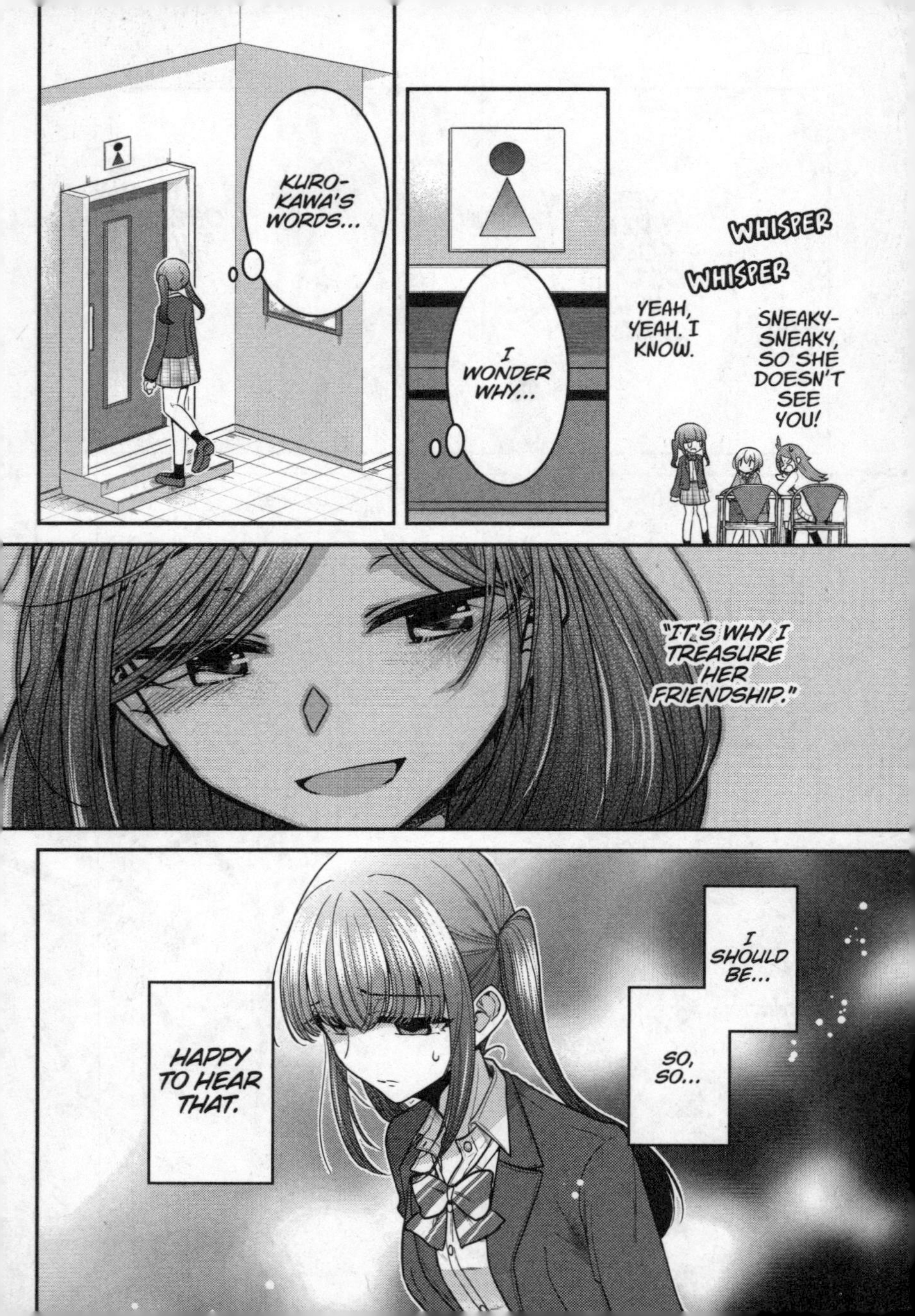
WHISPER
WHISPER
SNEAKY-SNEAKY, SO SHE DOESN'T SEE YOU!
YEAH, YEAH. I KNOW.
I WONDER WHY...
KURO-KAWA'S WORDS...
"IT'S WHY I TREASURE HER FRIENDSHIP."
I SHOULD BE...
SO, SO...
HAPPY TO HEAR THAT.

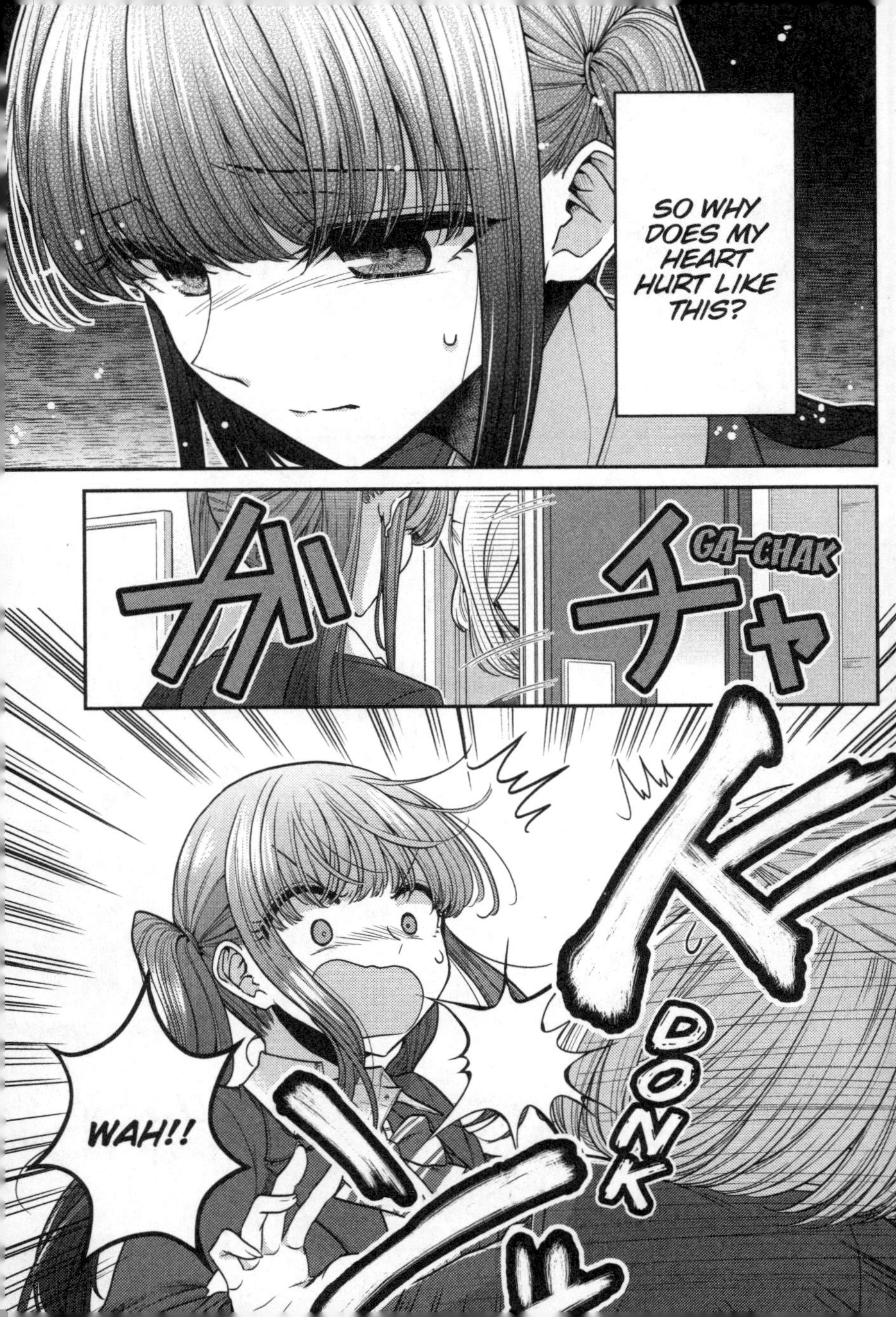
SO WHY DOES MY HEART HURT LIKE THIS?
GA-CHAK
DONK
WAH!!

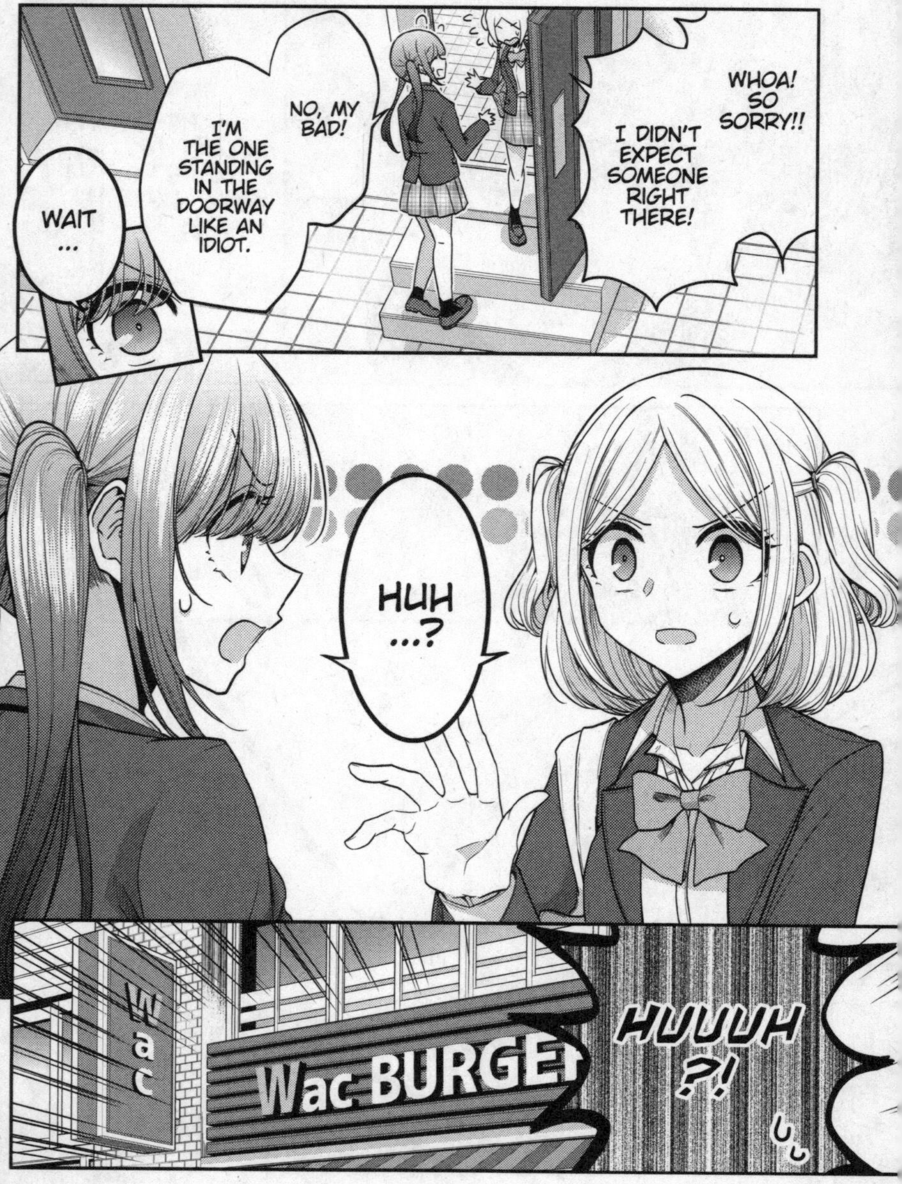
WHOA! SO SORRY!!
I DIDN'T EXPECT SOMEONE RIGHT THERE!
NO, MY BAD!
I'M THE ONE STANDING IN THE DOORWAY LIKE AN IDIOT.
WAIT ...
HUH ...?
HUUUH ?!
Wac BURGER
Wac

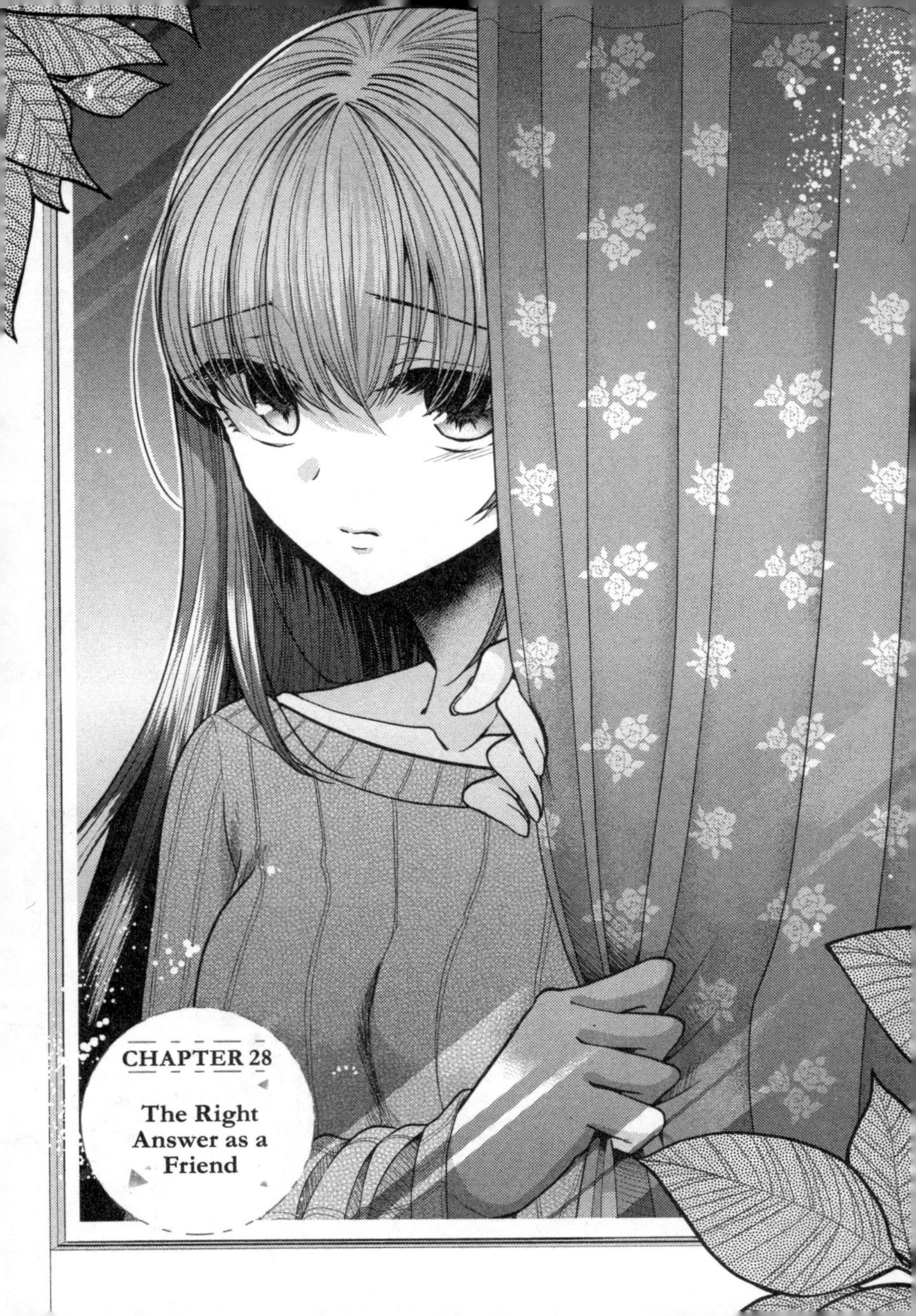
CHAPTER 28
The Right Answer as a Friend

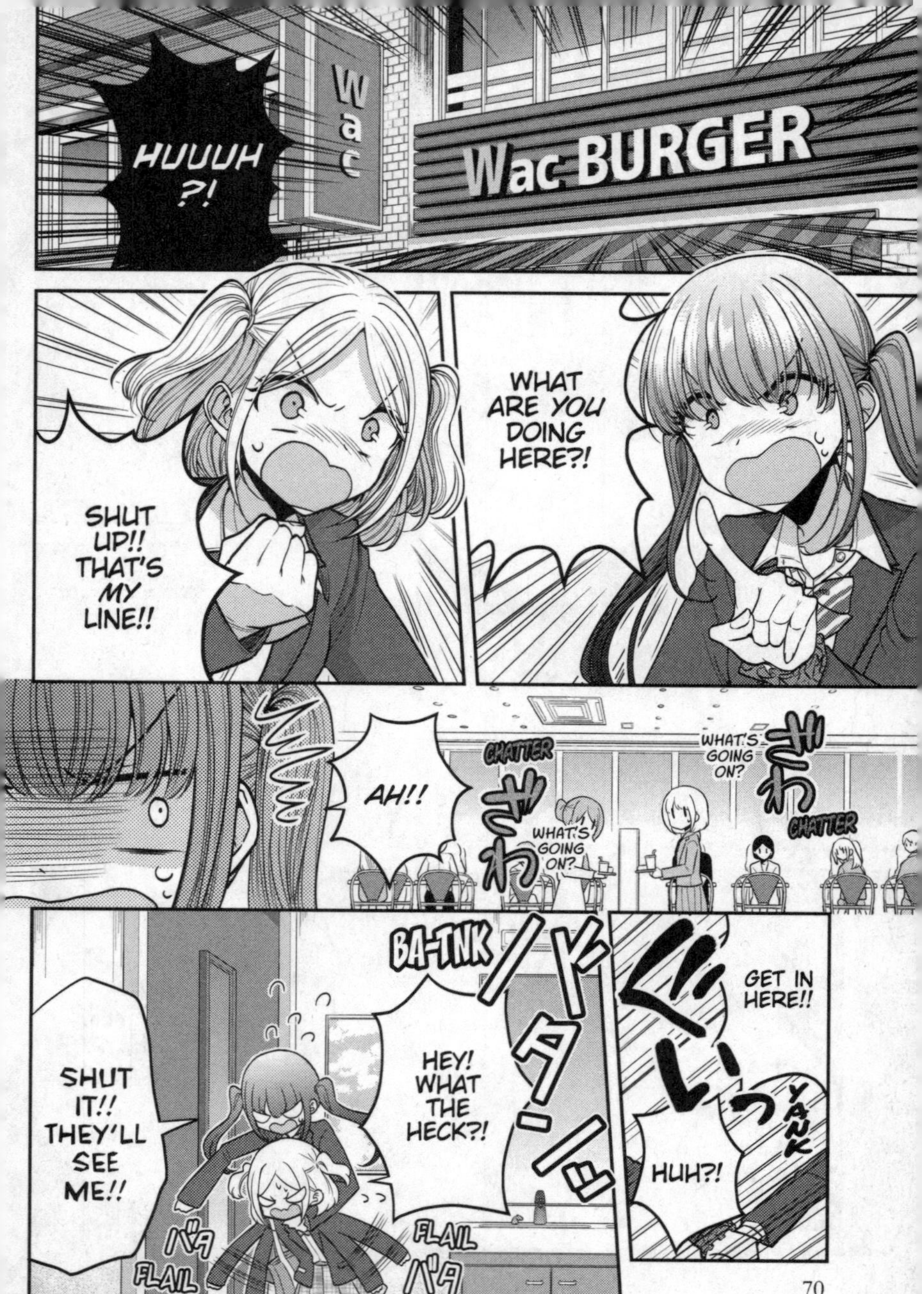
Wac BURGER
Wac
HUUUH ?!
WHAT ARE YOU DOING HERE?!
SHUT UP!! THAT'S MY LINE!!
ざわ
WHAT'S GOING ON?
CHATTER
ざわ
CHATTER
WHAT'S GOING ON?
AH!!
GET IN HERE!!
くいっ
YANK
HUH?!
ドターンッ
BA-TNK
HEY! WHAT THE HECK?!
SHUT IT!! THEY'LL SEE ME!!
FLAIL
バタ
バタ
FLAIL

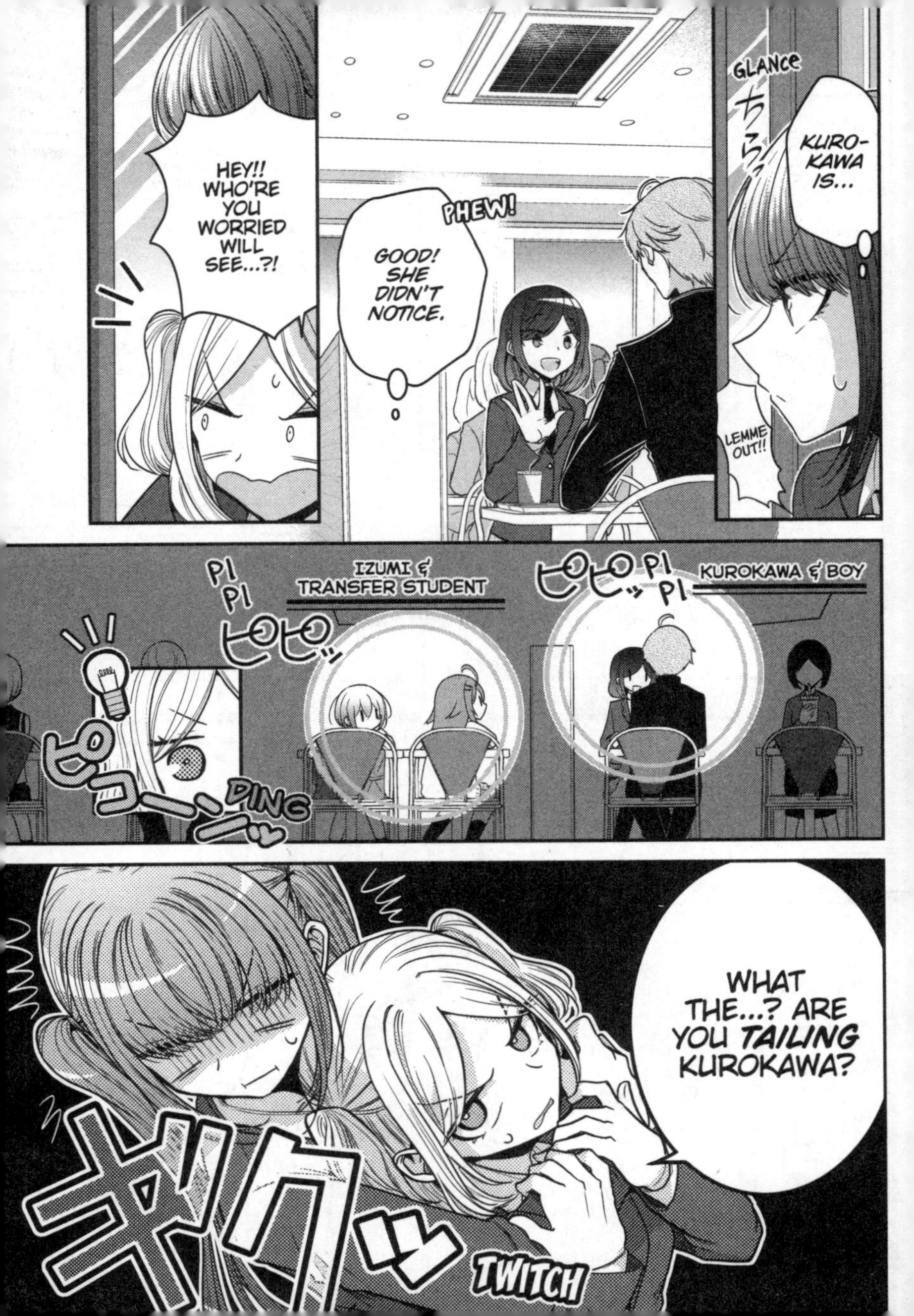
GLANCE
KURO-KAWA IS...
LEMME OUT!!
PHEW!
GOOD! SHE DIDN'T NOTICE.
HEY!! WHO'RE YOU WORRIED WILL SEE...?!
KUROKAWA & BOY
PI PI
IZUMI & TRANSFER STUDENT
PI PI
DING
WHAT THE...? ARE YOU *TAILING* KUROKAWA?
TWITCH

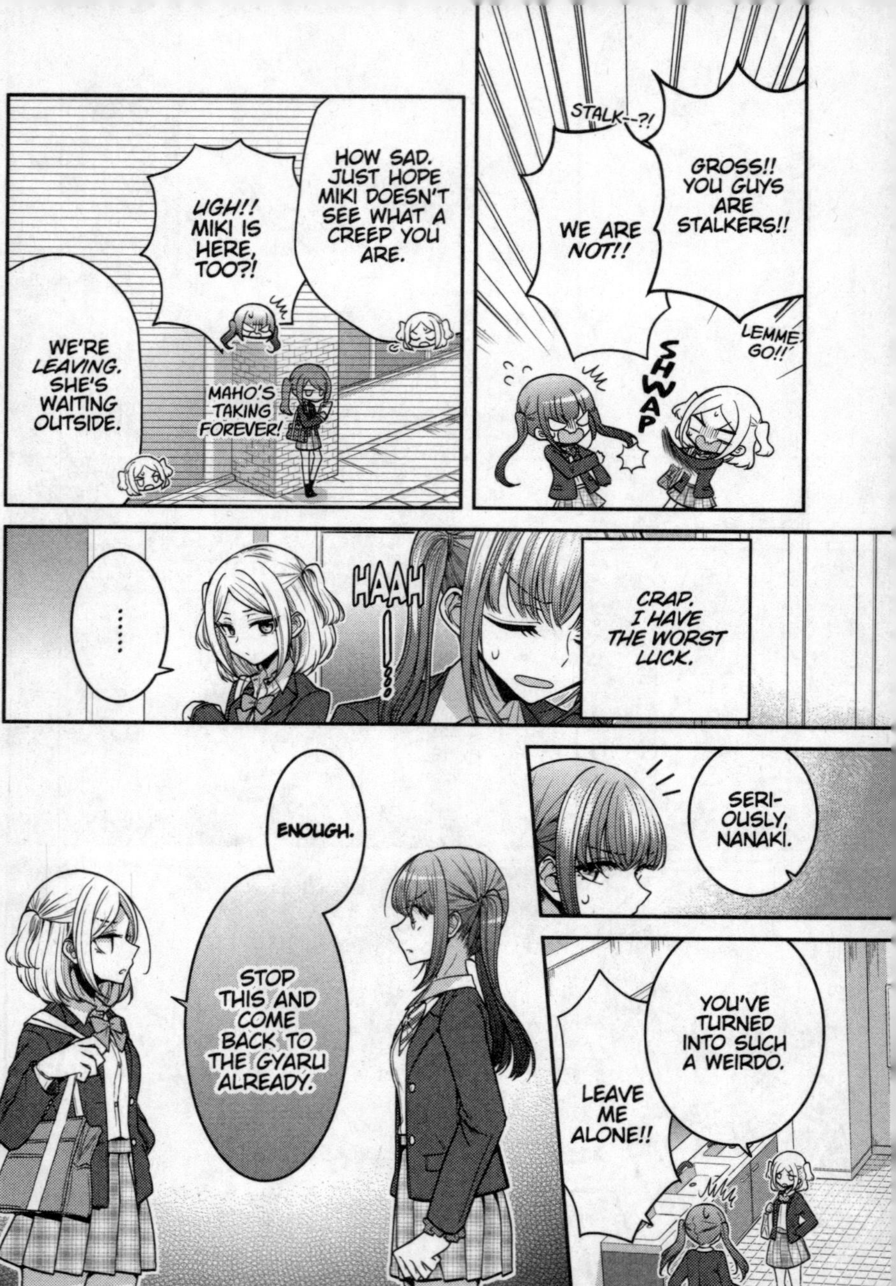
STALK--?!
GROSS!! YOU GUYS ARE STALKERS!!
WE ARE NOT!!
LEMME GO!!
SHWAP
HOW SAD. JUST HOPE MIKI DOESN'T SEE WHAT A CREEP YOU ARE.
UGH!! MIKI IS HERE, TOO?!
WE'RE LEAVING. SHE'S WAITING OUTSIDE.
MAHO'S TAKING FOREVER!
CRAP. I HAVE THE WORST LUCK.
HAAAH
......
SERI-OUSLY, NANAKI.
YOU'VE TURNED INTO SUCH A WEIRDO.
LEAVE ME ALONE!!
ENOUGH.
STOP THIS AND COME BACK TO THE GYARU ALREADY.

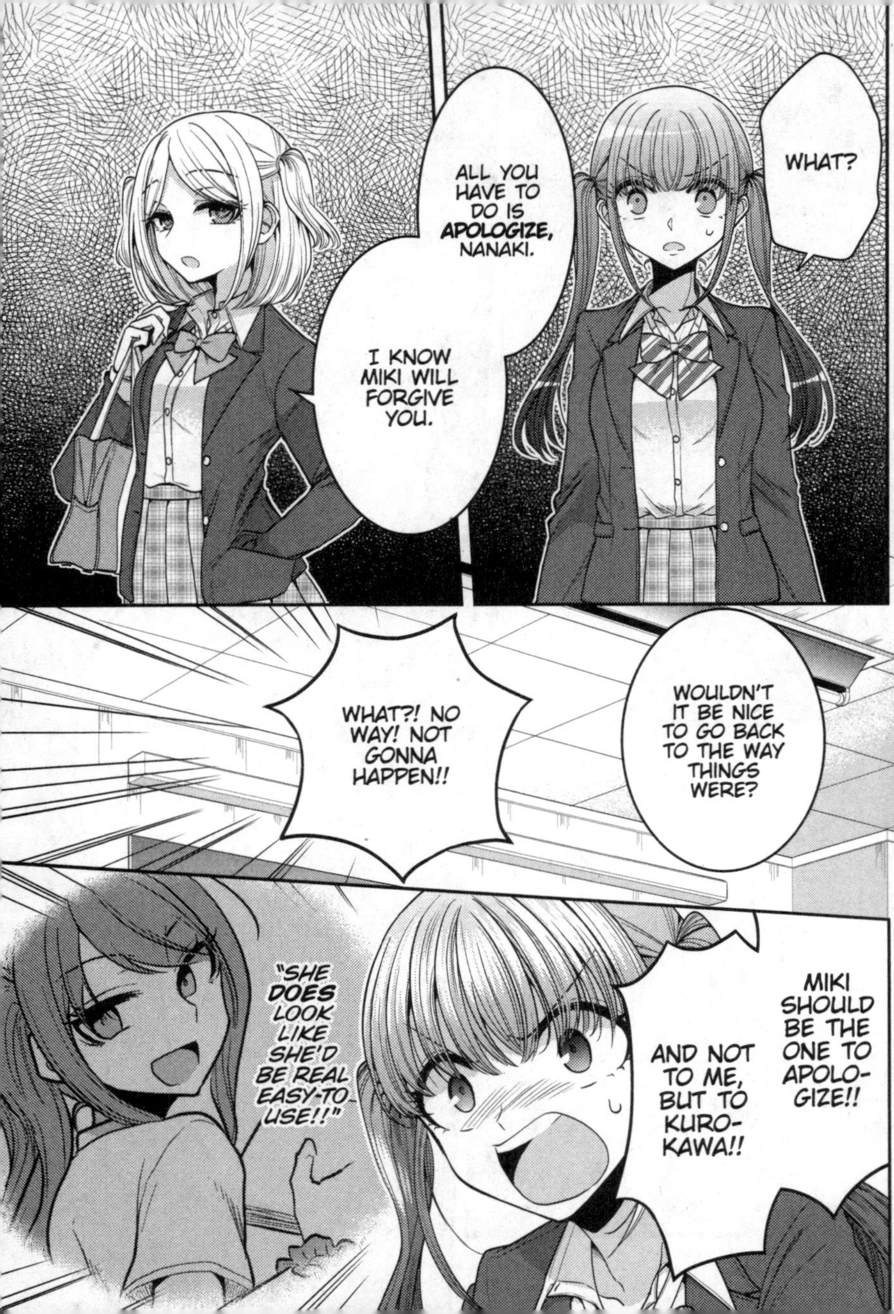
WHAT?
ALL YOU HAVE TO DO IS APOLOGIZE, NANAKI.
I KNOW MIKI WILL FORGIVE YOU.
WOULDN'T IT BE NICE TO GO BACK TO THE WAY THINGS WERE?
WHAT?! NO WAY! NOT GONNA HAPPEN!!
MIKI SHOULD BE THE ONE TO APOLOGIZE!!
AND NOT TO ME, BUT TO KUROKAWA!!
"SHE DOES LOOK LIKE SHE'D BE REAL EASY-TO-USE!!"

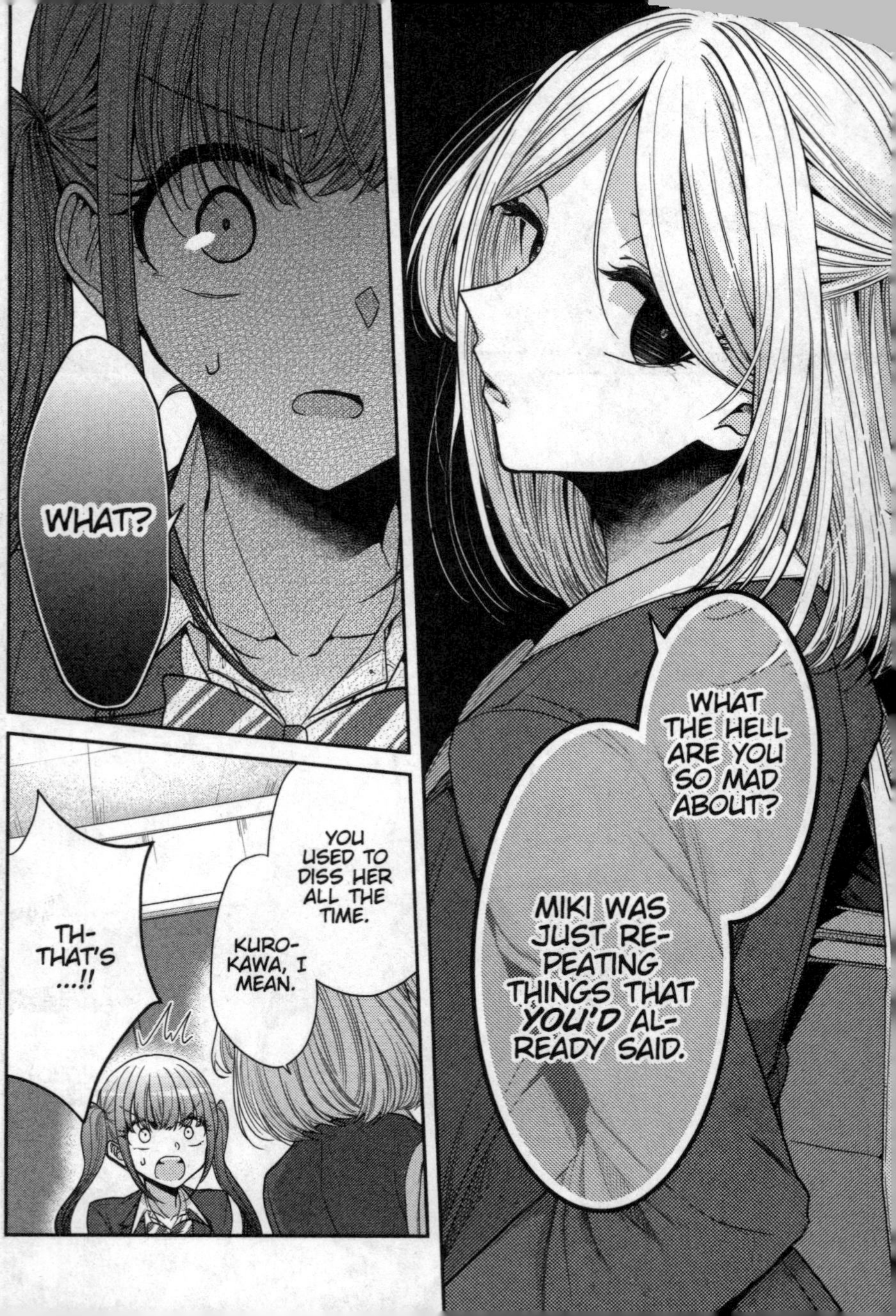
WHAT THE HELL ARE YOU SO MAD ABOUT?
MIKI WAS JUST RE-PEATING THINGS THAT *YOU'D* AL-READY SAID.
WHAT?
YOU USED TO DISS HER ALL THE TIME.
KURO-KAWA, I MEAN.
TH-THAT'S ...!!

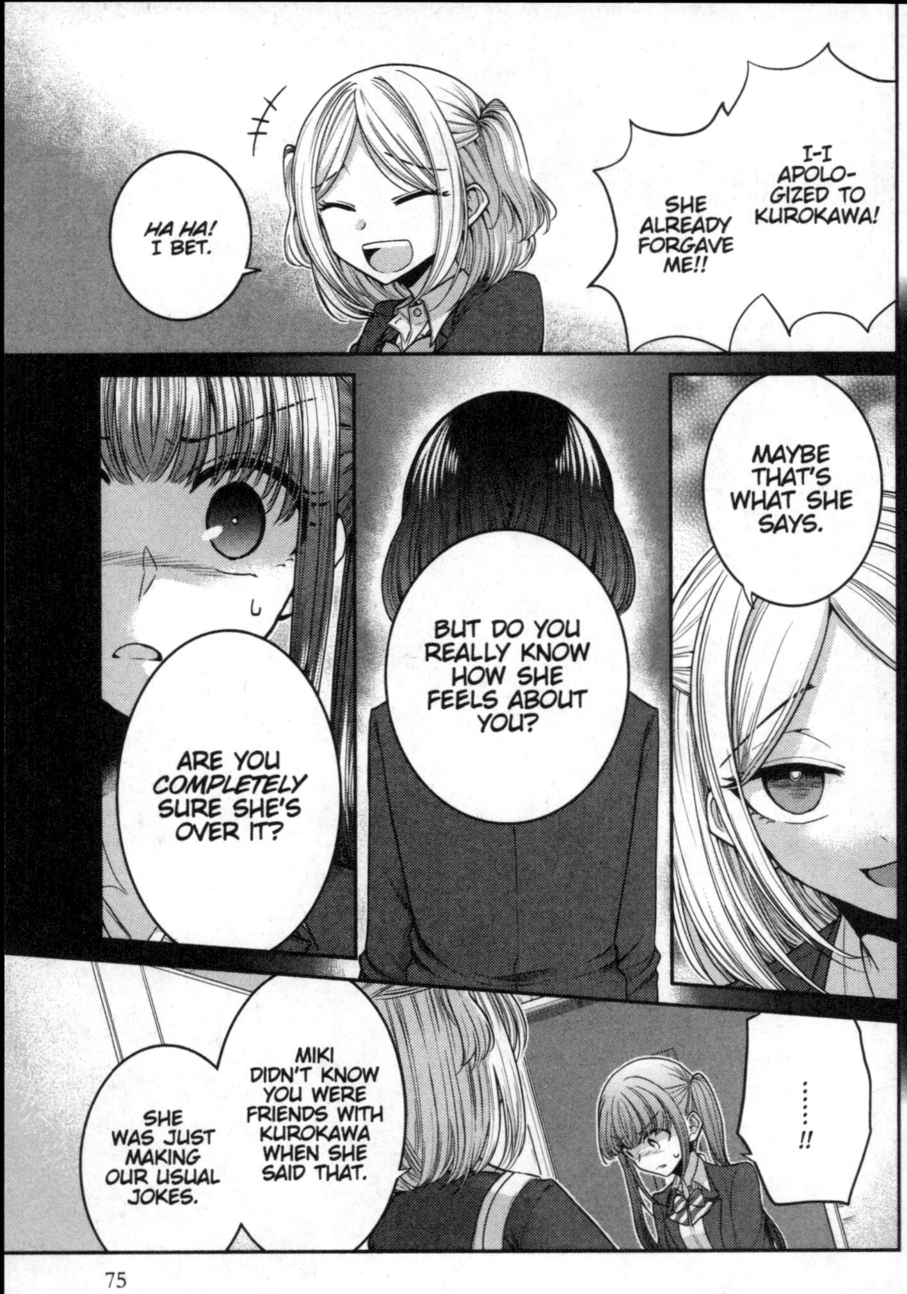
I-I APOLOGIZED TO KUROKAWA!
SHE ALREADY FORGAVE ME!!
HA HA! I BET.
MAYBE THAT'S WHAT SHE SAYS.
BUT DO YOU REALLY KNOW HOW SHE FEELS ABOUT YOU?
ARE YOU *COMPLETELY* SURE SHE'S OVER IT?
......!!
MIKI DIDN'T KNOW YOU WERE FRIENDS WITH KUROKAWA WHEN SHE SAID THAT.
SHE WAS JUST MAKING OUR USUAL JOKES.

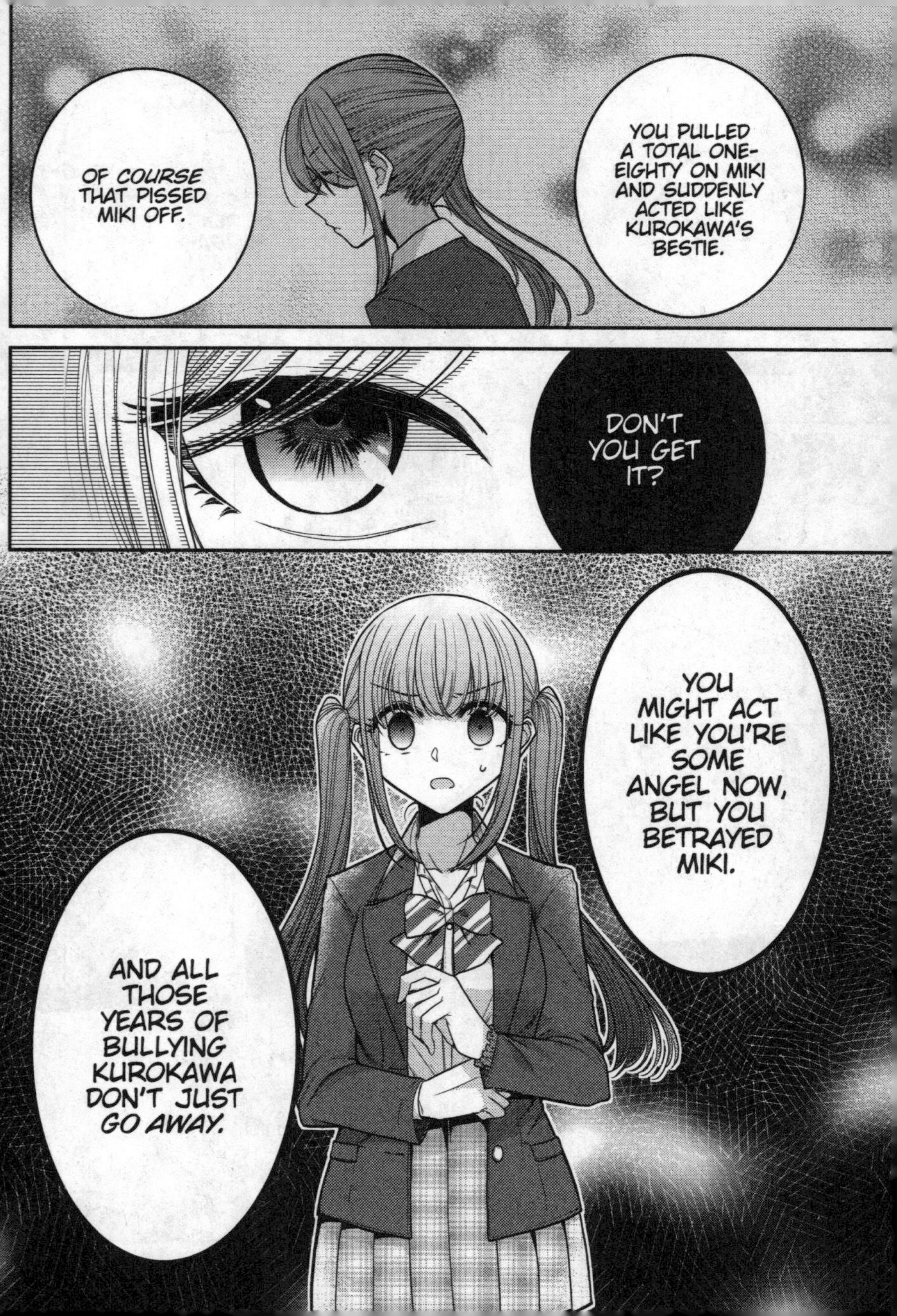
YOU PULLED A TOTAL ONE-EIGHTY ON MIKI AND SUDDENLY ACTED LIKE KUROKAWA'S BESTIE.
OF COURSE THAT PISSED MIKI OFF.
DON'T YOU GET IT?
YOU MIGHT ACT LIKE YOU'RE SOME ANGEL NOW, BUT YOU BETRAYED MIKI.
AND ALL THOSE YEARS OF BULLYING KUROKAWA DON'T JUST GO AWAY.

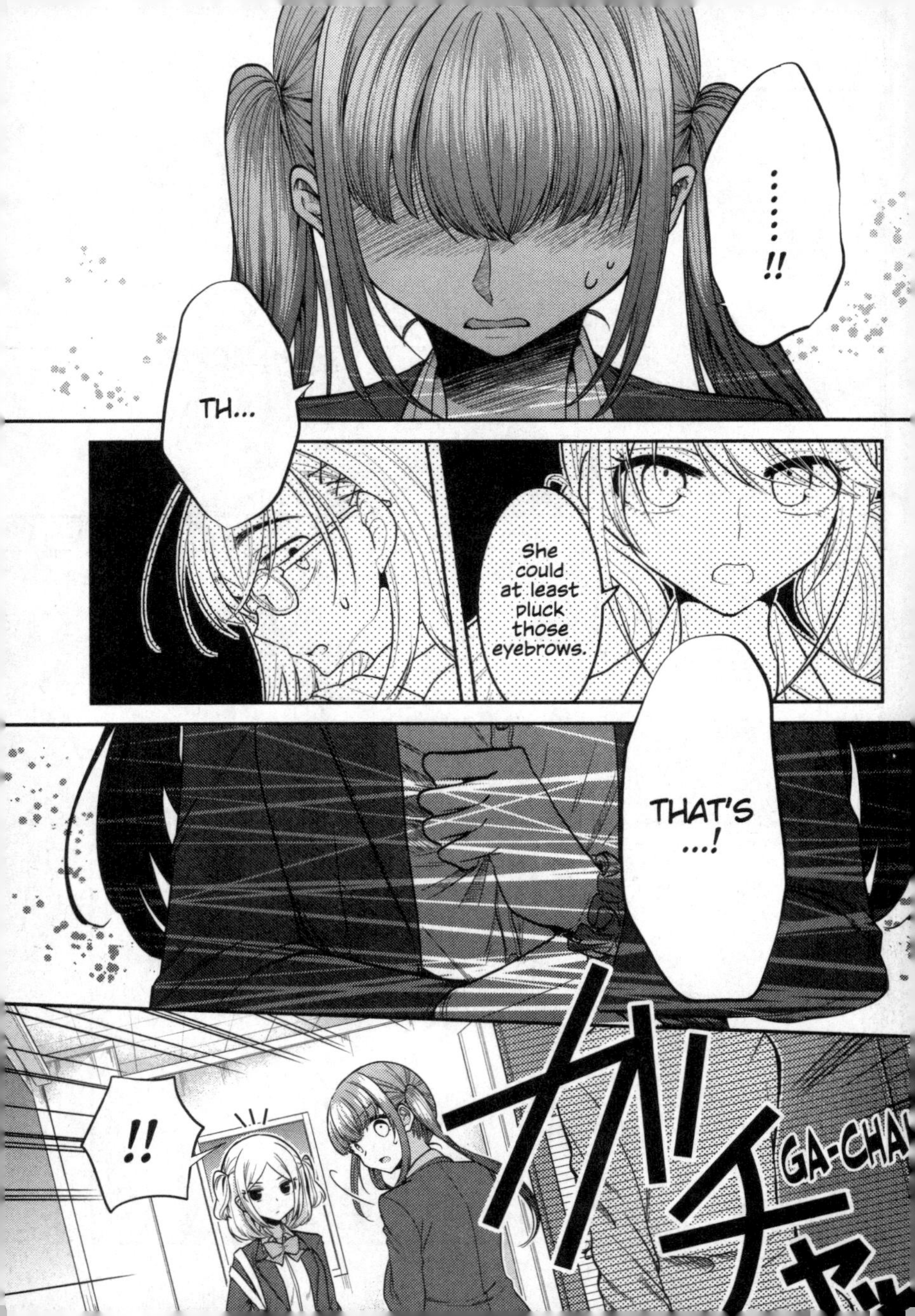
……!!
TH…
She could at least pluck those eyebrows.
THAT'S …!
GA-CHA
!!

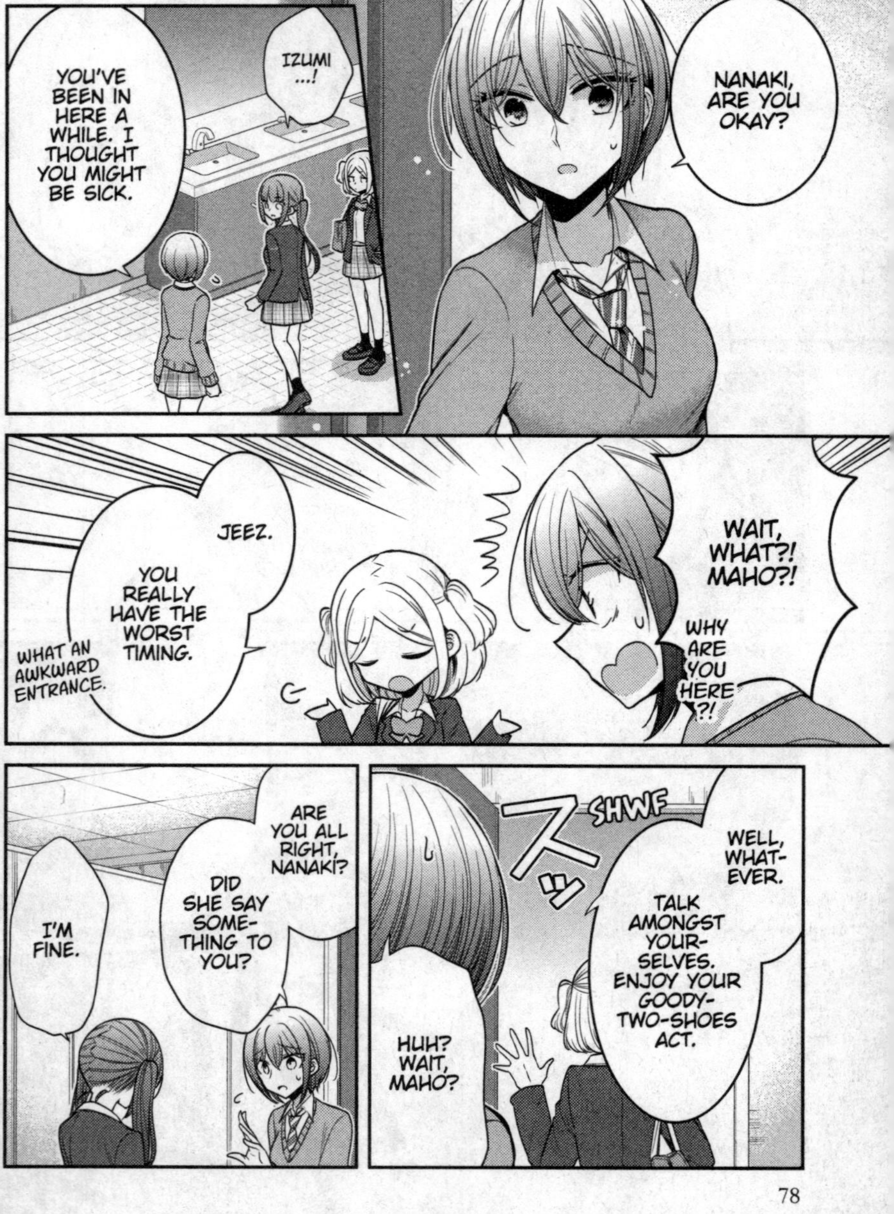
NANAKI, ARE YOU OKAY?
IZUMI ...!
YOU'VE BEEN IN HERE A WHILE. I THOUGHT YOU MIGHT BE SICK.
WAIT, WHAT?! MAHO?!
WHY ARE YOU HERE ?!
JEEZ.
YOU REALLY HAVE THE WORST TIMING.
WHAT AN AWKWARD ENTRANCE.
SHWF
WELL, WHAT-EVER.
TALK AMONGST YOUR-SELVES. ENJOY YOUR GOODY-TWO-SHOES ACT.
HUH? WAIT, MAHO?
ARE YOU ALL RIGHT, NANAKI?
DID SHE SAY SOME-THING TO YOU?
I'M FINE.

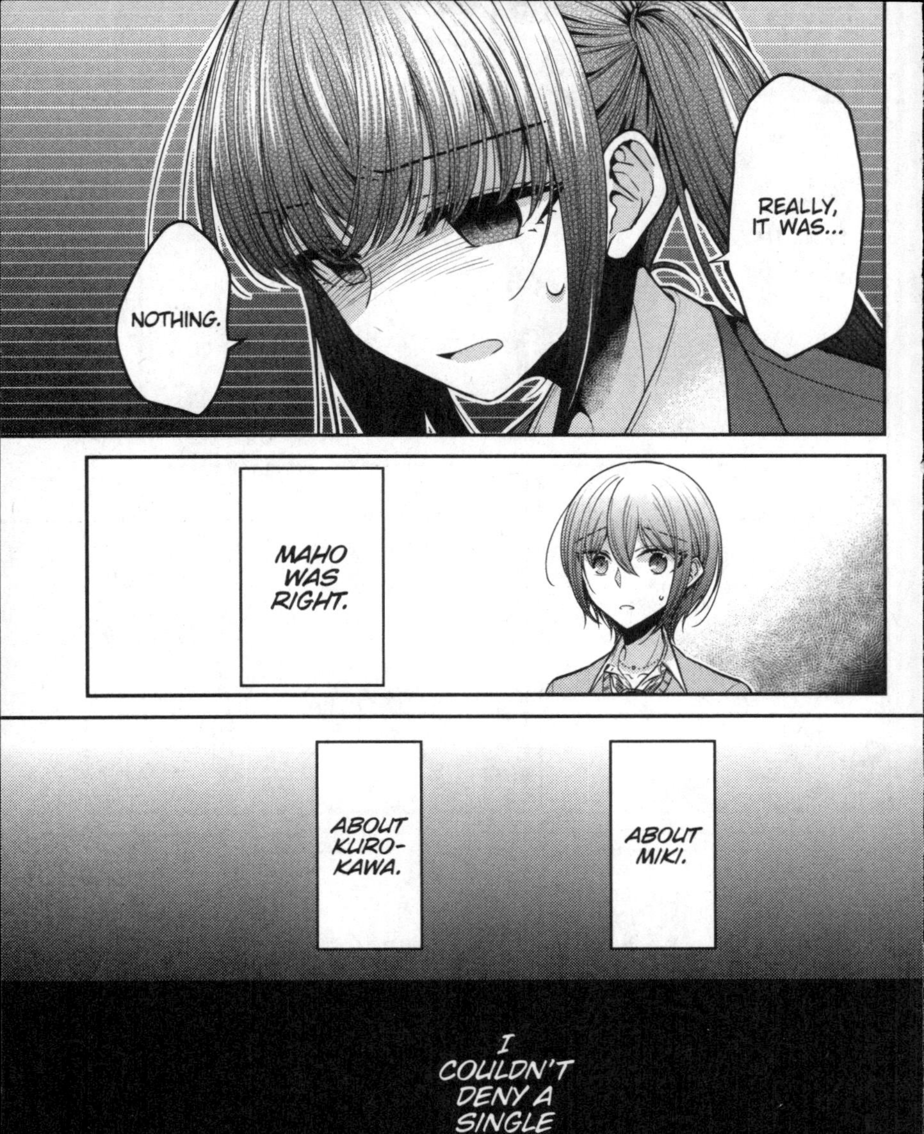
REALLY, IT WAS...
NOTHING.
MAHO WAS RIGHT.
ABOUT MIKI.
ABOUT KURO-KAWA.
I COULDN'T DENY A SINGLE

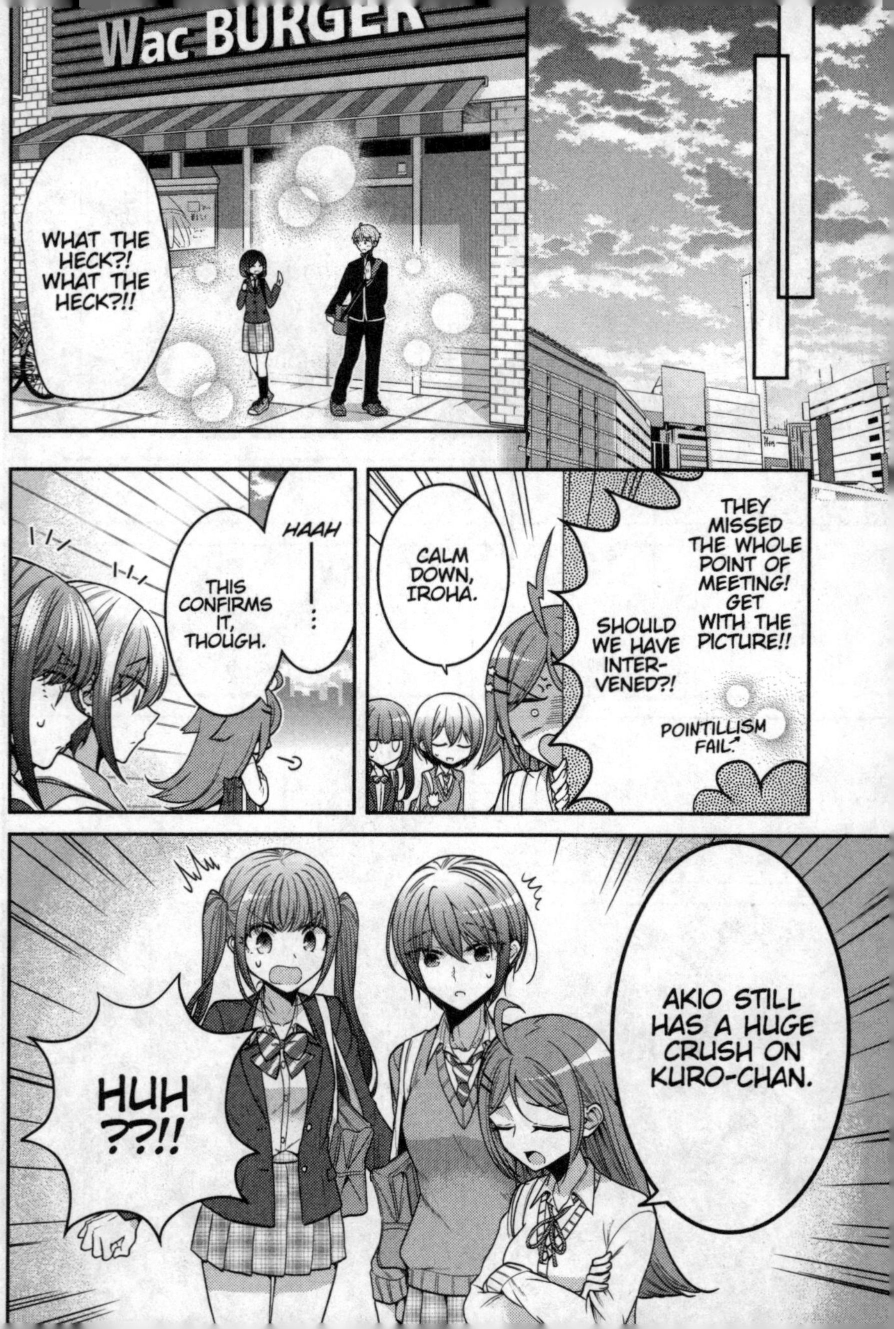
Wac BURGER
WHAT THE HECK?! WHAT THE HECK?!!
THEY MISSED THE WHOLE POINT OF MEETING! GET WITH THE PICTURE!!
SHOULD WE HAVE INTER-VENED?!
CALM DOWN, IROHA.
POINTILLISM FAIL.
HAAH—…
THIS CONFIRMS IT, THOUGH.
AKIO STILL HAS A HUGE CRUSH ON KURO-CHAN.
HUH ??!!

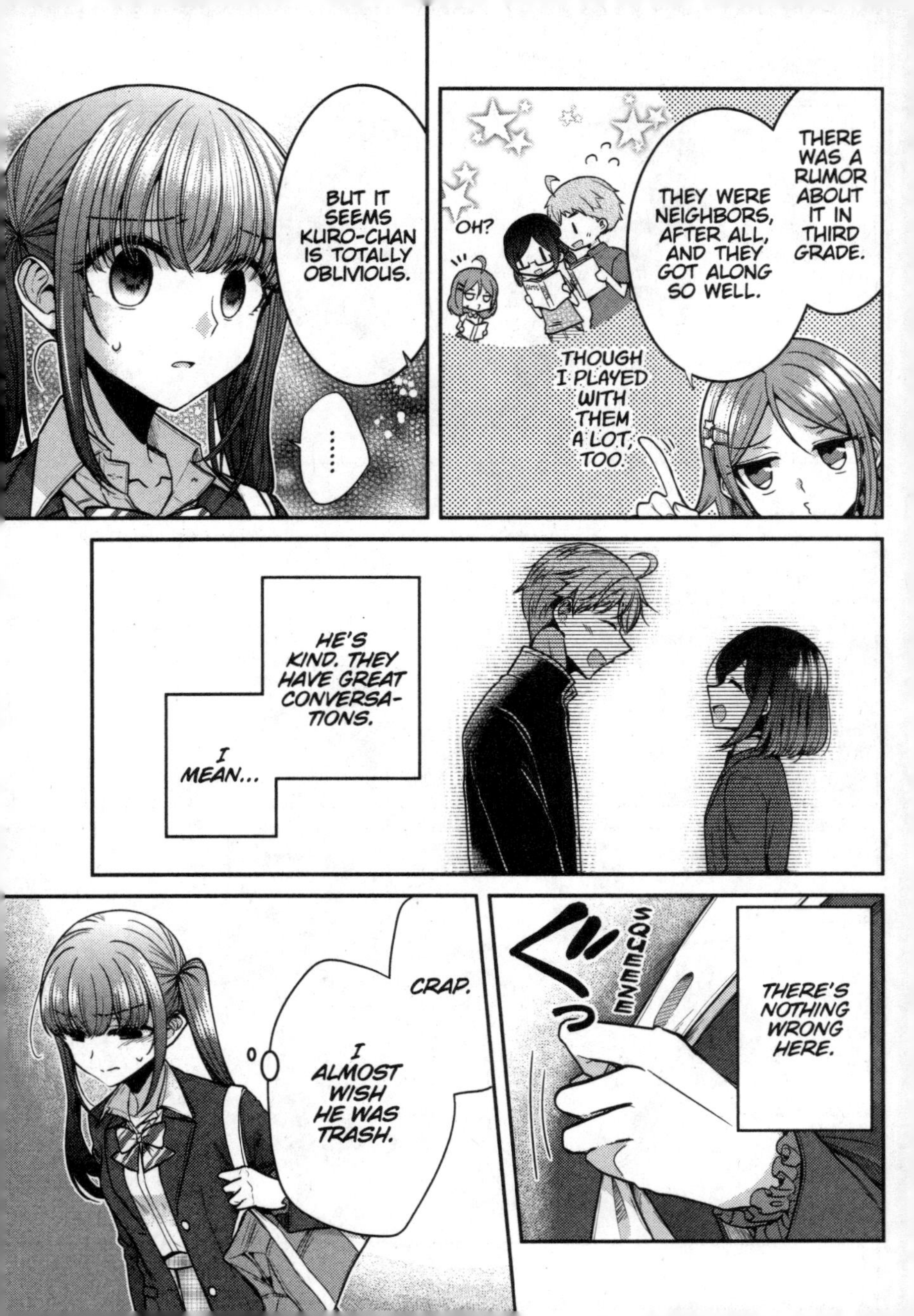
THERE WAS A RUMOR ABOUT IT IN THIRD GRADE.
THEY WERE NEIGHBORS, AFTER ALL, AND THEY GOT ALONG SO WELL.
OH?
THOUGH I PLAYED WITH THEM A LOT, TOO.
BUT IT SEEMS KURO-CHAN IS TOTALLY OBLIVIOUS.
......
HE'S KIND. THEY HAVE GREAT CONVERSA-TIONS.
I MEAN...
SQUEEZE
THERE'S NOTHING WRONG HERE.
CRAP.
I ALMOST WISH HE WAS TRASH.

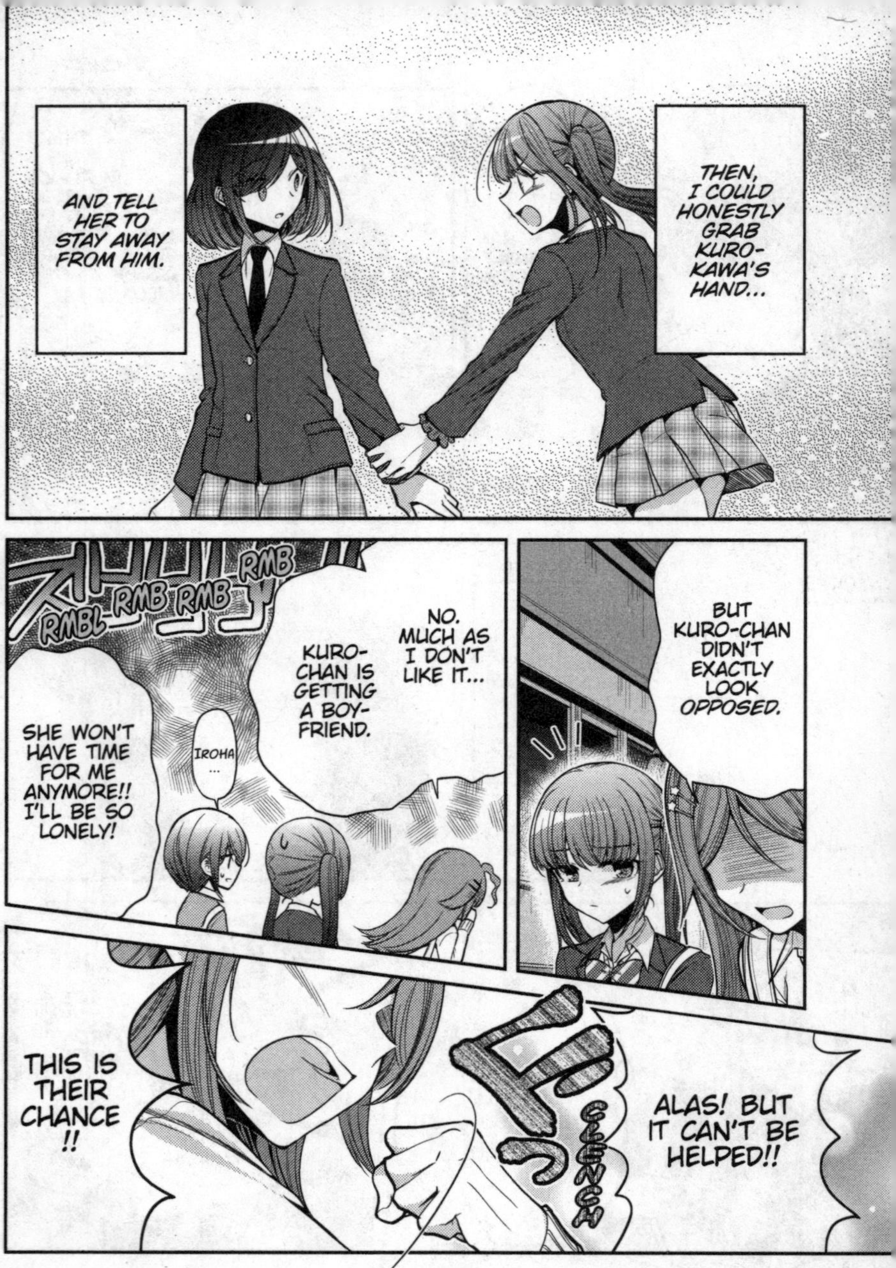
THEN, I COULD HONESTLY GRAB KURO-KAWA'S HAND...
AND TELL HER TO STAY AWAY FROM HIM.
BUT KURO-CHAN DIDN'T EXACTLY LOOK OPPOSED.
RMBL-RMB RMB RMB
NO. MUCH AS I DON'T LIKE IT...
KURO-CHAN IS GETTING A BOY-FRIEND.
SHE WON'T HAVE TIME FOR ME ANYMORE!! I'LL BE SO LONELY!
IROHA ...
ALAS! BUT IT CAN'T BE HELPED!!
CLENCH
THIS IS THEIR CHANCE!!

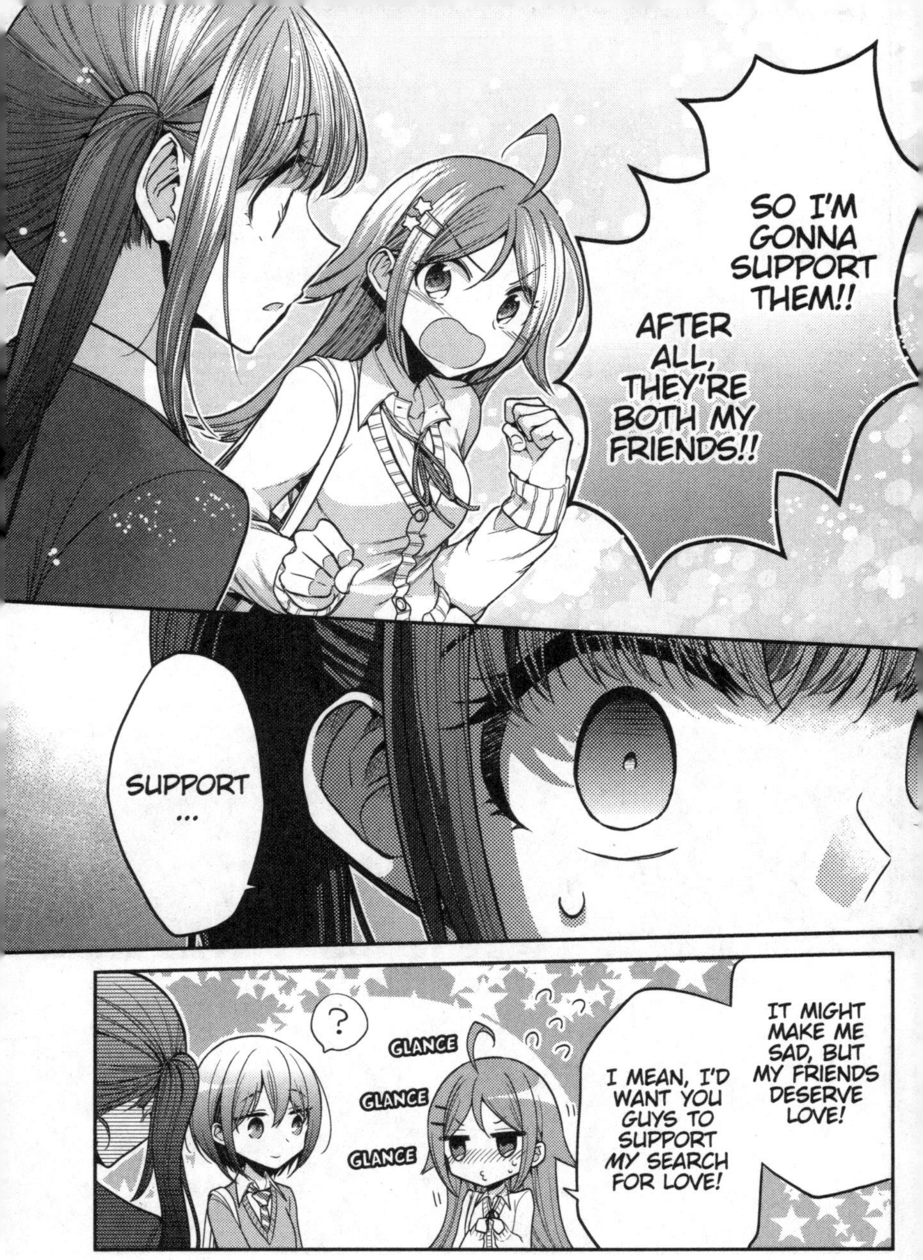
SO I'M GONNA SUPPORT THEM!!
AFTER ALL, THEY'RE BOTH MY FRIENDS!!
SUPPORT ...
IT MIGHT MAKE ME SAD, BUT MY FRIENDS DESERVE LOVE!
I MEAN, I'D WANT YOU GUYS TO SUPPORT MY SEARCH FOR LOVE!
GLANCE
GLANCE
GLANCE
?

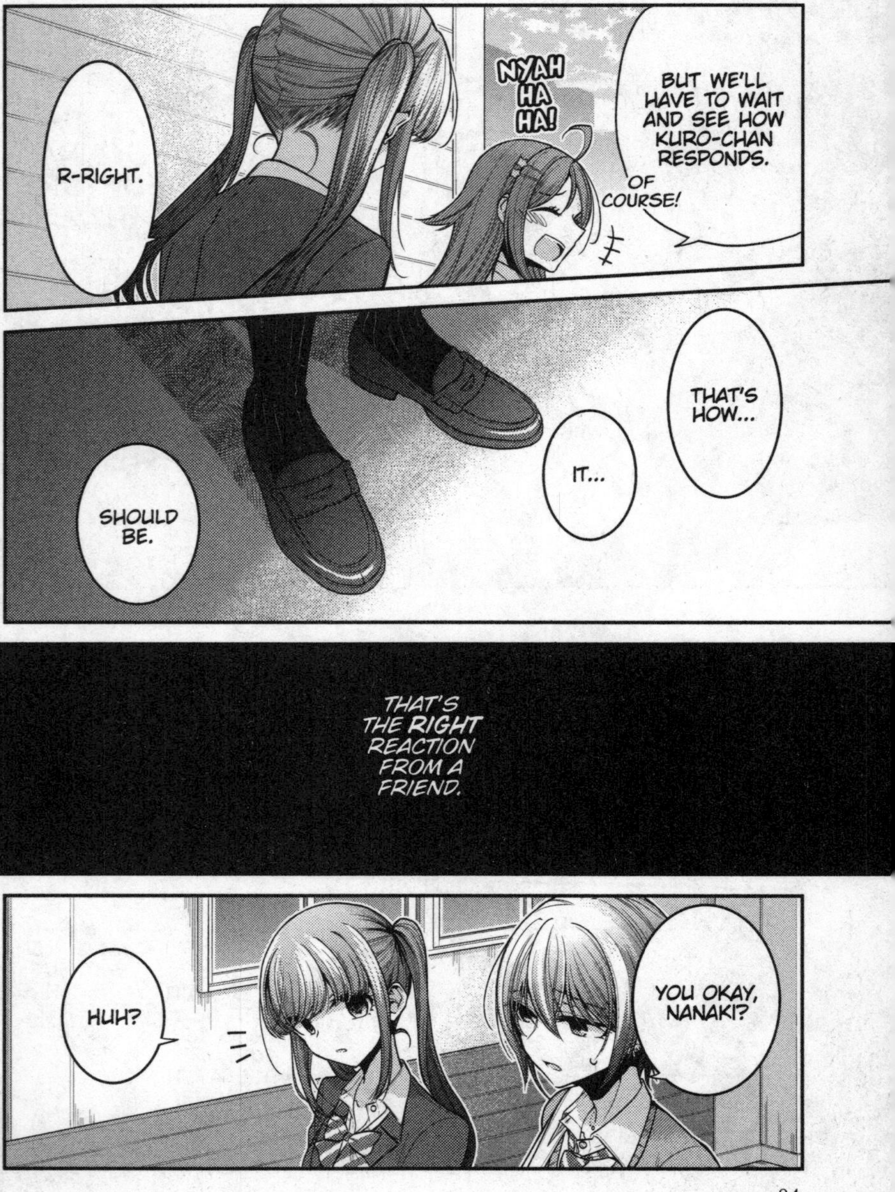
BUT WE'LL HAVE TO WAIT AND SEE HOW KURO-CHAN RESPONDS.
NYAH HA HA!
OF COURSE!
R-RIGHT.
THAT'S HOW...
IT...
SHOULD BE.
THAT'S THE RIGHT REACTION FROM A FRIEND.
YOU OKAY, NANAKI?
HUH?

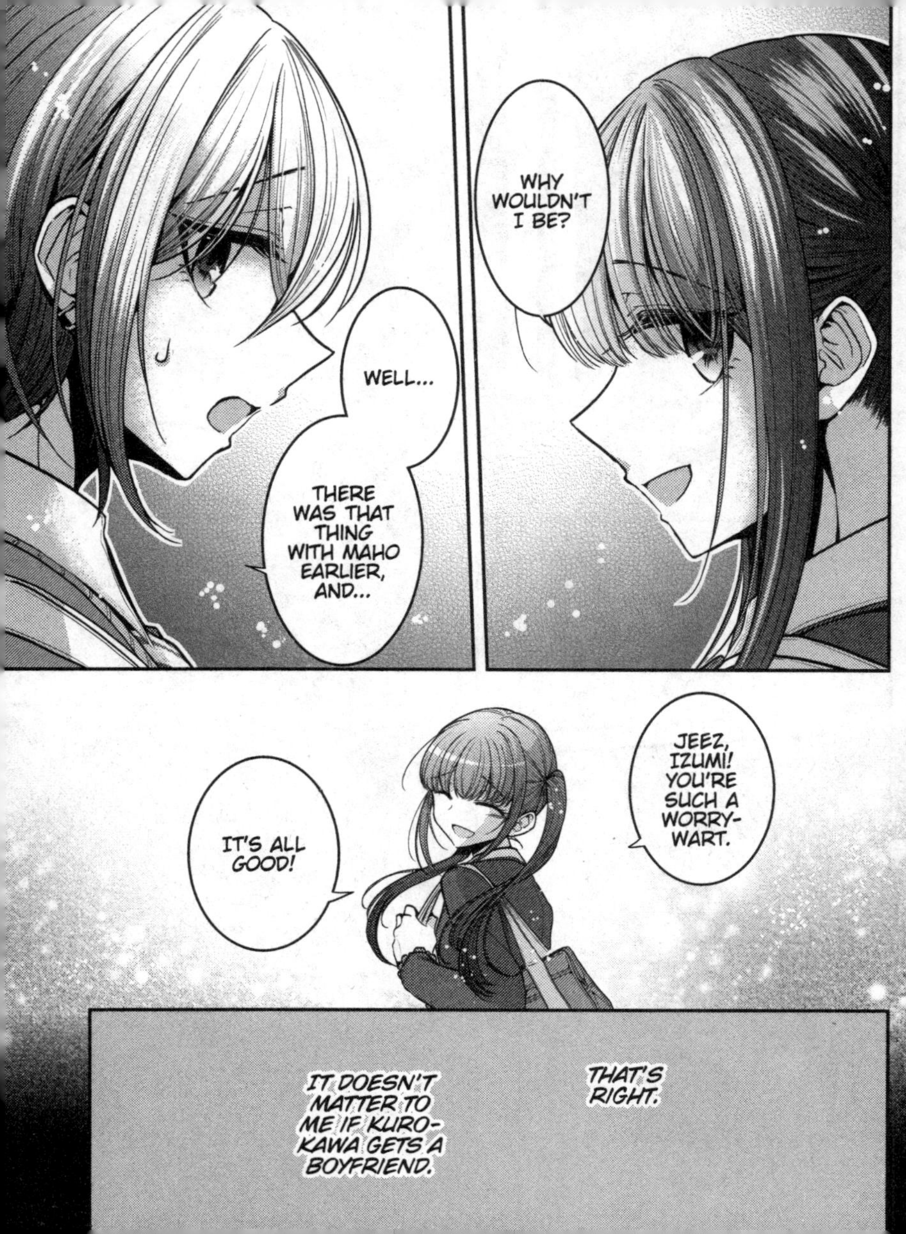
WHY WOULDN'T I BE?
WELL...
THERE WAS THAT THING WITH MAHO EARLIER, AND...
JEEZ, IZUMI! YOU'RE SUCH A WORRY-WART.
IT'S ALL GOOD!
THAT'S RIGHT.
IT DOESN'T MATTER TO ME IF KURO-KAWA GETS A BOYFRIEND.

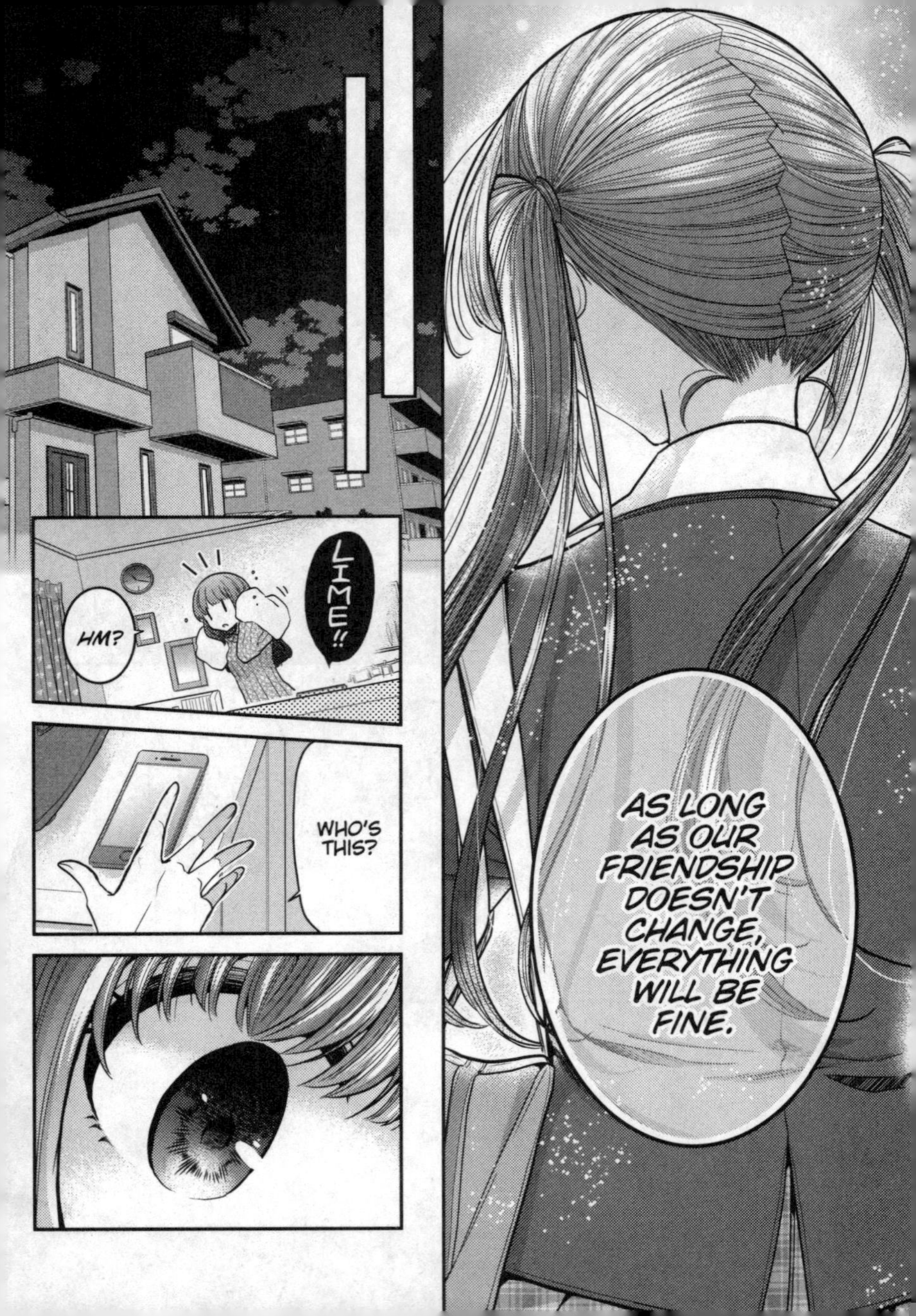
AS LONG AS OUR FRIENDSHIP DOESN'T CHANGE, EVERYTHING WILL BE FINE.
LIME!!
HM?
WHO'S THIS?

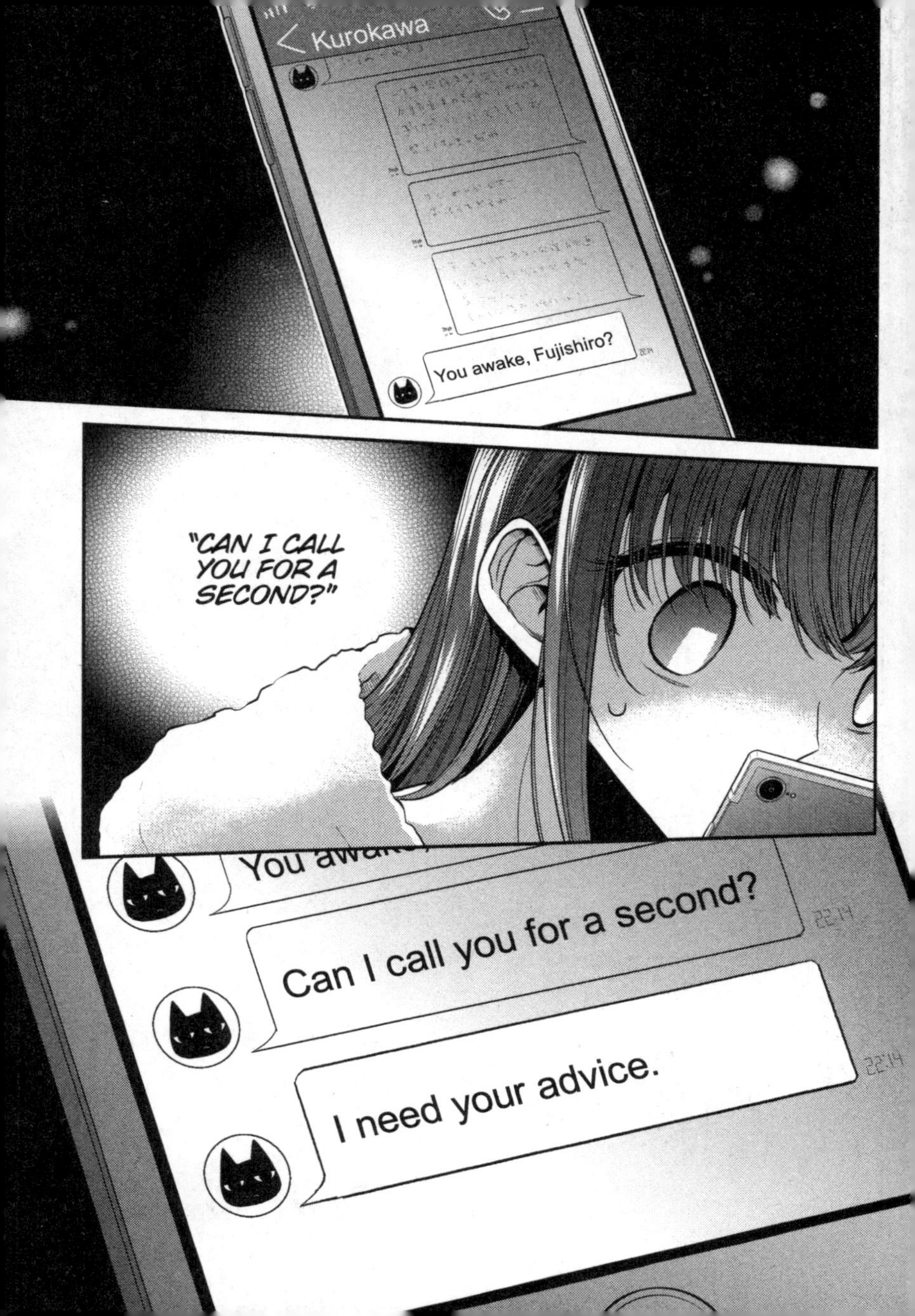
Kurokawa
You awake, Fujishiro?
"CAN I CALL YOU FOR A SECOND?"
Can I call you for a second?
22:14
I need your advice.
22:14

Failed Princesses

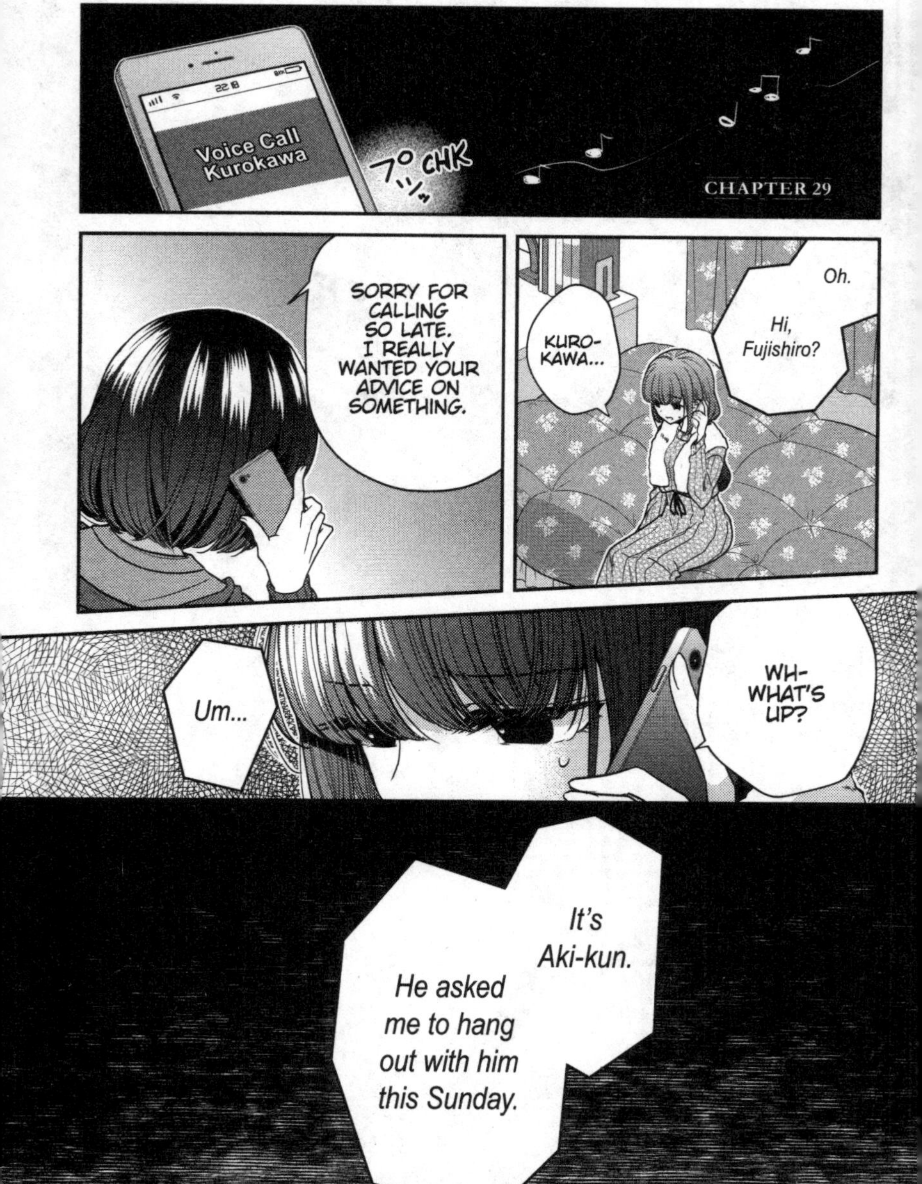
Voice Call
Kurokawa
CHK
CHAPTER 29
Oh.
Hi, Fujishiro?
KURO-KAWA...
SORRY FOR CALLING SO LATE. I REALLY WANTED YOUR ADVICE ON SOMETHING.
WH-WHAT'S UP?
Um...
It's Aki-kun.
He asked me to hang out with him this Sunday.

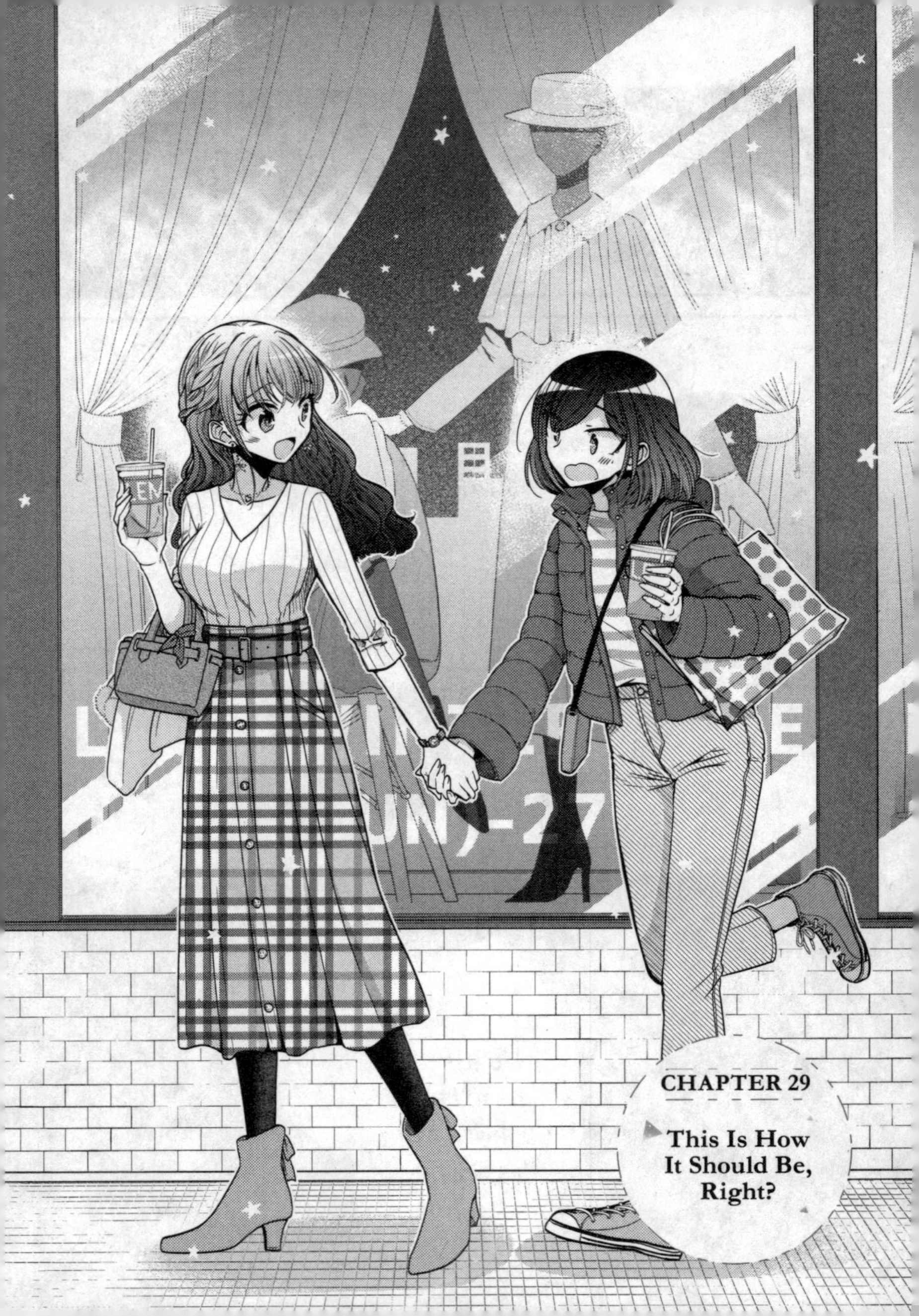
CHAPTER 29
This Is How It Should Be, Right?

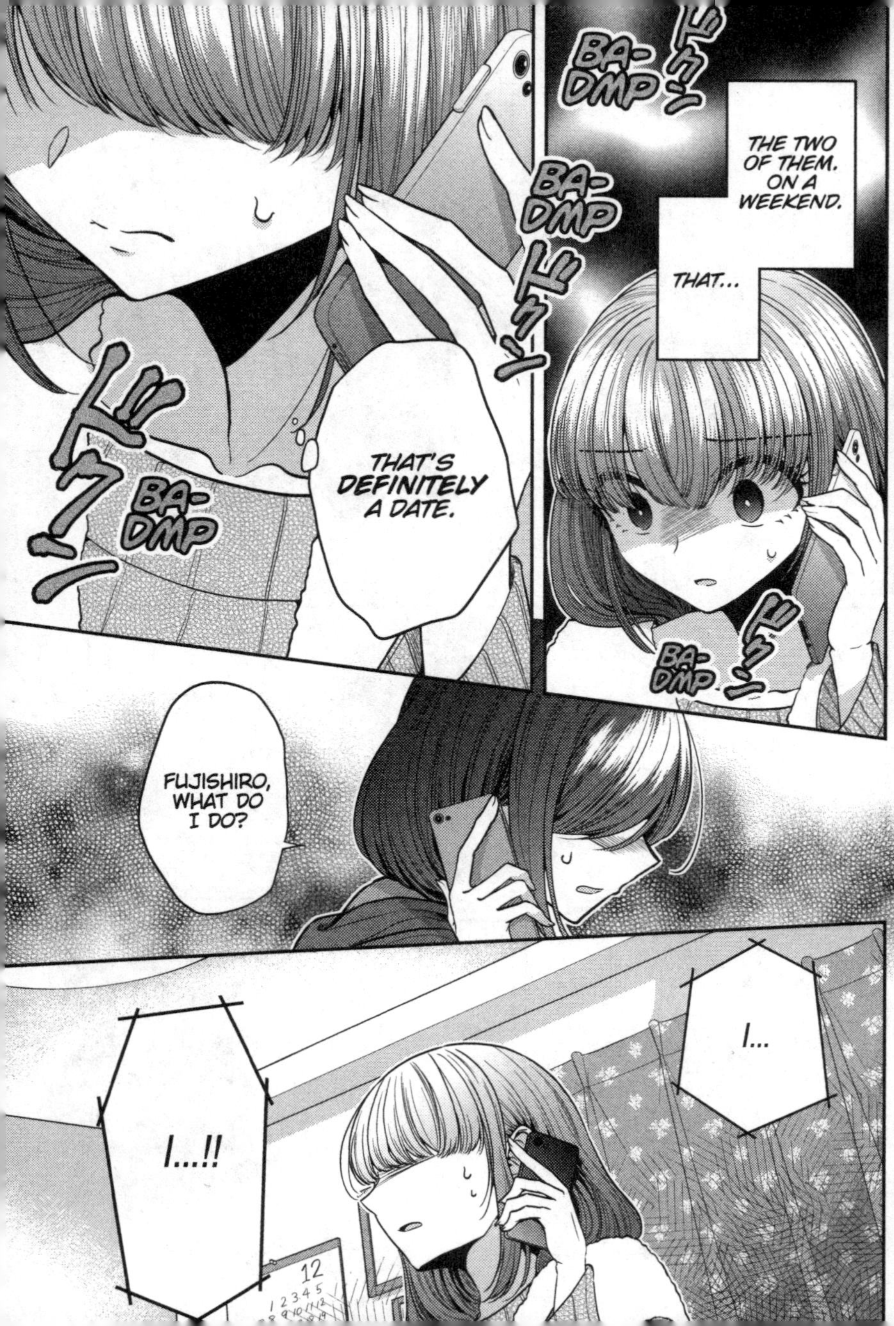
BA-DMP
THE TWO OF THEM. ON A WEEKEND.
THAT...
BA-DMP
BA-DMP
THAT'S DEFINITELY A DATE.
BA-DMP
FUJISHIRO, WHAT DO I DO?
I...
I...!!

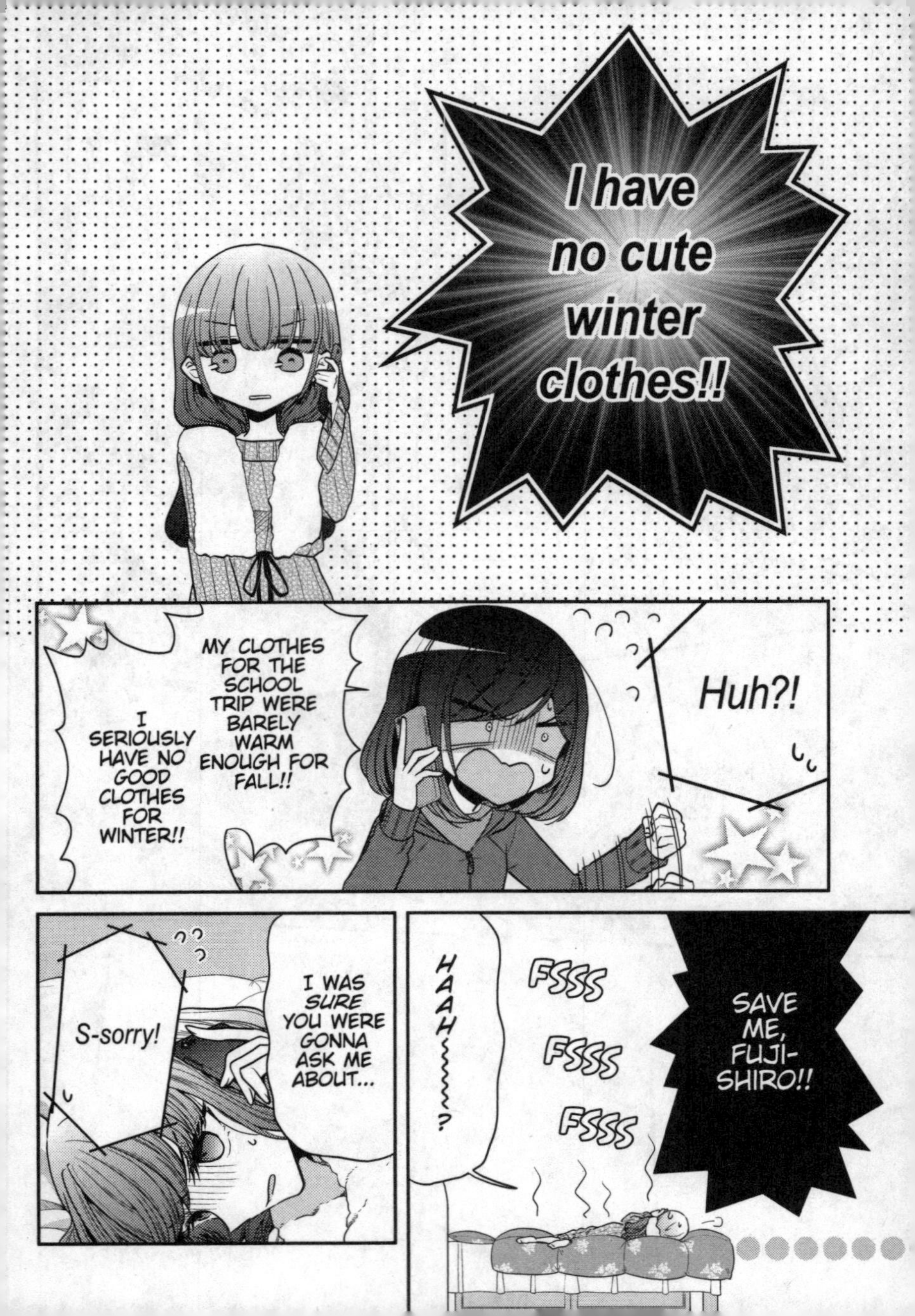
I have no cute winter clothes!!
Huh?!
MY CLOTHES FOR THE SCHOOL TRIP WERE BARELY WARM ENOUGH FOR FALL!!
I SERIOUSLY HAVE NO GOOD CLOTHES FOR WINTER!!
SAVE ME, FUJI-SHIRO!!
FSSS
FSSS
FSSS
HAAAH~~~?
I WAS SURE YOU WERE GONNA ASK ME ABOUT...
S-sorry!

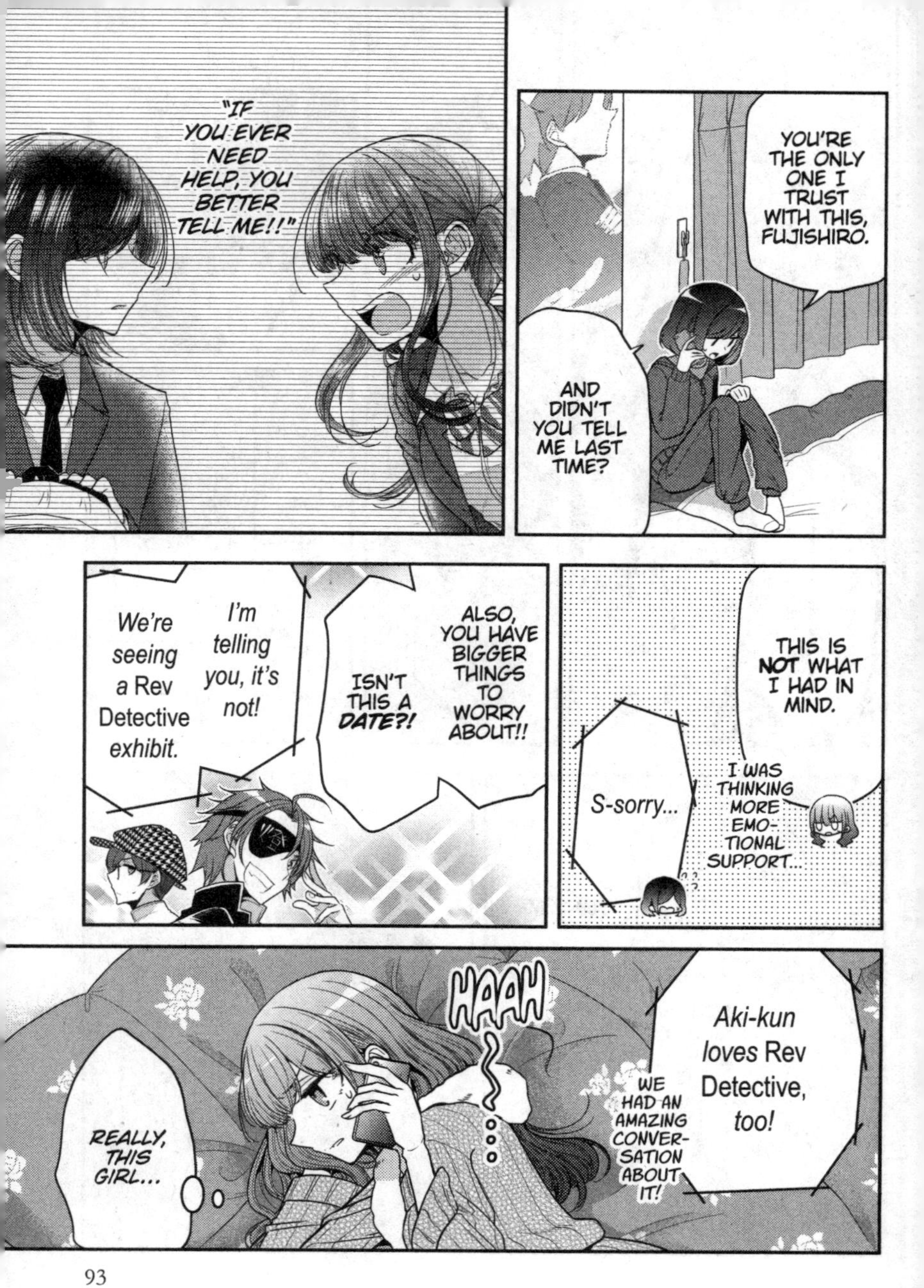
YOU'RE THE ONLY ONE I TRUST WITH THIS, FUJISHIRO.
AND DIDN'T YOU TELL ME LAST TIME?
"IF YOU EVER NEED HELP, YOU BETTER TELL ME!!"
THIS IS NOT WHAT I HAD IN MIND.
I WAS THINKING MORE EMO-TIONAL SUPPORT...
S-sorry...
ALSO, YOU HAVE BIGGER THINGS TO WORRY ABOUT!!
ISN'T THIS A DATE?!
I'm telling you, it's not!
We're seeing a Rev Detective exhibit.
Aki-kun loves Rev Detective, too!
WE HAD AN AMAZING CONVER-SATION ABOUT IT!
HAAH~~...
REALLY, THIS GIRL...

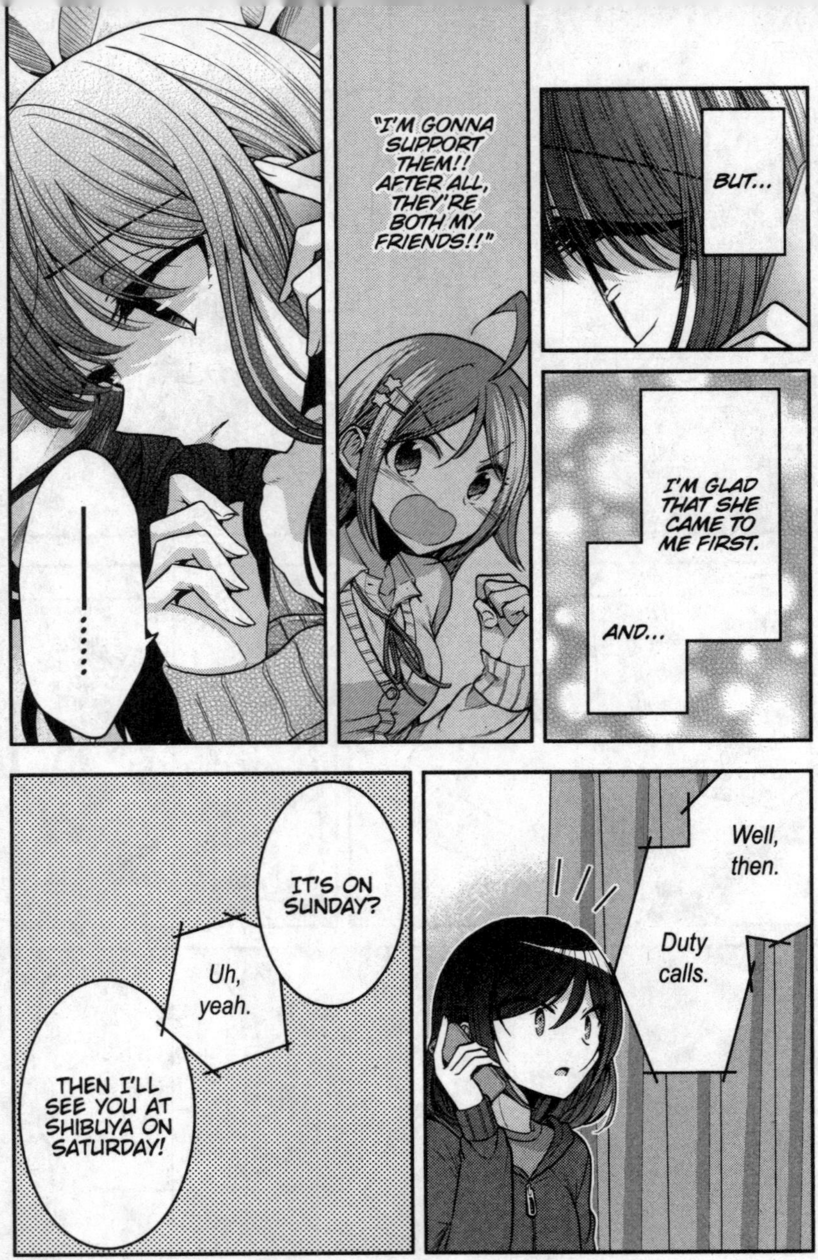
BUT...
I'M GLAD THAT SHE CAME TO ME FIRST.
AND...
"I'M GONNA SUPPORT THEM!! AFTER ALL, THEY'RE BOTH MY FRIENDS!!"
—......
Well, then.
Duty calls.
IT'S ON SUNDAY?
Uh, yeah.
THEN I'LL SEE YOU AT SHIBUYA ON SATURDAY!

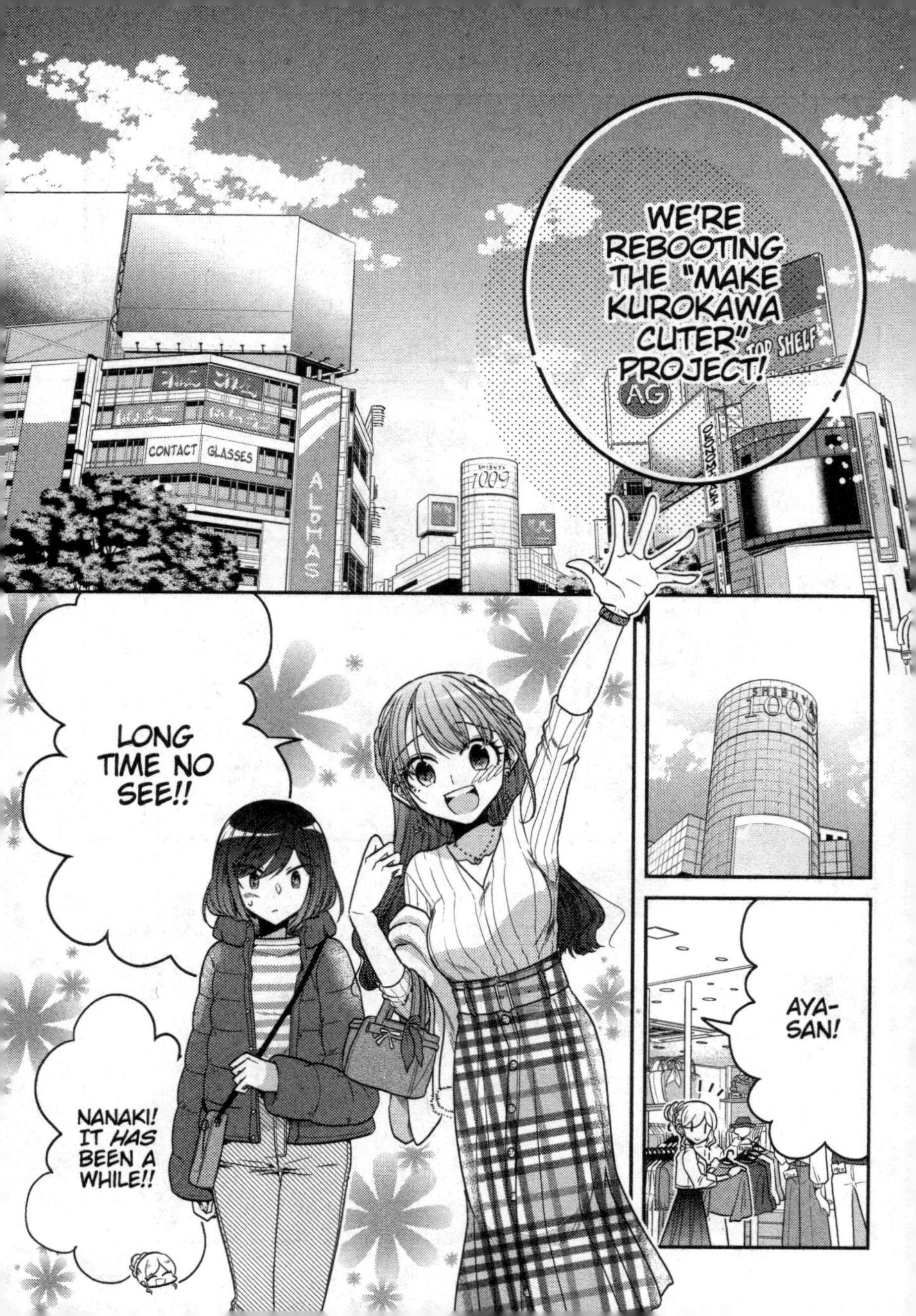
WE'RE REBOOTING THE "MAKE KUROKAWA CUTER" PROJECT!
TOP SHELF
AG
CONTACT
GLASSES
ALOHAS
AYA-SAN!
LONG TIME NO SEE!!
NANAKI! IT *HAS* BEEN A WHILE!!

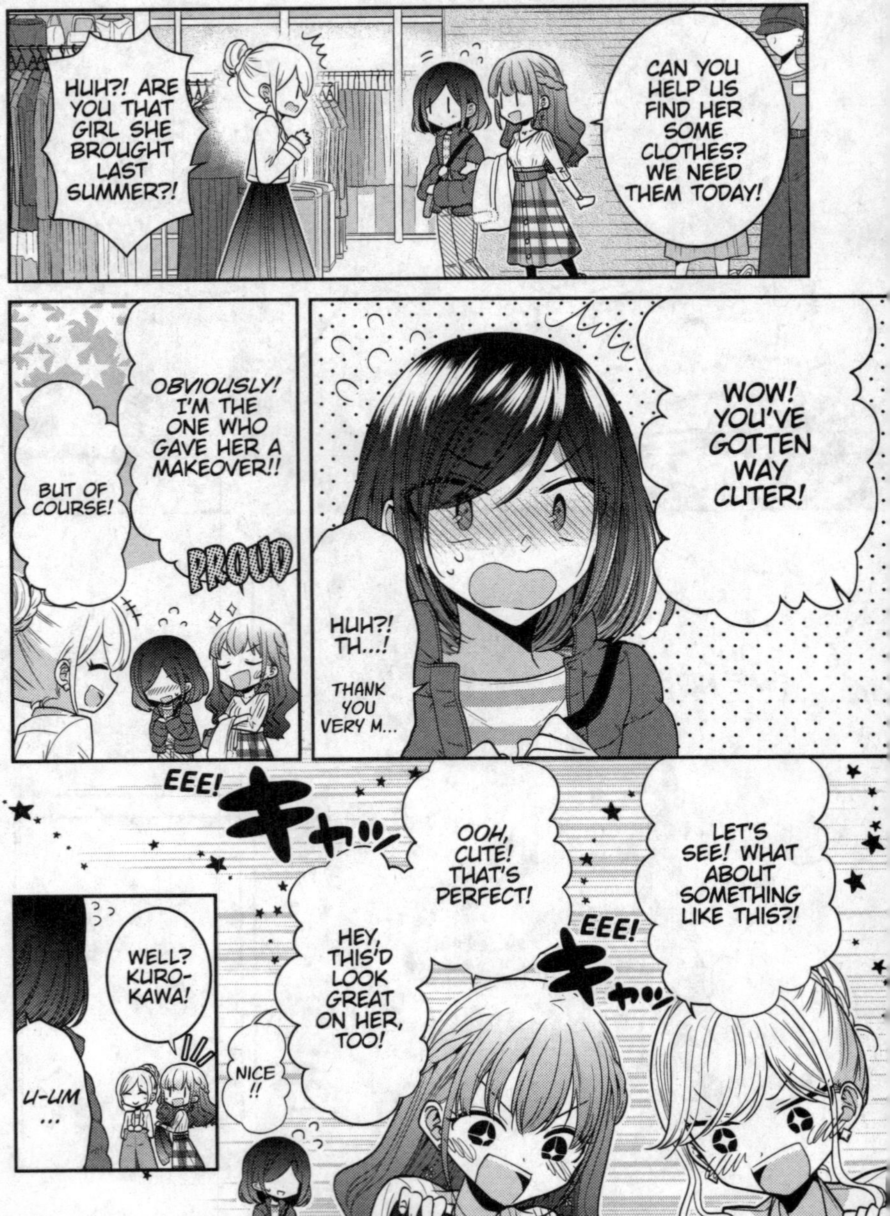

CAN YOU HELP US FIND HER SOME CLOTHES? WE NEED THEM TODAY!
HUH?! ARE YOU THAT GIRL SHE BROUGHT LAST SUMMER?!
WOW! YOU'VE GOTTEN WAY CUTER!
HUH?! TH...!
THANK YOU VERY M...
OBVIOUSLY! I'M THE ONE WHO GAVE HER A MAKEOVER!!
BUT OF COURSE!
PROUD
LET'S SEE! WHAT ABOUT SOMETHING LIKE THIS?!
EEE!
キャッ
OOH, CUTE! THAT'S PERFECT!
EEE!
キャッ
HEY, THIS'D LOOK GREAT ON HER, TOO!
NICE!!
WELL? KURO-KAWA!
U-UM...

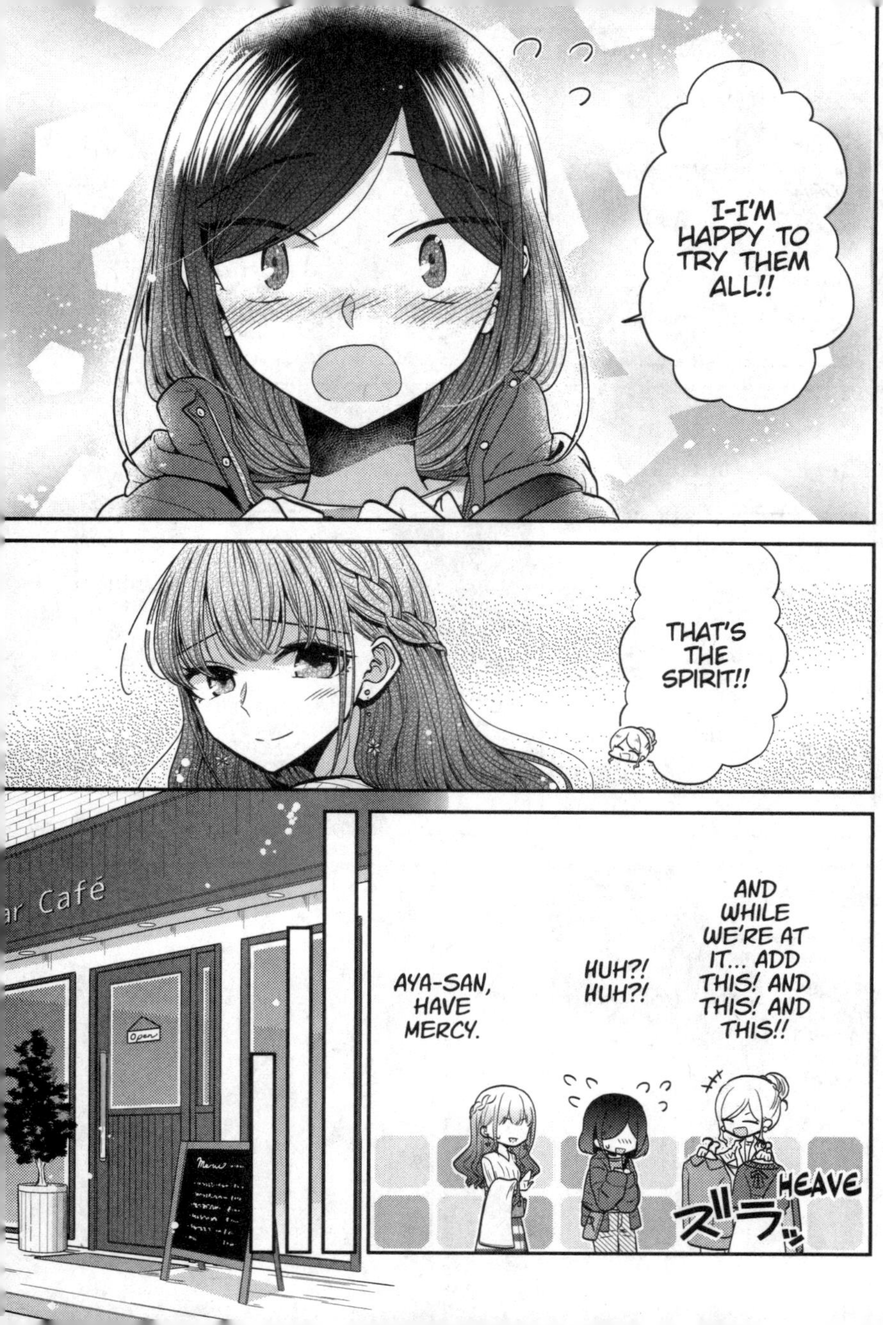
I-I'M HAPPY TO TRY THEM ALL!!
THAT'S THE SPIRIT!!
AND WHILE WE'RE AT IT... ADD THIS! AND THIS! AND THIS!!
HUH?! HUH?!
AYA-SAN, HAVE MERCY.
HEAVE
ズラッ
ar Café

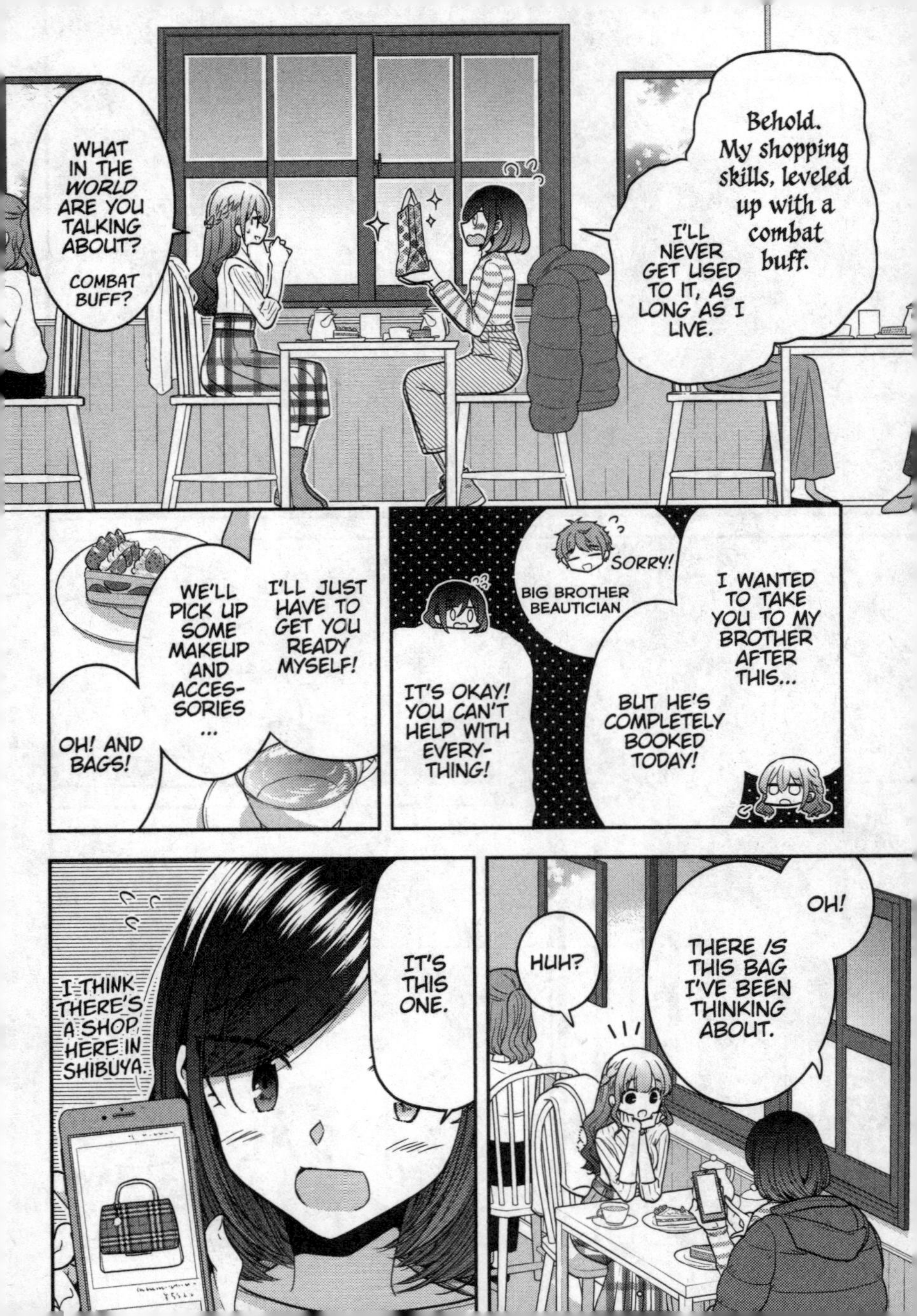
Behold. My shopping skills, leveled up with a combat buff.
WHAT IN THE *WORLD* ARE YOU TALKING ABOUT?
COMBAT BUFF?
I'LL NEVER GET USED TO IT, AS LONG AS I LIVE.
I WANTED TO TAKE YOU TO MY BROTHER AFTER THIS...
BUT HE'S COMPLETELY BOOKED TODAY!
SORRY!
BIG BROTHER BEAUTICIAN
IT'S OKAY! YOU CAN'T HELP WITH EVERY-THING!
I'LL JUST HAVE TO GET YOU READY MYSELF!
WE'LL PICK UP SOME MAKEUP AND ACCES-SORIES...
OH! AND BAGS!
OH!
THERE *IS* THIS BAG I'VE BEEN THINKING ABOUT.
HUH?
IT'S THIS ONE.
I THINK THERE'S A SHOP HERE IN SHIBUYA.

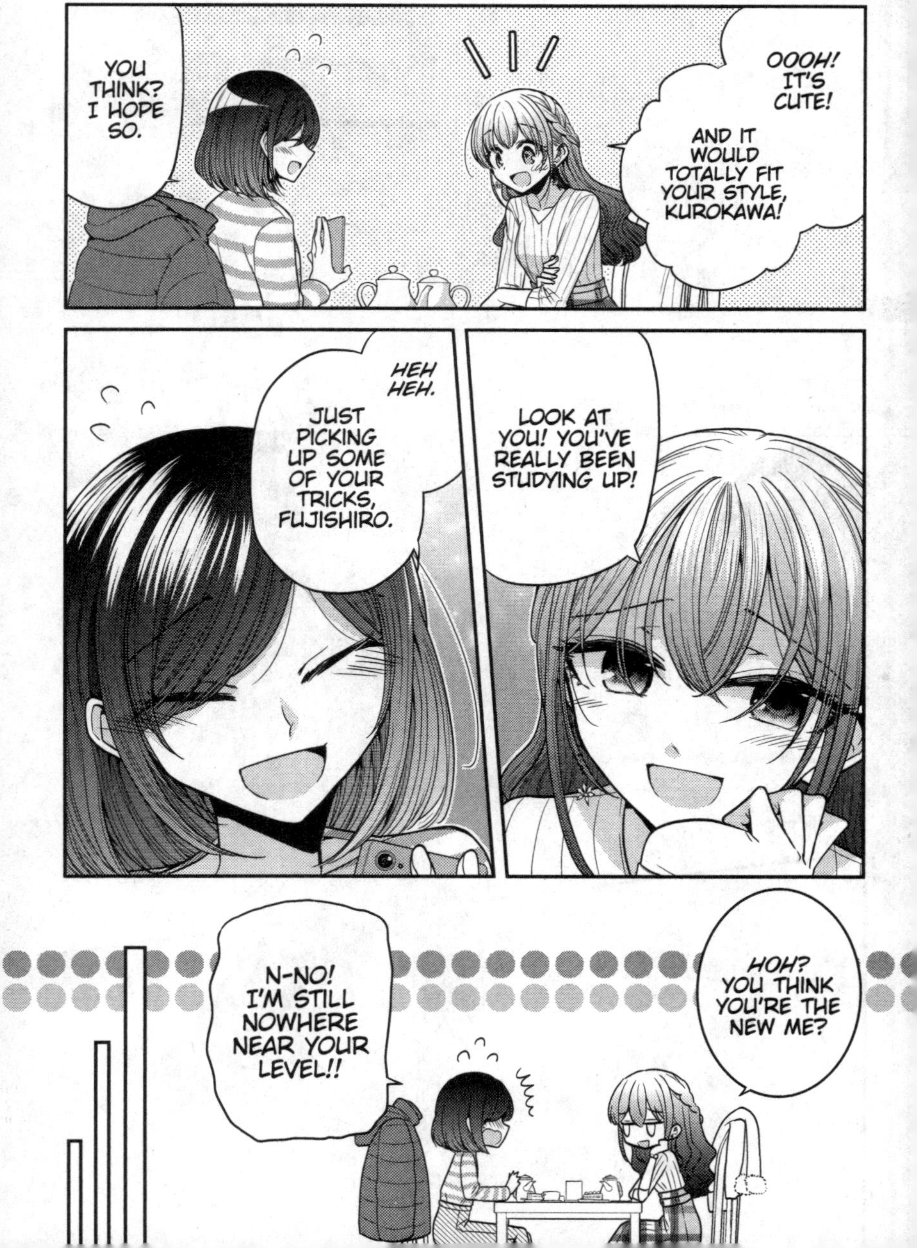
OOOH! IT'S CUTE!
AND IT WOULD TOTALLY FIT YOUR STYLE, KUROKAWA!
YOU THINK? I HOPE SO.
LOOK AT YOU! YOU'VE REALLY BEEN STUDYING UP!
HEH HEH.
JUST PICKING UP SOME OF YOUR TRICKS, FUJISHIRO.
HOH? YOU THINK YOU'RE THE NEW ME?
N-NO! I'M STILL NOWHERE NEAR YOUR LEVEL!!

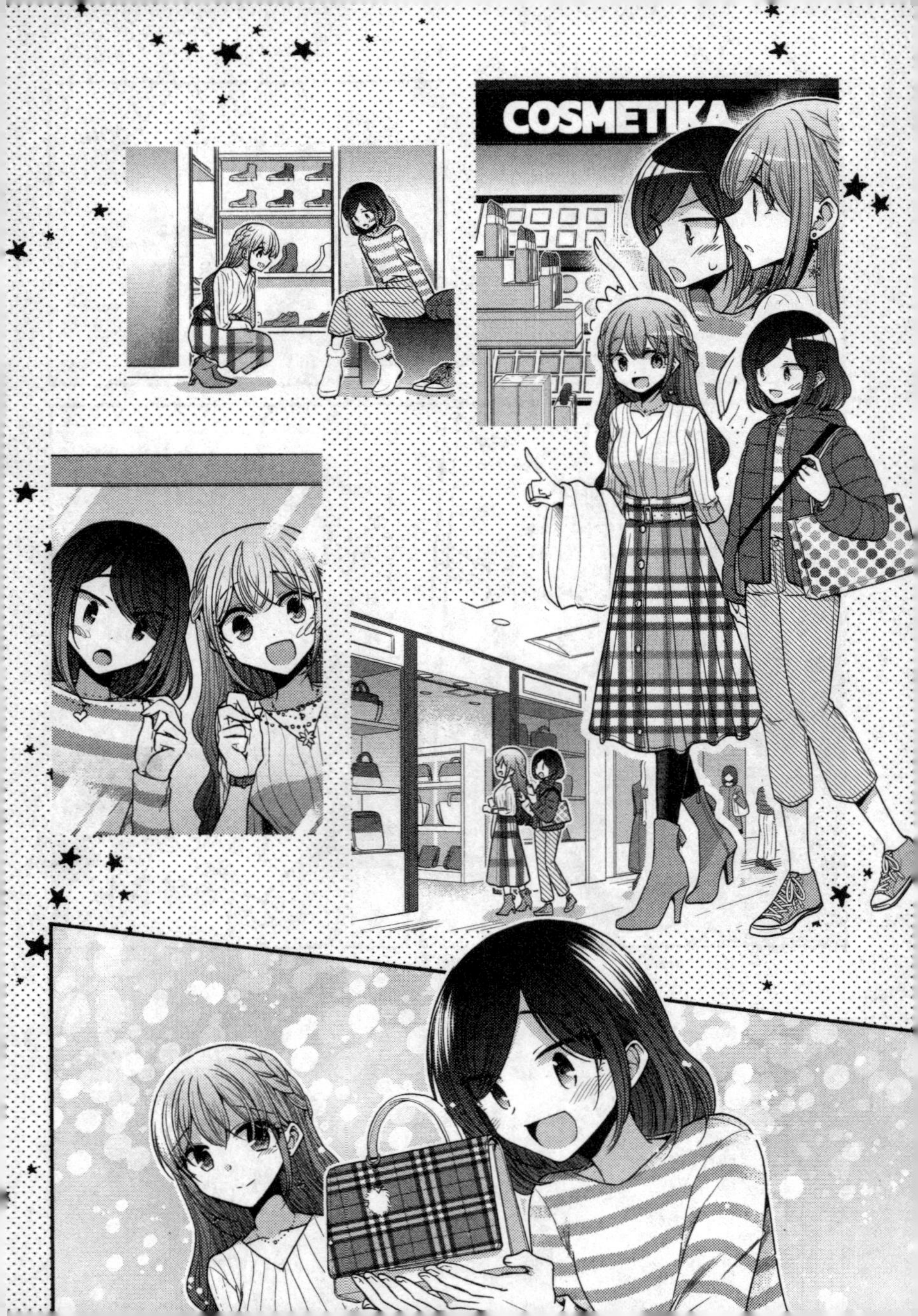
COSMETIKA

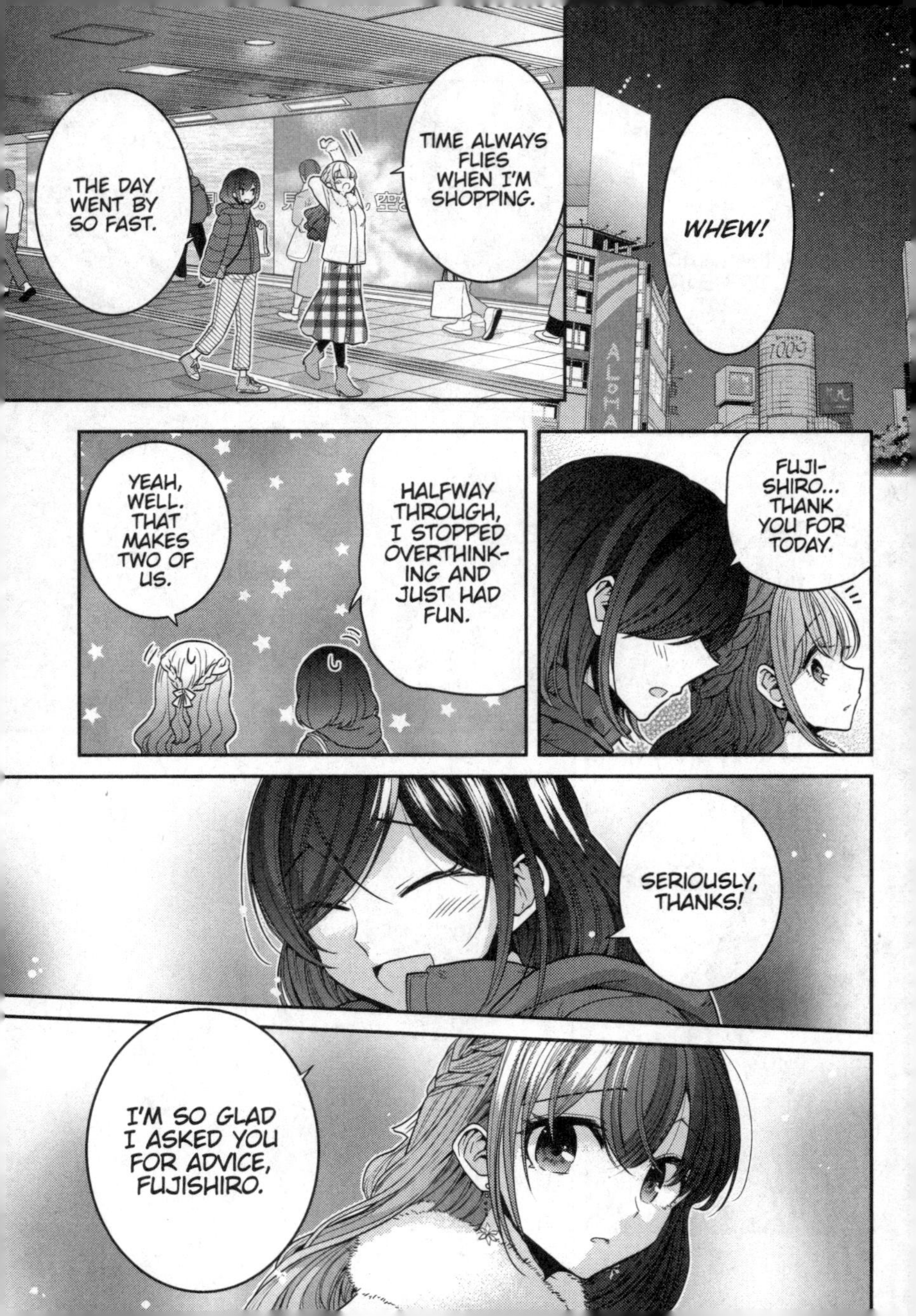
WHEW!
TIME ALWAYS FLIES WHEN I'M SHOPPING.
THE DAY WENT BY SO FAST.
FUJI-SHIRO... THANK YOU FOR TODAY.
HALFWAY THROUGH, I STOPPED OVERTHINK-ING AND JUST HAD FUN.
YEAH, WELL. THAT MAKES TWO OF US.
SERIOUSLY, THANKS!
I'M SO GLAD I ASKED YOU FOR ADVICE, FUJISHIRO.

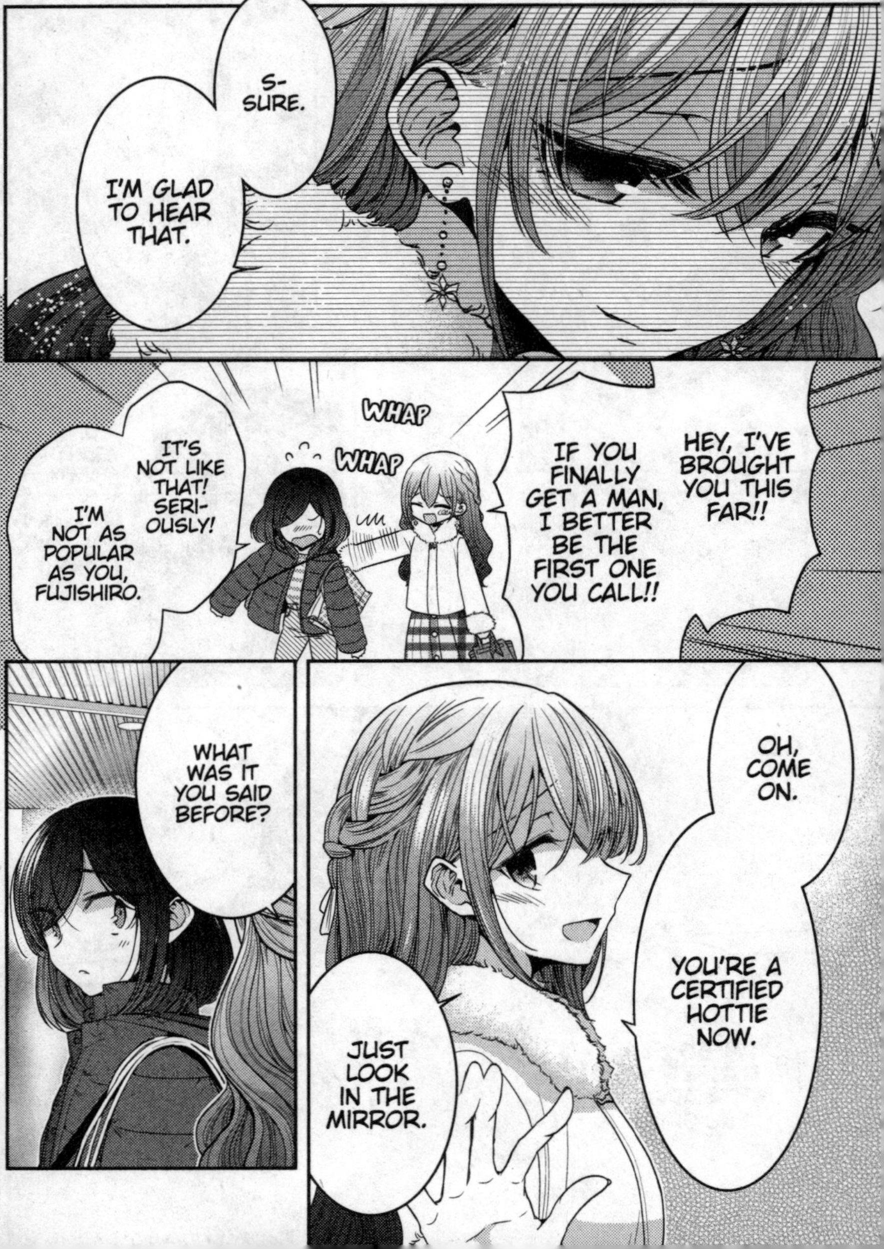
S- SURE.
I'M GLAD TO HEAR THAT.
HEY, I'VE BROUGHT YOU THIS FAR!!
IF YOU FINALLY GET A MAN, I BETTER BE THE FIRST ONE YOU CALL!!
WHAP
WHAP
IT'S NOT LIKE THAT! SERI-OUSLY!
I'M NOT AS POPULAR AS YOU, FUJISHIRO.
OH, COME ON.
YOU'RE A CERTIFIED HOTTIE NOW.
JUST LOOK IN THE MIRROR.
WHAT WAS IT YOU SAID BEFORE?

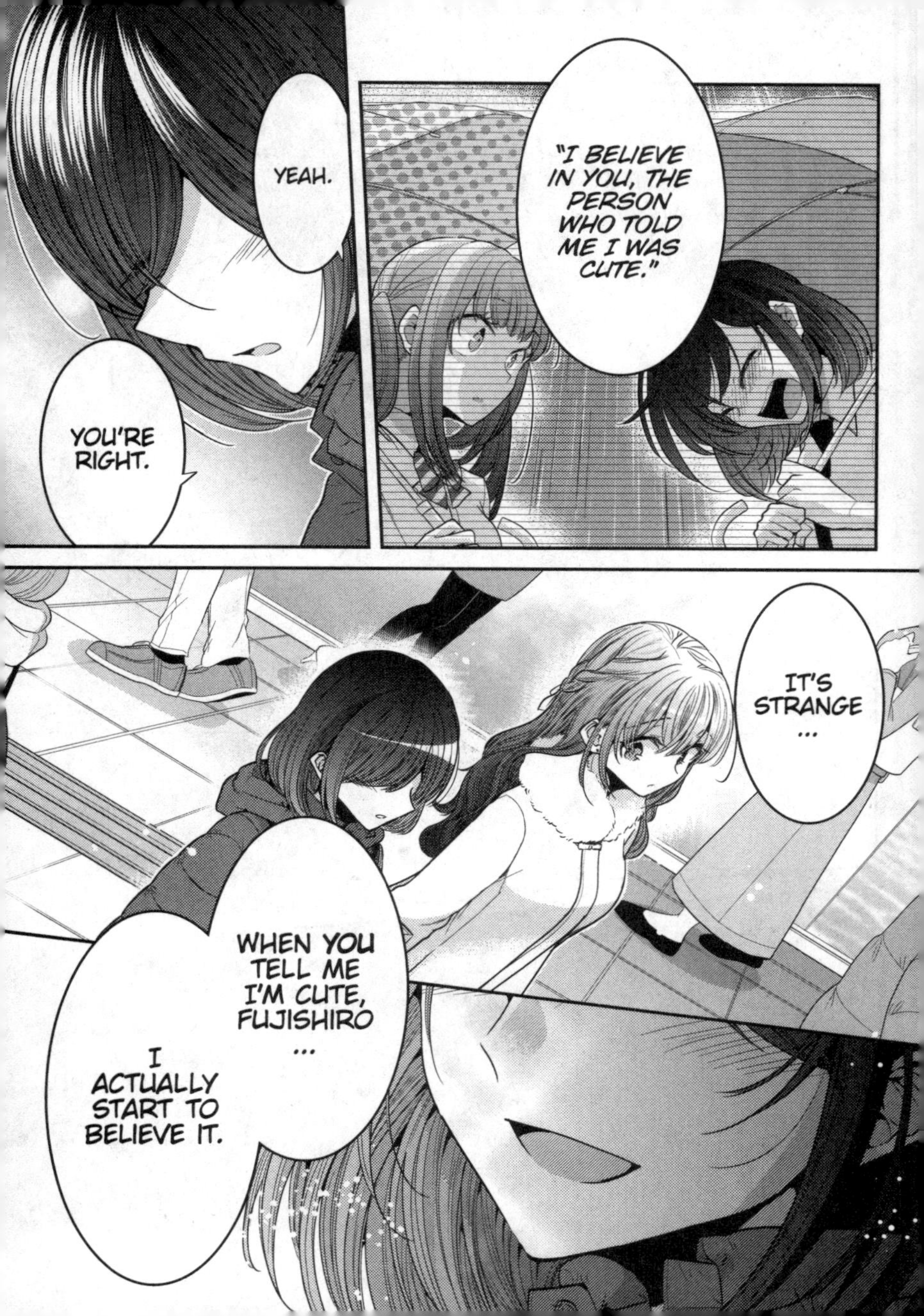
"I BELIEVE IN YOU, THE PERSON WHO TOLD ME I WAS CUTE."
YEAH.
YOU'RE RIGHT.
IT'S STRANGE...
WHEN YOU TELL ME I'M CUTE, FUJISHIRO...
I ACTUALLY START TO BELIEVE IT.

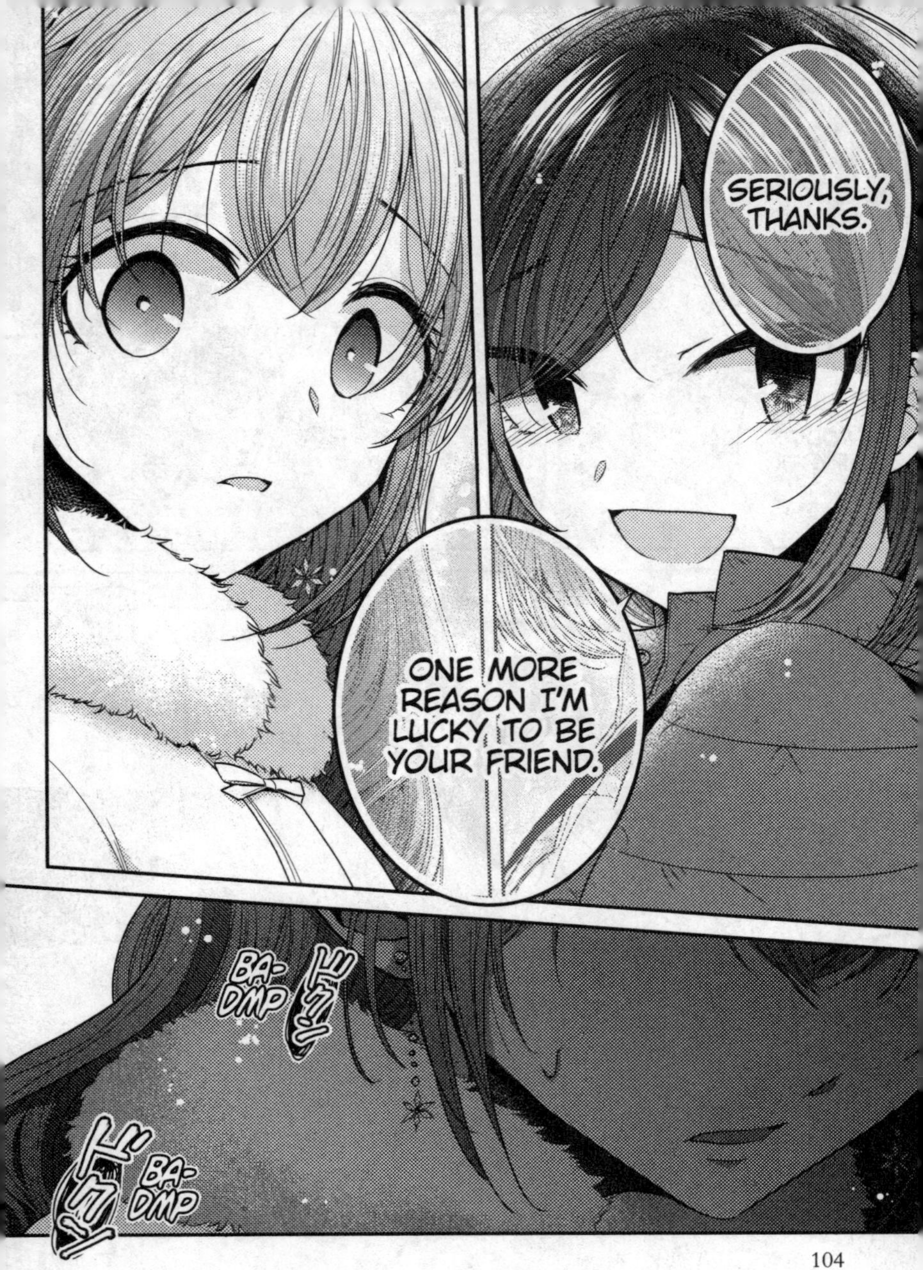
SERIOUSLY, THANKS.
ONE MORE REASON I'M LUCKY TO BE YOUR FRIEND.
BA-DMP
BA-DMP

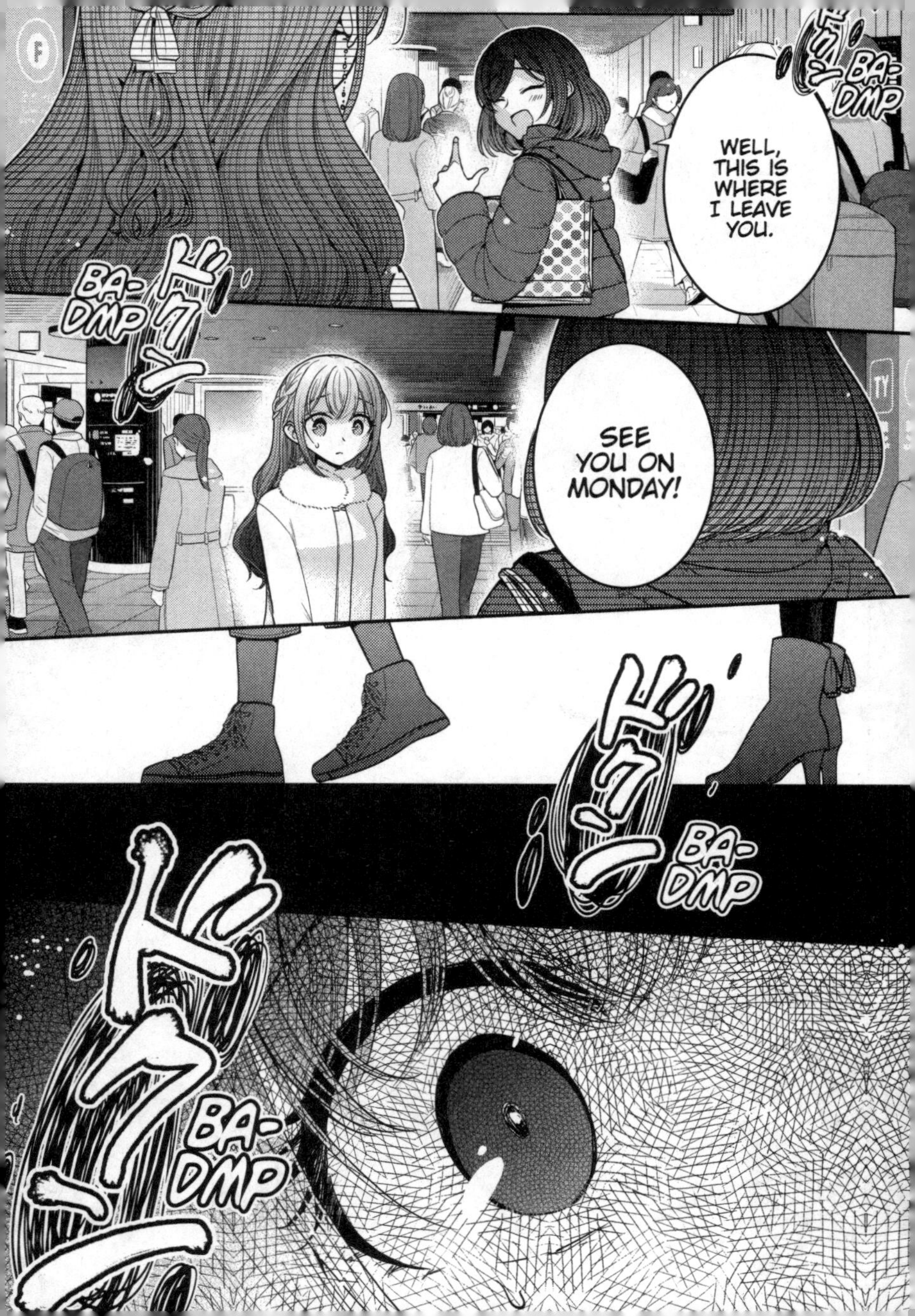
ドクン
BA-DMP
WELL, THIS IS WHERE I LEAVE YOU.
BA-DMP
ドクン
SEE YOU ON MONDAY!
ドクン
BA-DMP
ドクン
BA-DMP

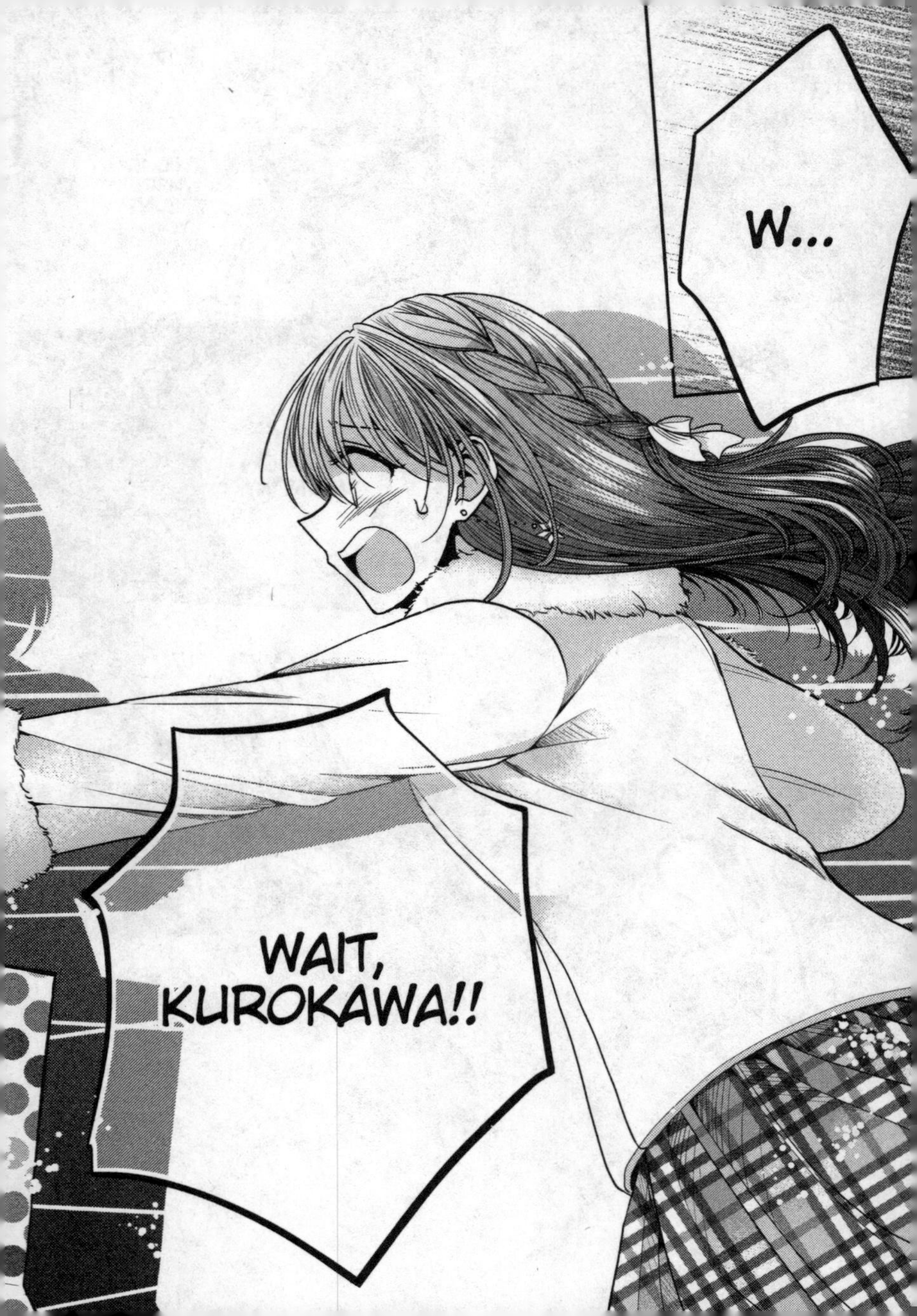
W...
WAIT, KUROKAWA!!

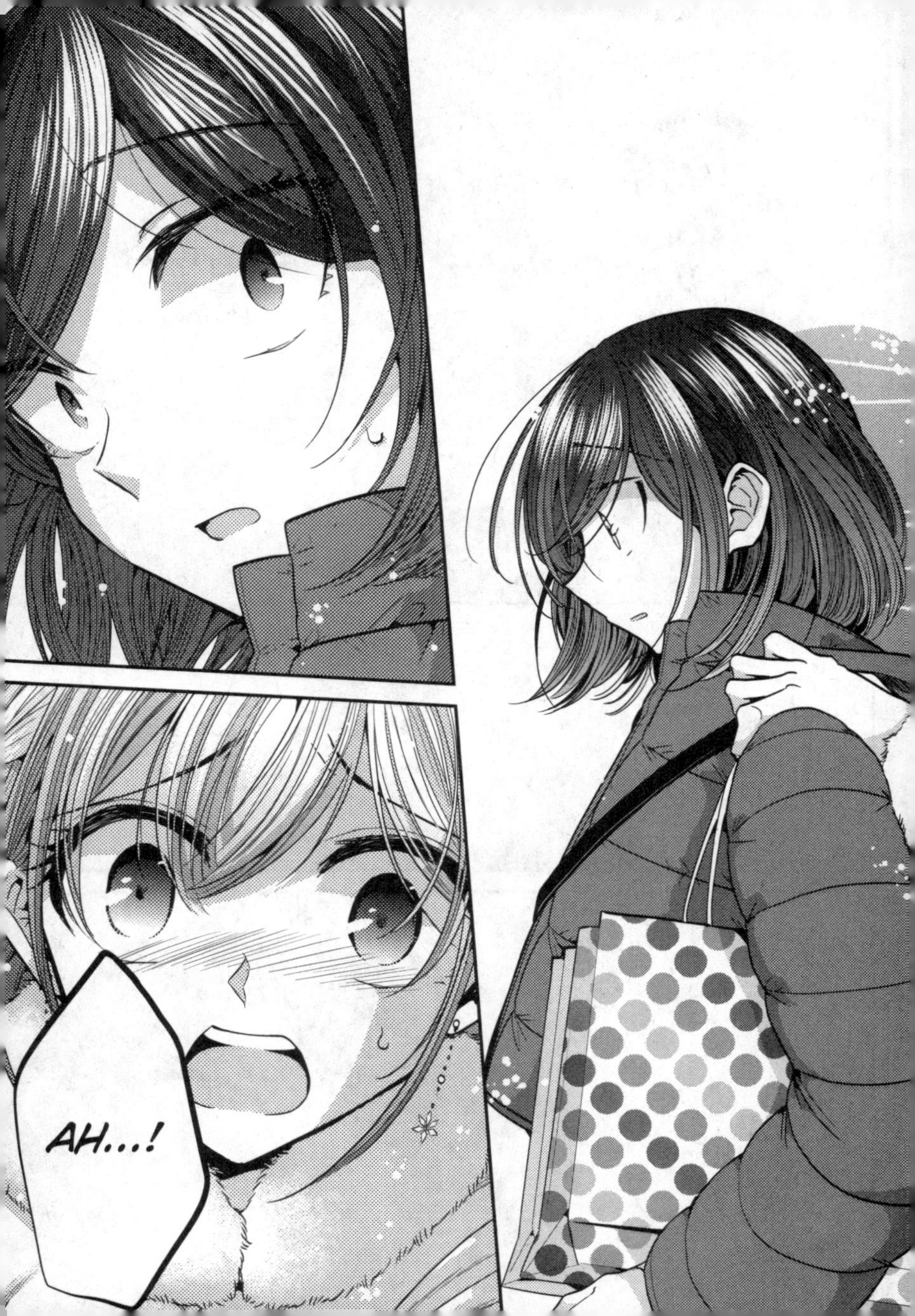
AH...!

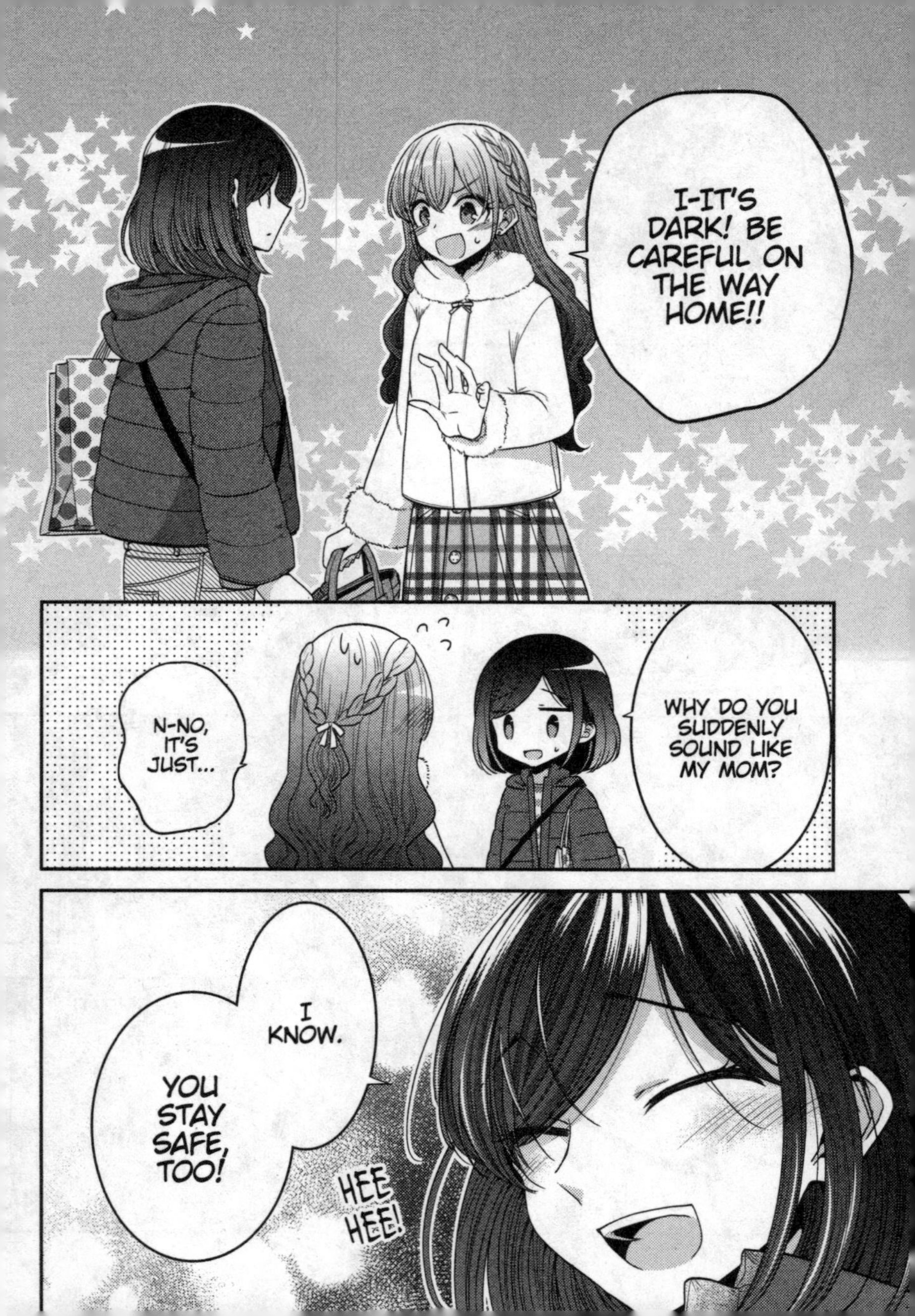
I-IT'S DARK! BE CAREFUL ON THE WAY HOME!!
WHY DO YOU SUDDENLY SOUND LIKE MY MOM?
N-NO, IT'S JUST...
I KNOW.
YOU STAY SAFE, TOO!
HEE HEE!

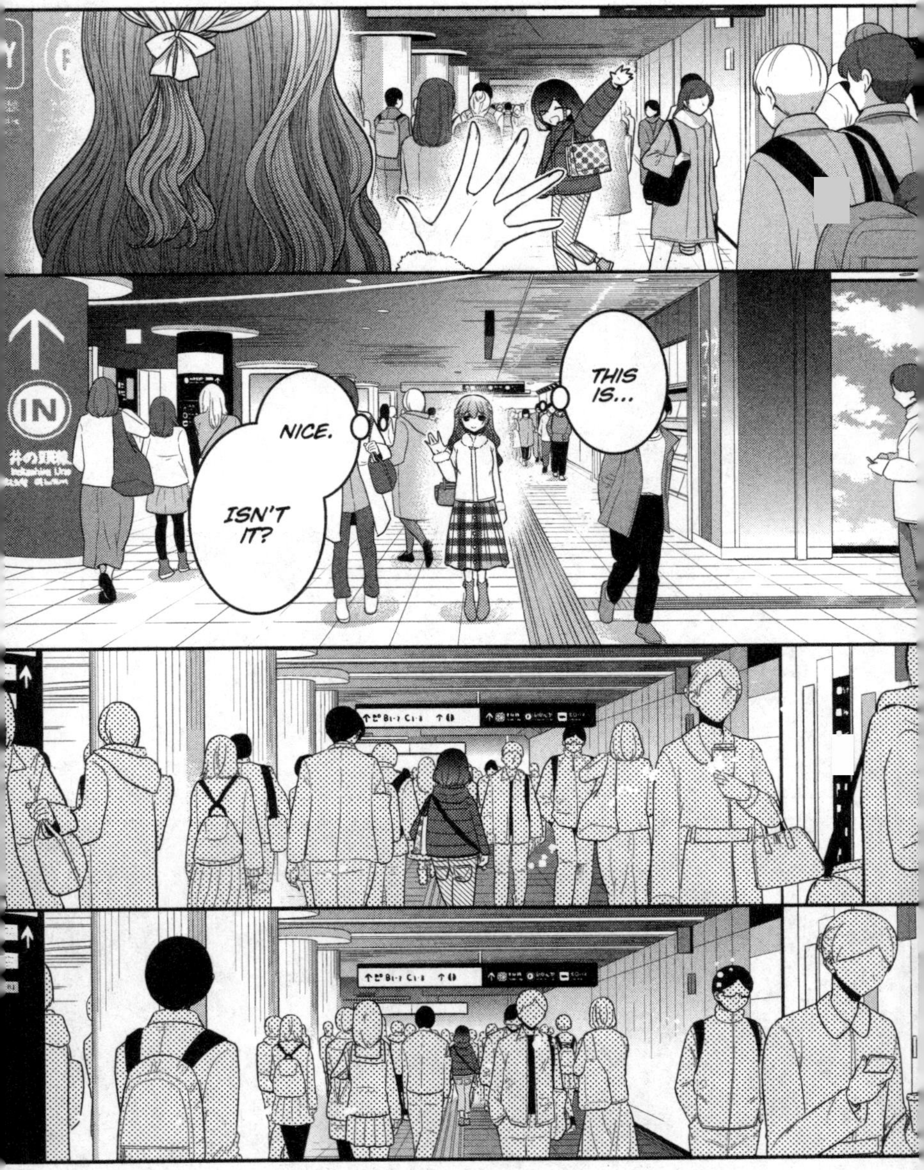
THIS IS...
NICE.
ISN'T IT?

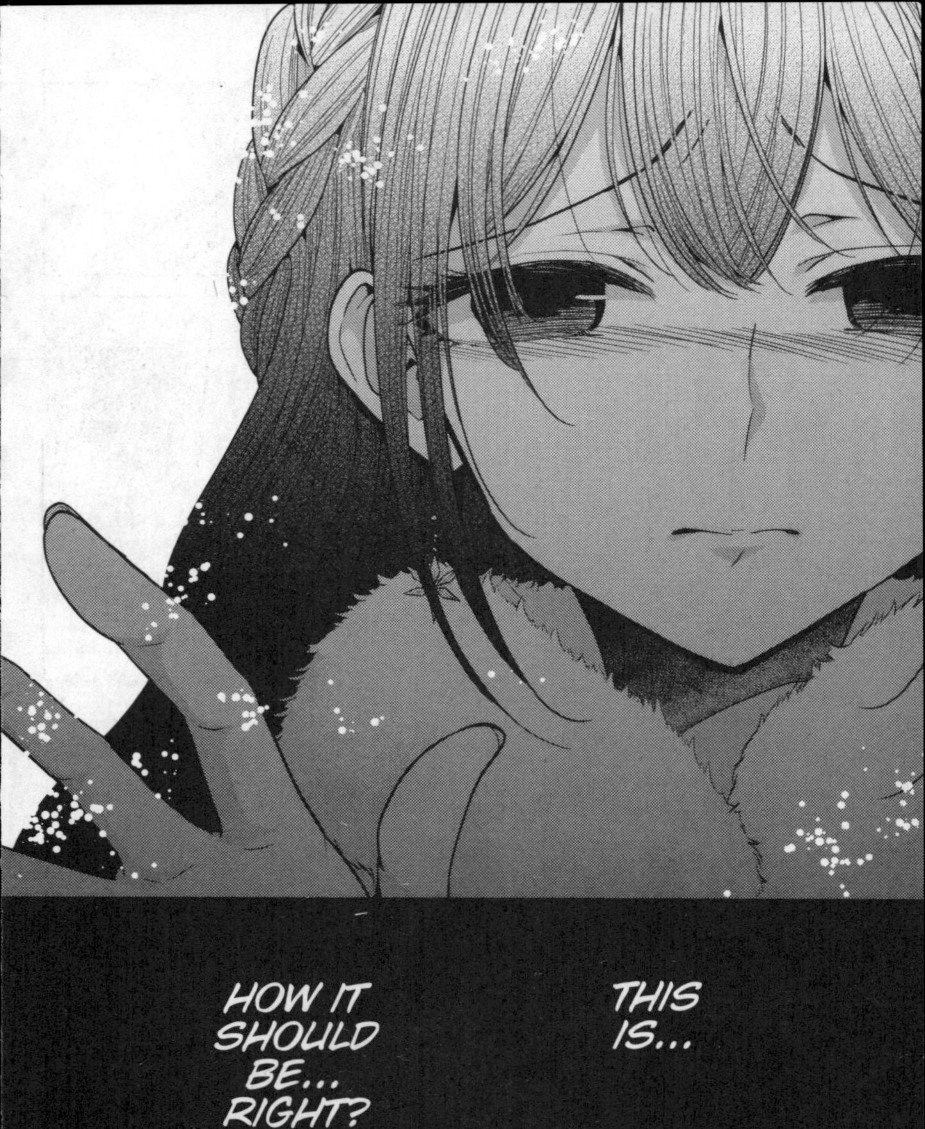
THIS IS...
HOW IT SHOULD BE... RIGHT?

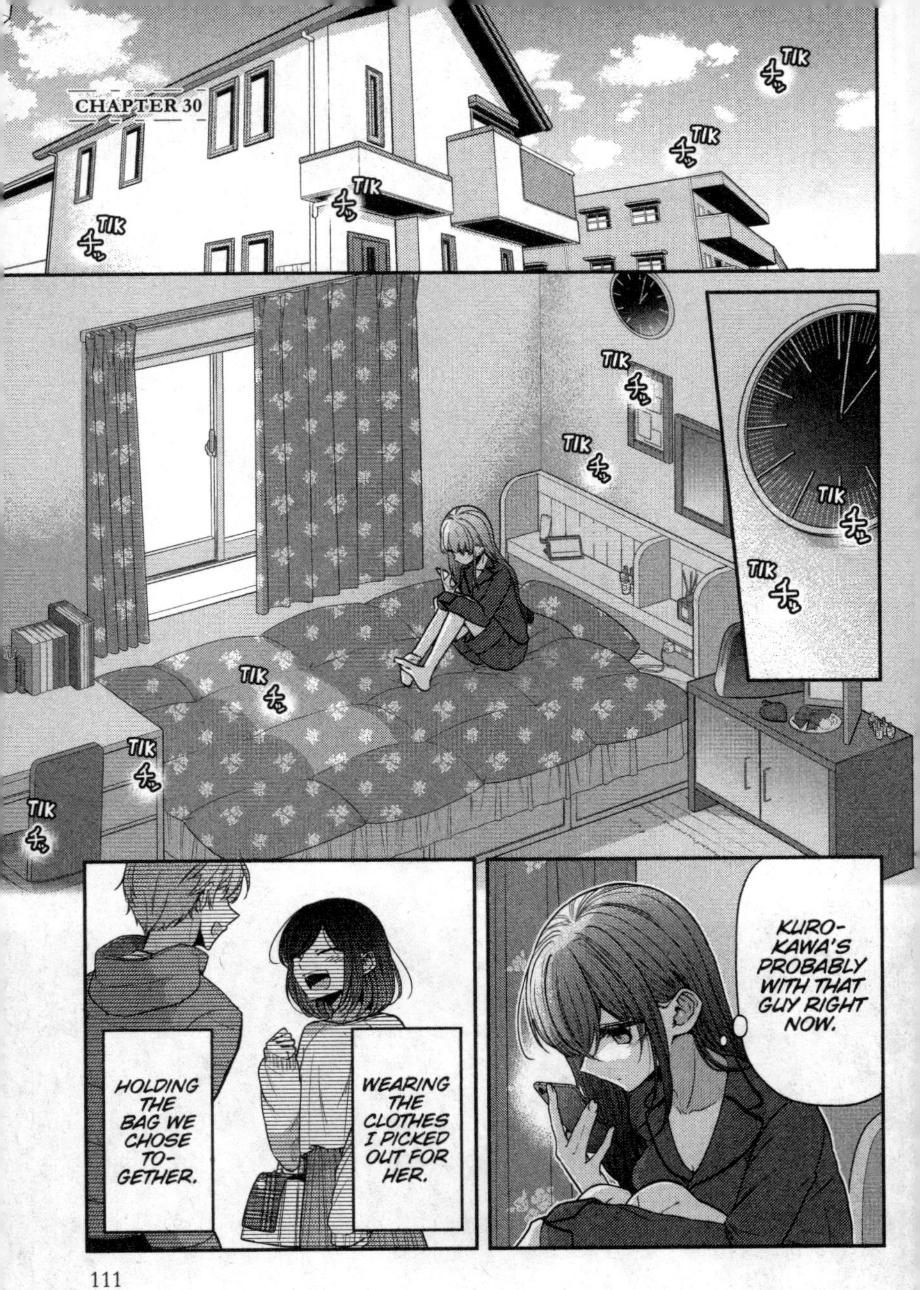
CHAPTER 30
TIK チッ
TIK チッ
TIK チッ
TIK チッ
TIK チッ
TIK チッ
TIK チッ
TIK チッ
TIK チッ
TIK チッ
TIK チッ
KURO-KAWA'S PROBABLY WITH THAT GUY RIGHT NOW.
WEARING THE CLOTHES I PICKED OUT FOR HER.
HOLDING THE BAG WE CHOSE TO-GETHER.

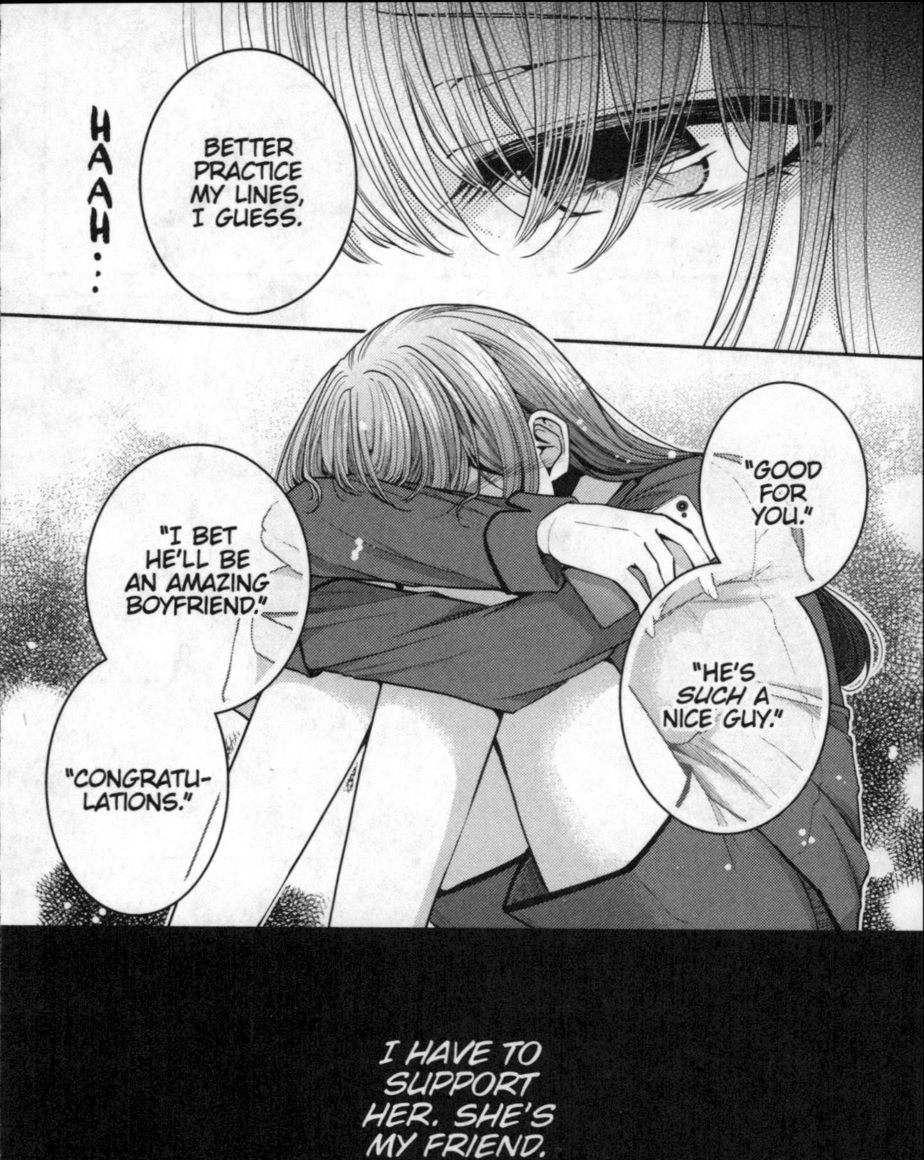
BETTER PRACTICE MY LINES, I GUESS.
HAAAH...
"GOOD FOR YOU."
"I BET HE'LL BE AN AMAZING BOYFRIEND."
"HE'S SUCH A NICE GUY."
"CONGRATULATIONS."
I HAVE TO SUPPORT HER. SHE'S MY FRIEND.

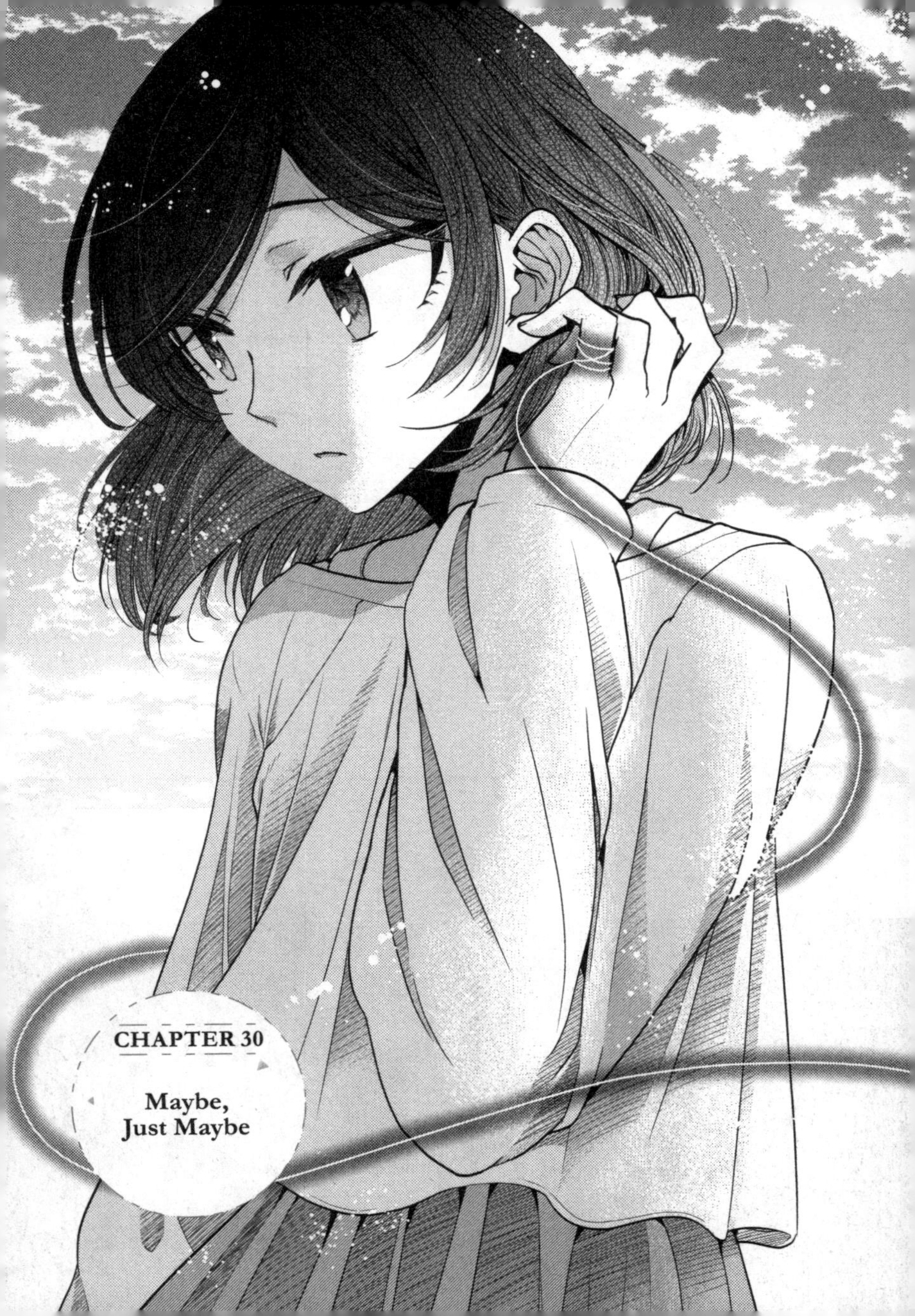
CHAPTER 30
Maybe, Just Maybe

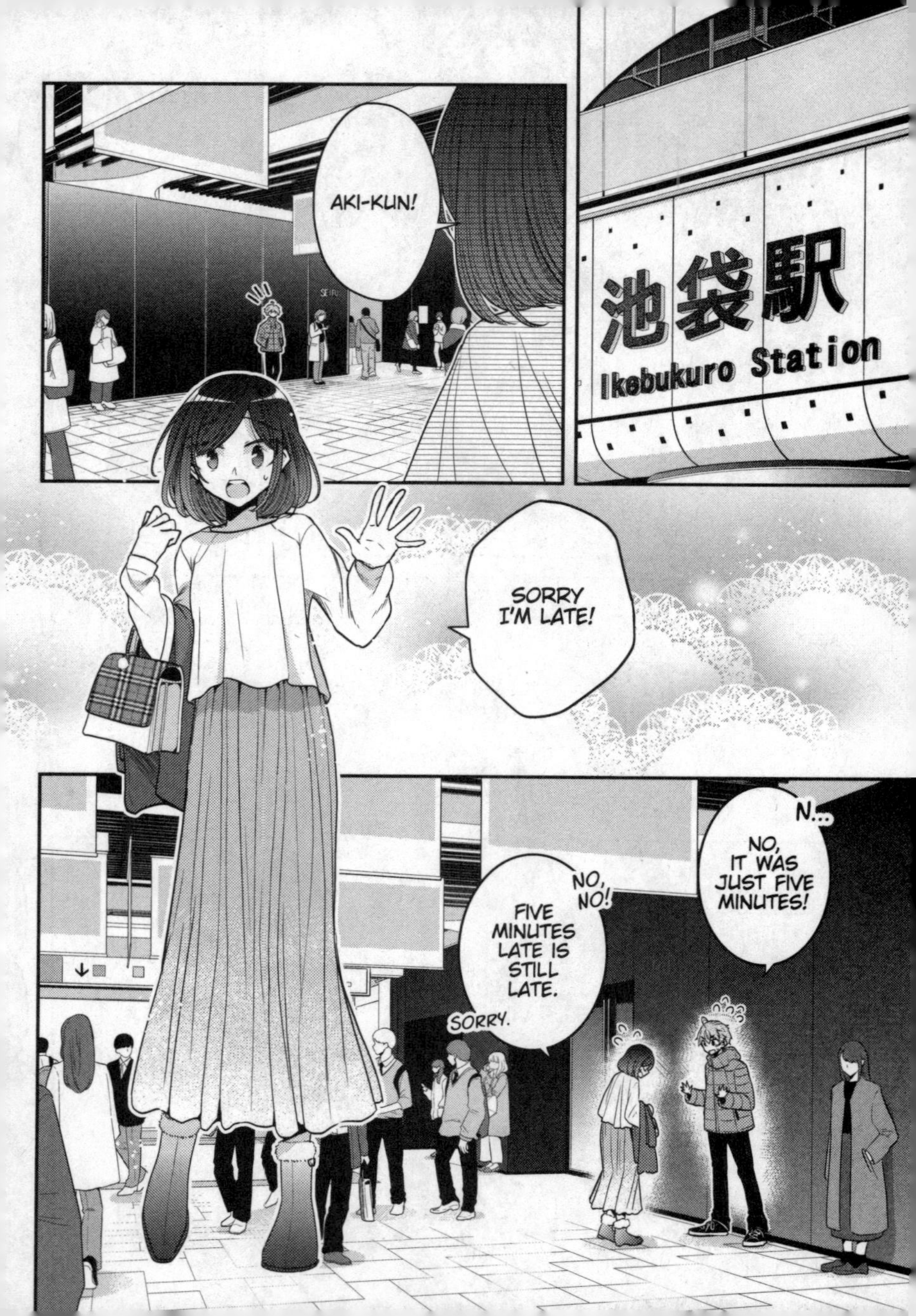
池袋駅
Ikebukuro Station
AKI-KUN!
SORRY I'M LATE!
N...
NO, IT WAS JUST FIVE MINUTES!
NO, NO!
FIVE MINUTES LATE IS STILL LATE.
SORRY.

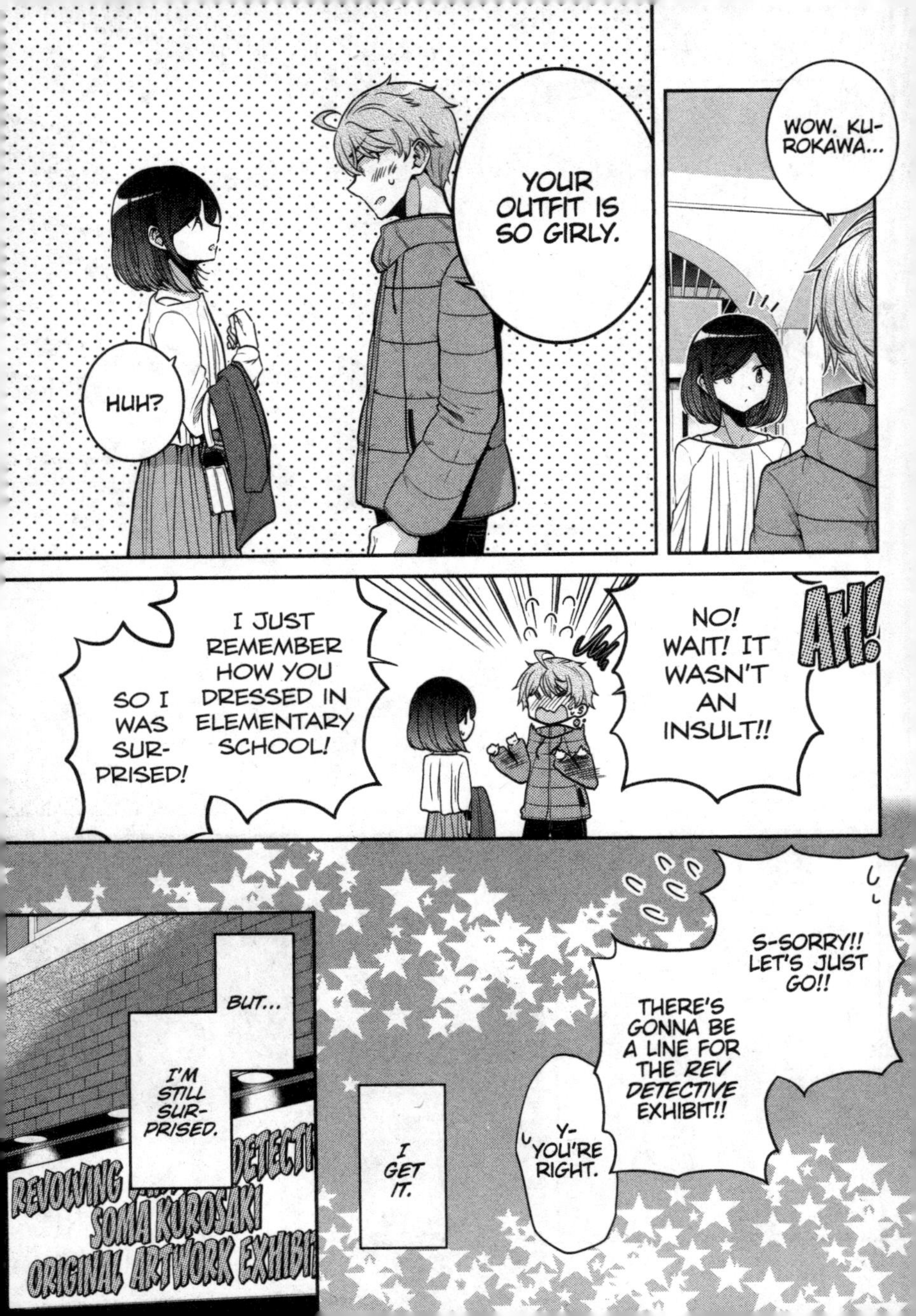
WOW. KU-ROKAWA...
YOUR OUTFIT IS SO GIRLY.
HUH?
AH!
NO! WAIT! IT WASN'T AN INSULT!!
I JUST REMEMBER HOW YOU DRESSED IN ELEMENTARY SCHOOL!
SO I WAS SUR-PRISED!
S-SORRY!! LET'S JUST GO!!
THERE'S GONNA BE A LINE FOR THE *REV DETECTIVE* EXHIBIT!!
Y-YOU'RE RIGHT.
I GET IT.
BUT...
I'M STILL SUR-PRISED.
REVOLVING
SOMA KUROSAKI
ORIGINAL ARTWORK

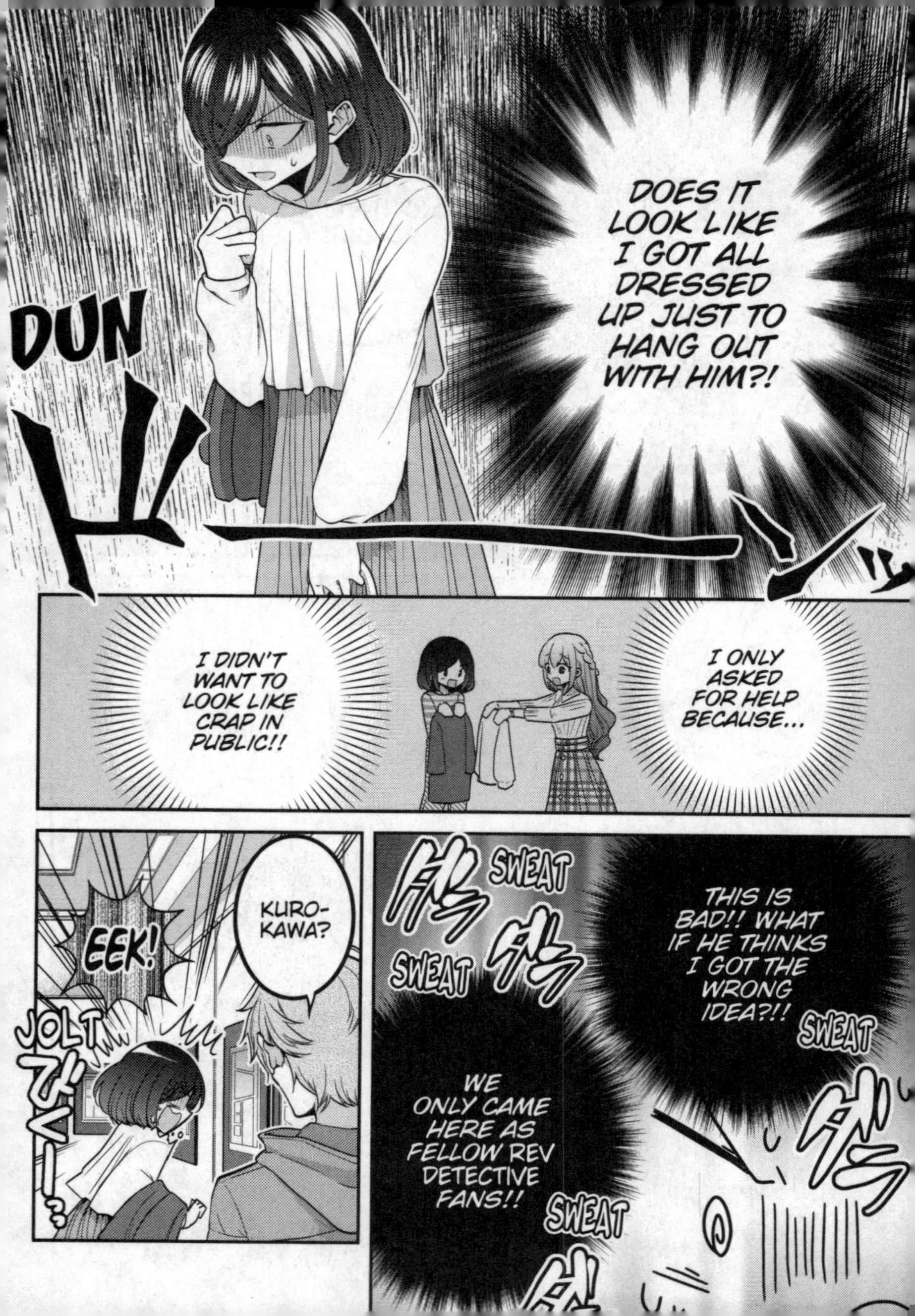
DOES IT LOOK LIKE I GOT ALL DRESSED UP JUST TO HANG OUT WITH HIM?!
DUN
I ONLY ASKED FOR HELP BECAUSE...
I DIDN'T WANT TO LOOK LIKE CRAP IN PUBLIC!!
SWEAT
SWEAT
THIS IS BAD!! WHAT IF HE THINKS I GOT THE WRONG IDEA?!!
SWEAT
WE ONLY CAME HERE AS FELLOW REV DETECTIVE FANS!!
SWEAT
KURO-KAWA?
EEK!
JOLT

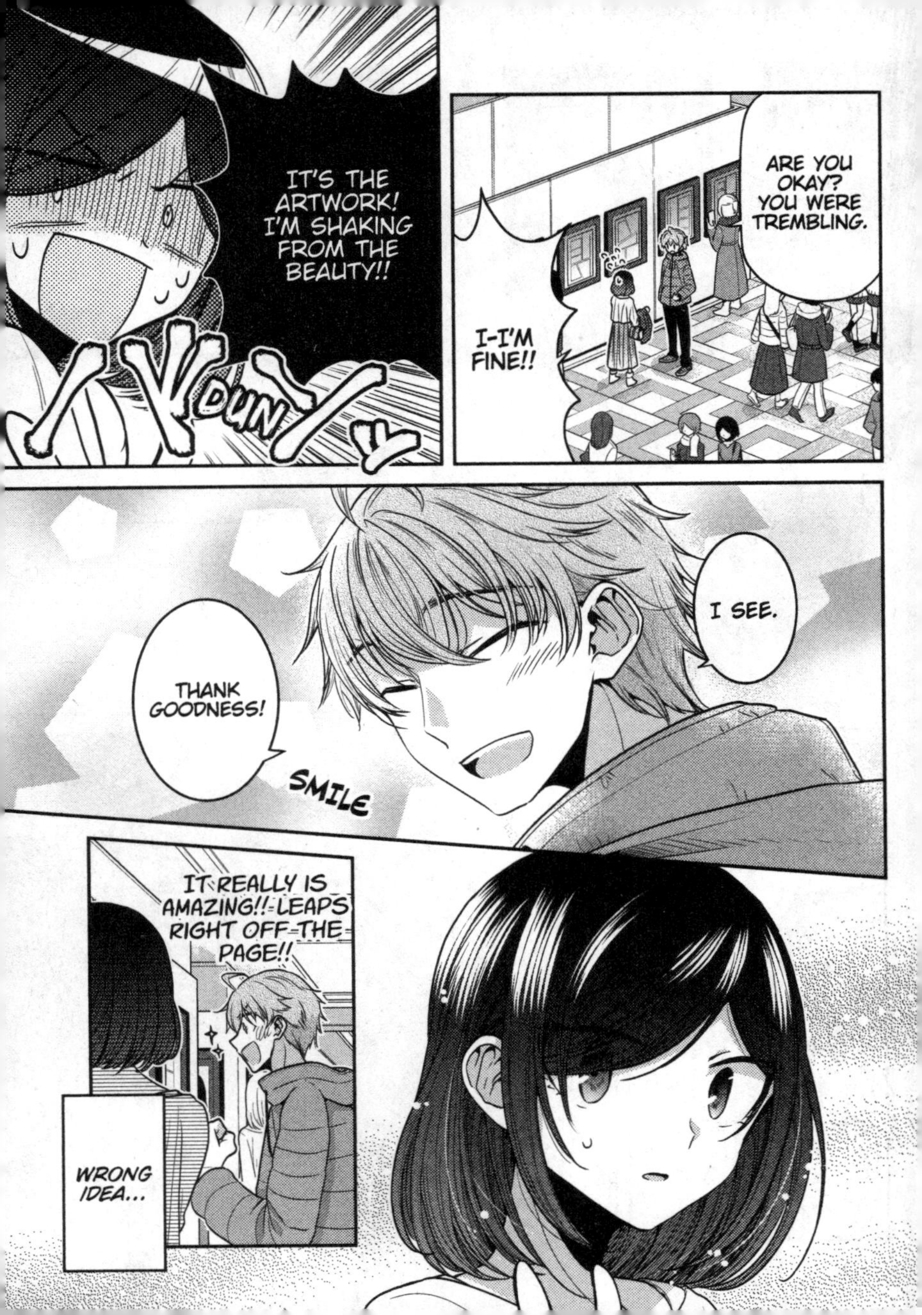
ARE YOU OKAY? YOU WERE TREMBLING.
I-I'M FINE!!
IT'S THE ARTWORK! I'M SHAKING FROM THE BEAUTY!!
DUN
DUN
I SEE.
THANK GOODNESS!
SMILE
IT REALLY IS AMAZING!! LEAPS RIGHT OFF THE PAGE!!
WRONG IDEA...

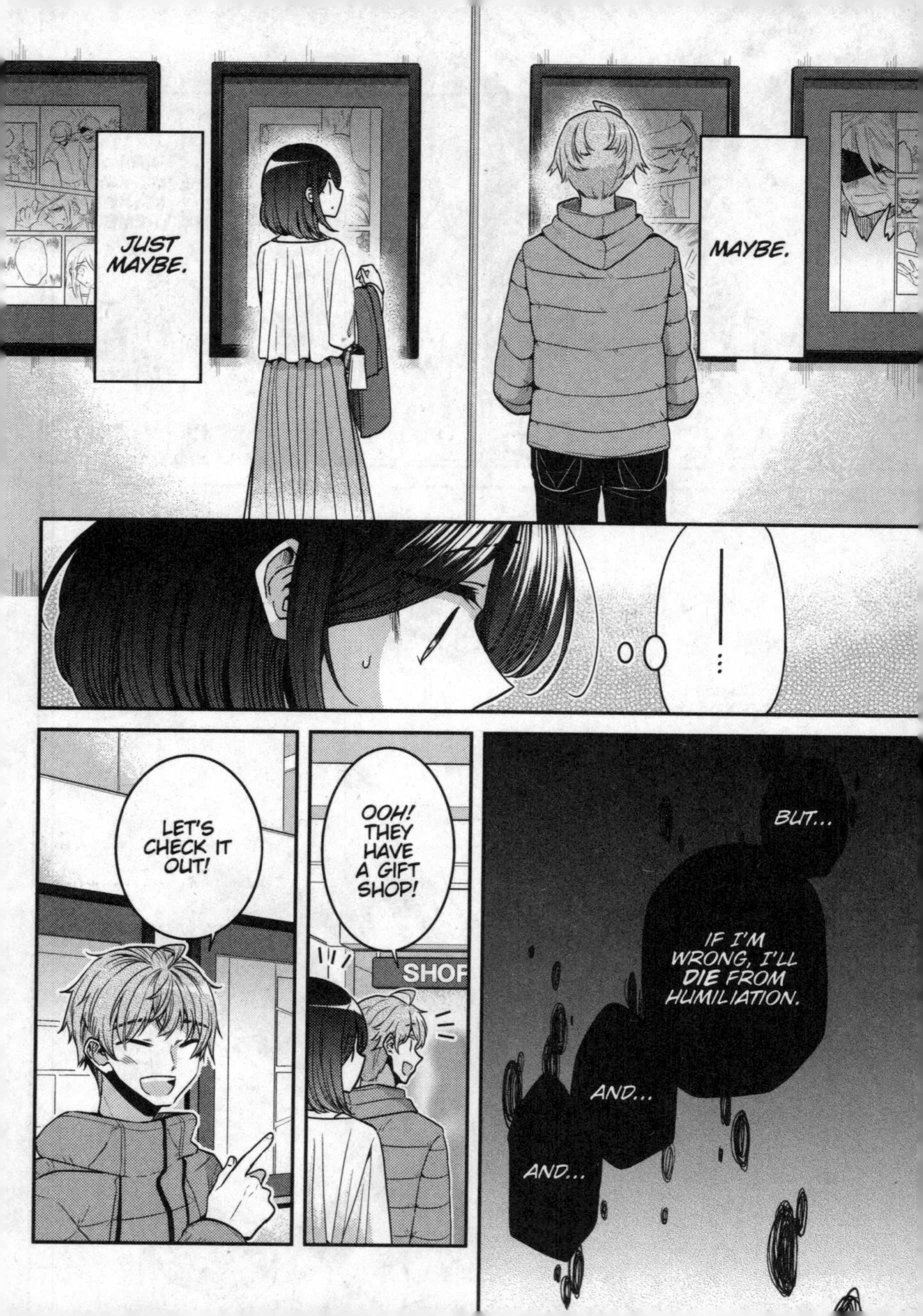
MAYBE.
JUST MAYBE.
BUT...
IF I'M WRONG, I'LL DIE FROM HUMILIATION.
AND...
AND...
OOH! THEY HAVE A GIFT SHOP!
SHOP
LET'S CHECK IT OUT!

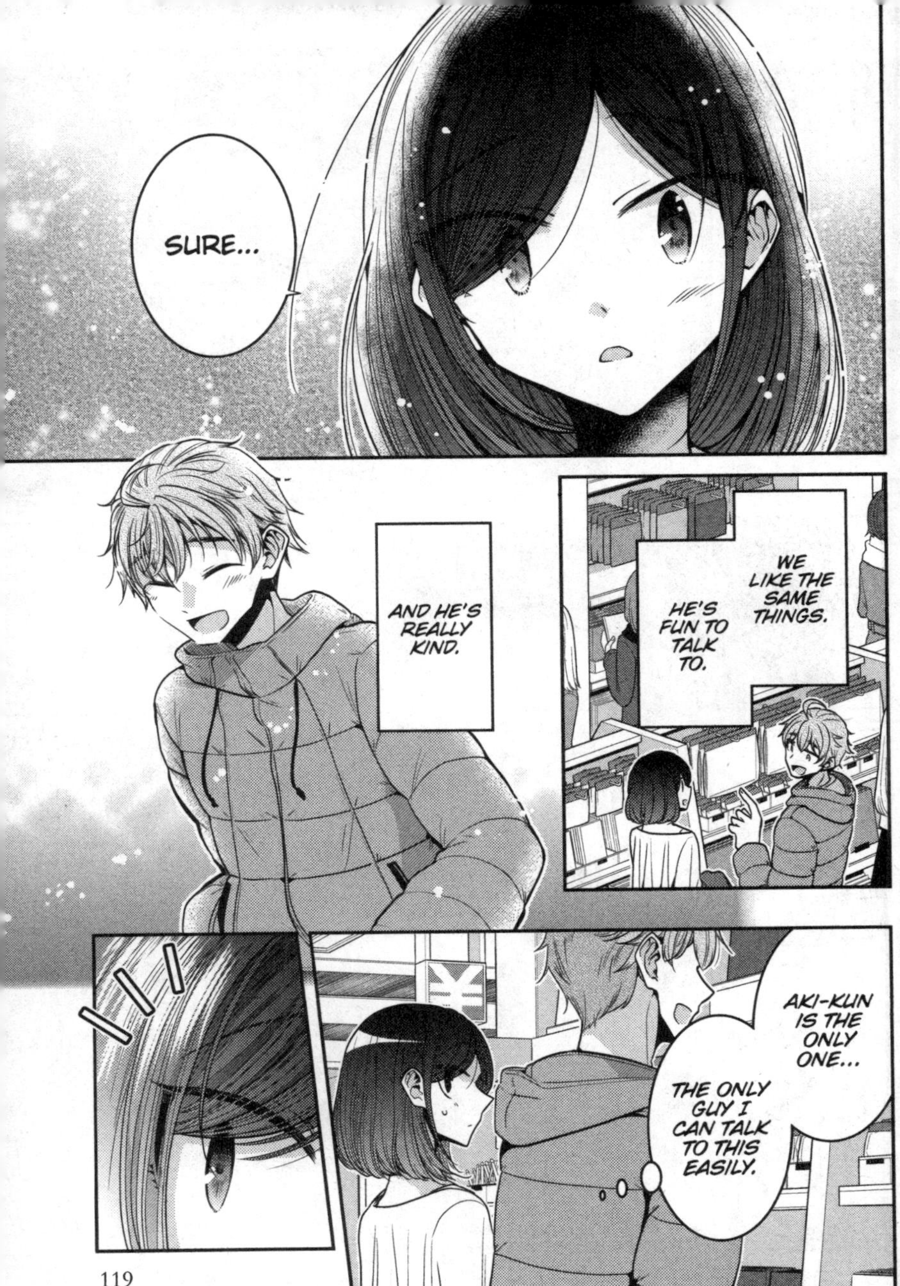
SURE...
WE LIKE THE SAME THINGS.
HE'S FUN TO TALK TO.
AND HE'S REALLY KIND.
AKI-KUN IS THE ONLY ONE...
THE ONLY GUY I CAN TALK TO THIS EASILY.

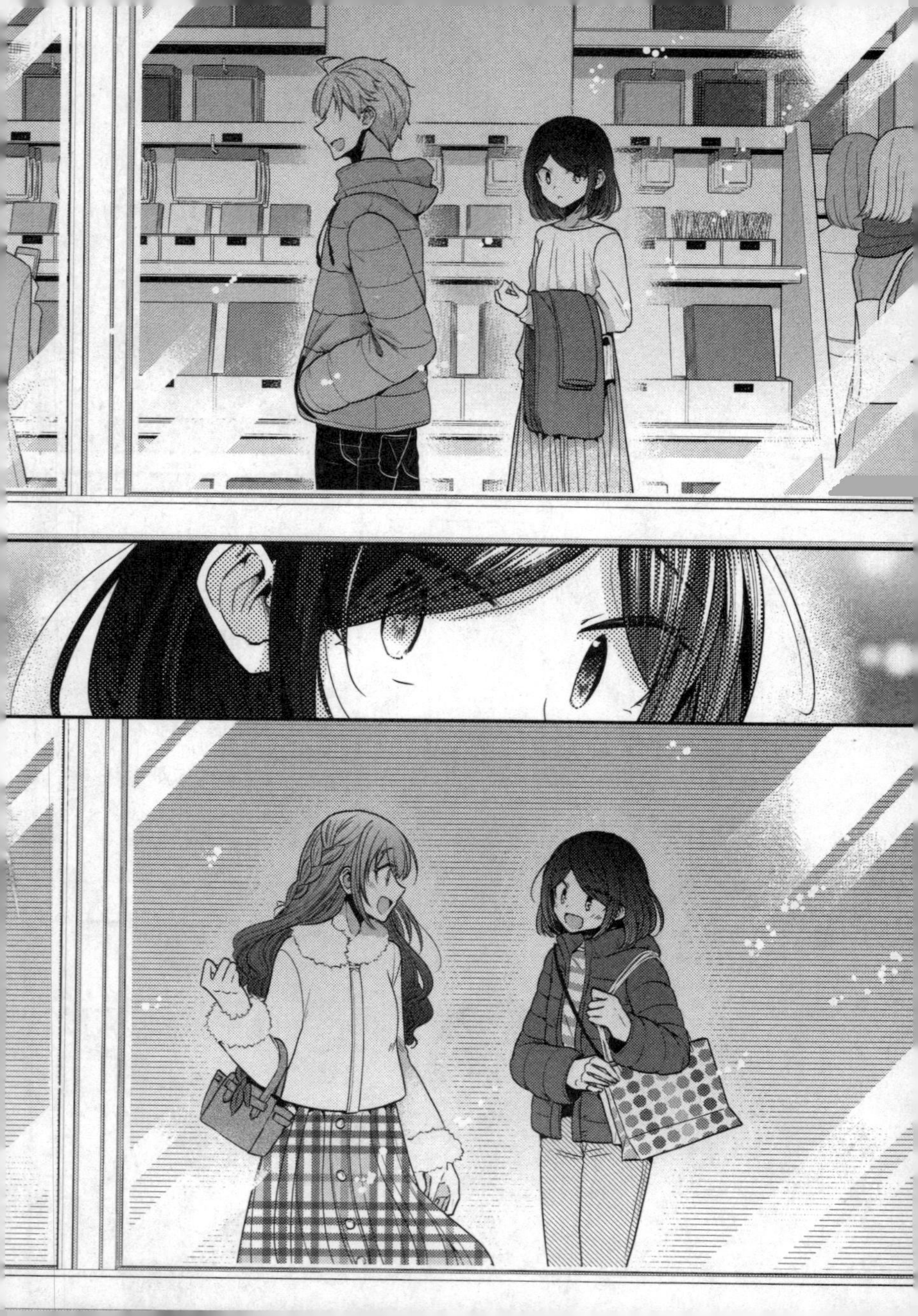

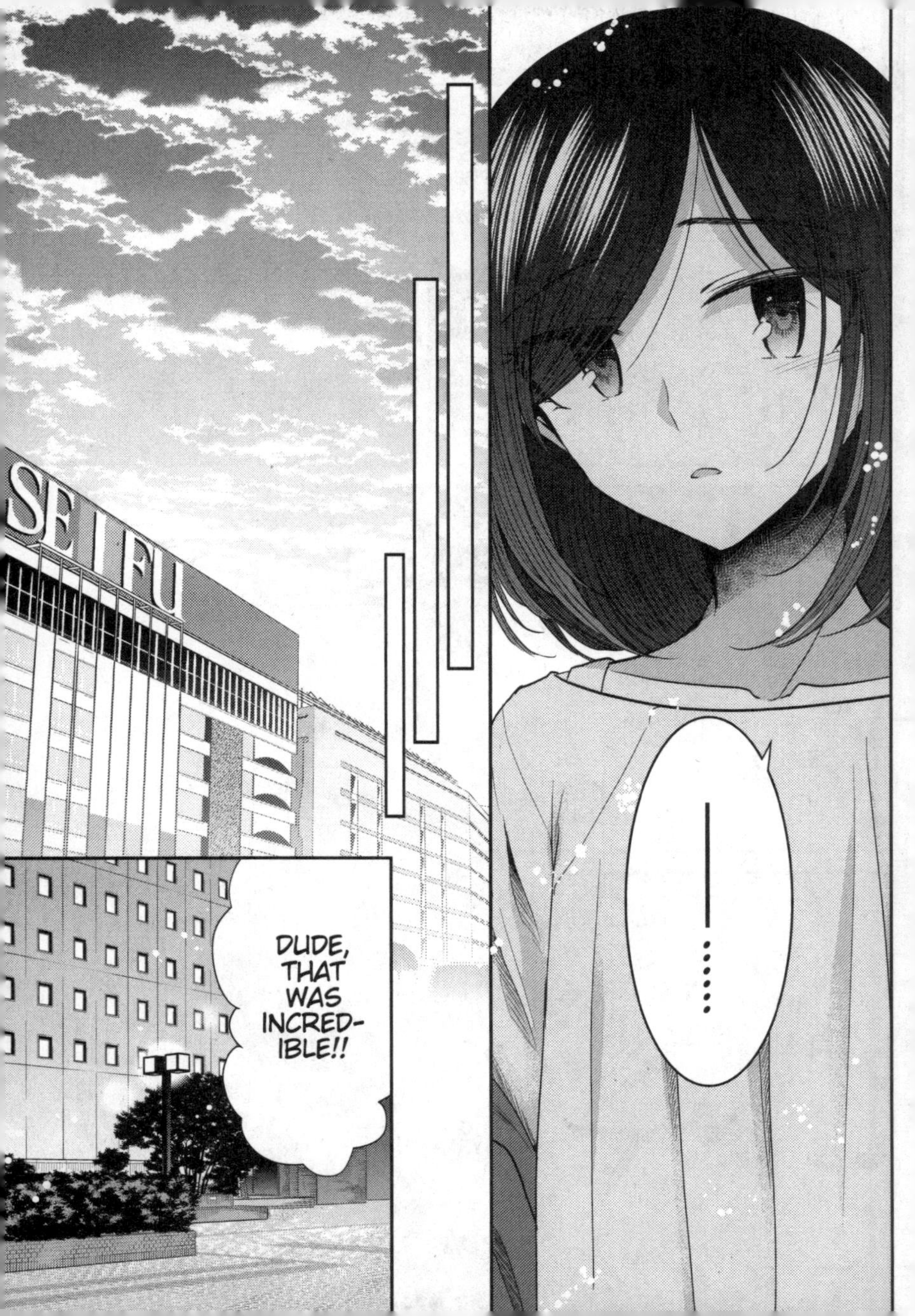
SEIFU
——……
DUDE, THAT WAS INCRED-IBLE!!

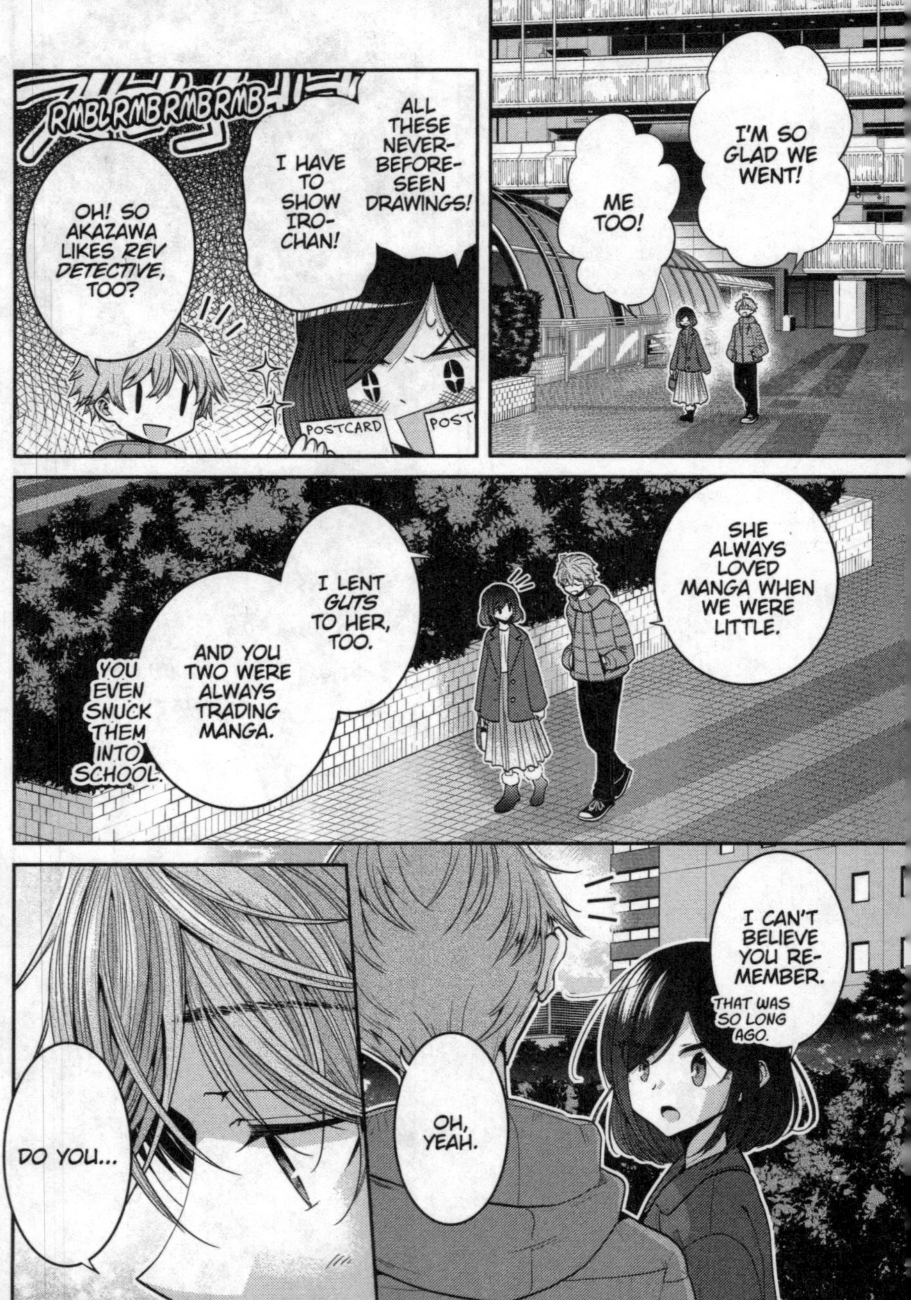
I'M SO GLAD WE WENT!
ME TOO!
ALL THESE NEVER-BEFORE-SEEN DRAWINGS!
I HAVE TO SHOW IRO-CHAN!
RMBL RMB RMB RMB
OH! SO AKAZAWA LIKES *REV DETECTIVE*, TOO?
POSTCARD
POST
SHE ALWAYS LOVED MANGA WHEN WE WERE LITTLE.
I LENT *GUTS* TO HER, TOO.
AND YOU TWO WERE ALWAYS TRADING MANGA.
YOU EVEN SNUCK THEM INTO SCHOOL.
I CAN'T BELIEVE YOU RE-MEMBER.
THAT WAS SO LONG AGO.
OH, YEAH.
DO YOU...

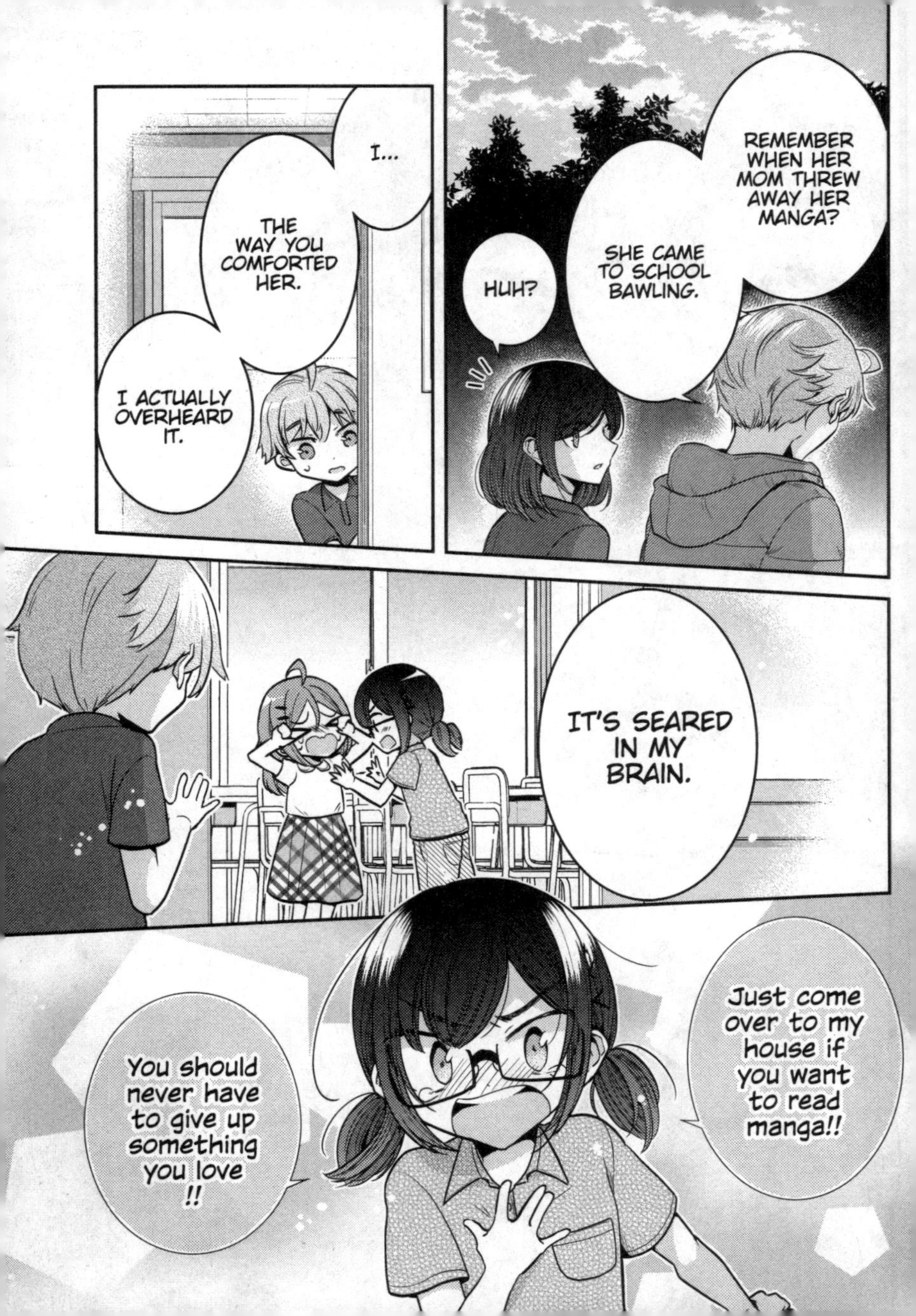
REMEMBER WHEN HER MOM THREW AWAY HER MANGA?
SHE CAME TO SCHOOL BAWLING.
HUH?
I...
THE WAY YOU COMFORTED HER.
I ACTUALLY OVERHEARD IT.
IT'S SEARED IN MY BRAIN.
Just come over to my house if you want to read manga!!
You should never have to give up something you love !!

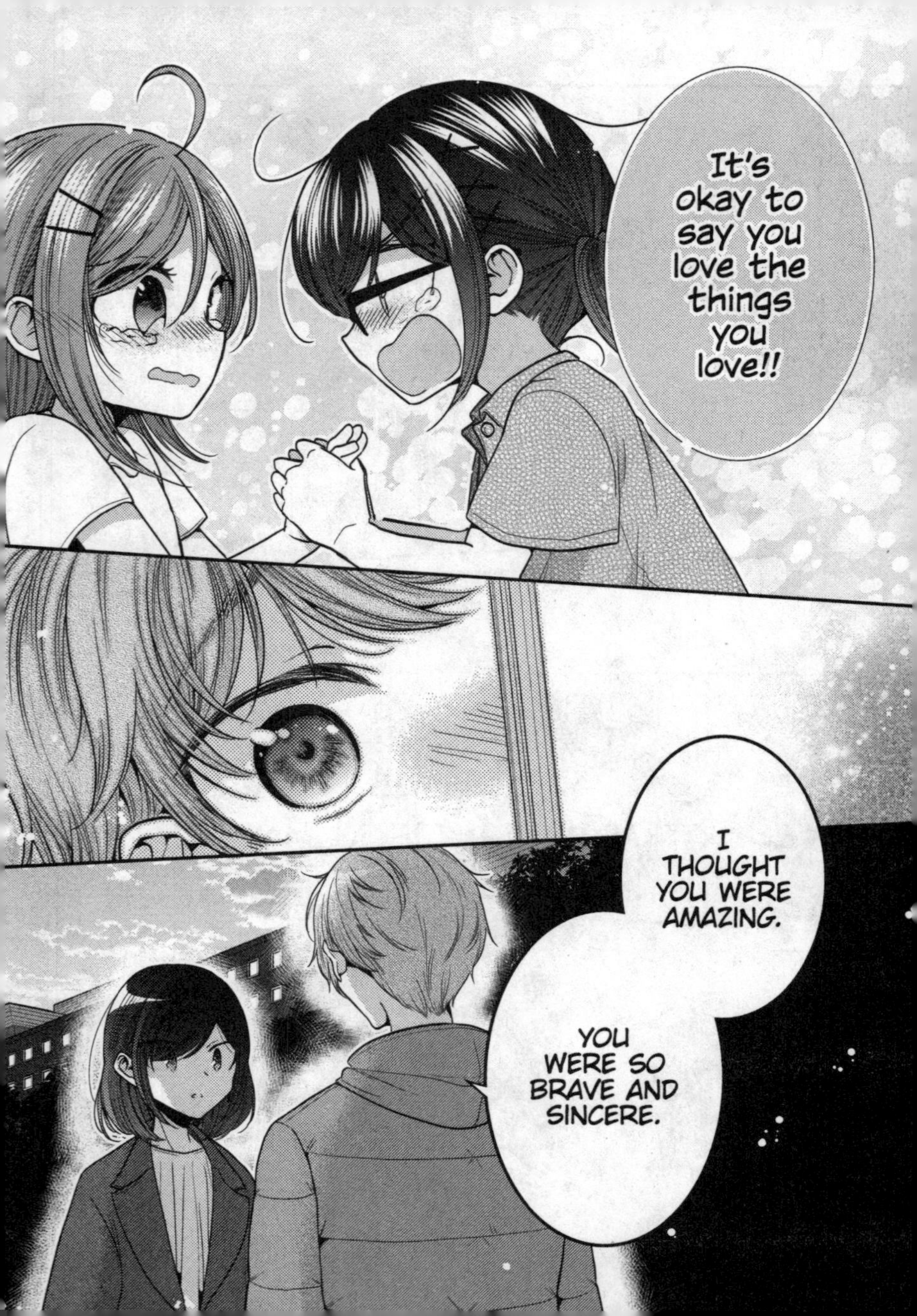
It's okay to say you love the things you love!!
I THOUGHT YOU WERE AMAZING.
YOU WERE SO BRAVE AND SINCERE.

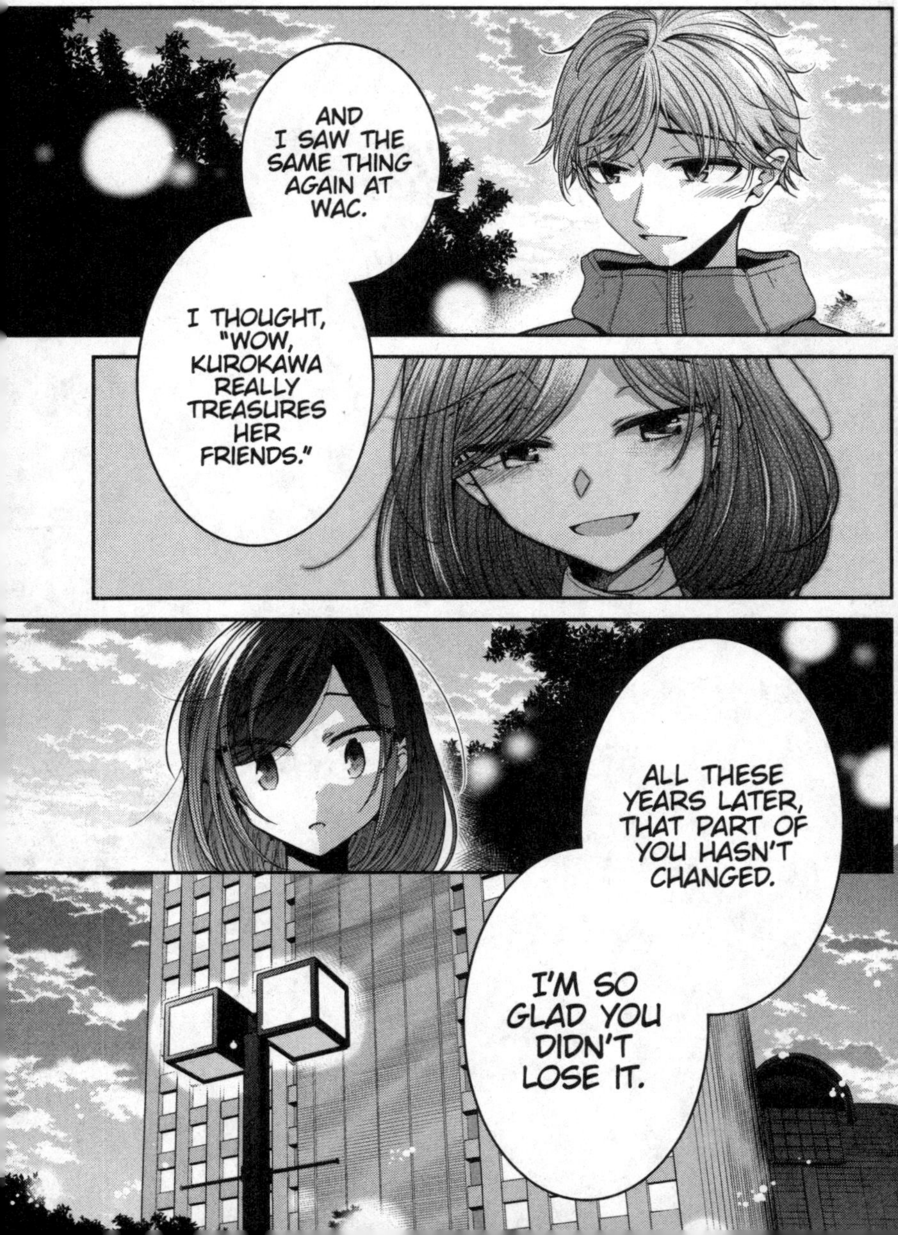
AND I SAW THE SAME THING AGAIN AT WAC.
I THOUGHT, "WOW, KUROKAWA REALLY TREASURES HER FRIENDS."
ALL THESE YEARS LATER, THAT PART OF YOU HASN'T CHANGED.
I'M SO GLAD YOU DIDN'T LOSE IT.

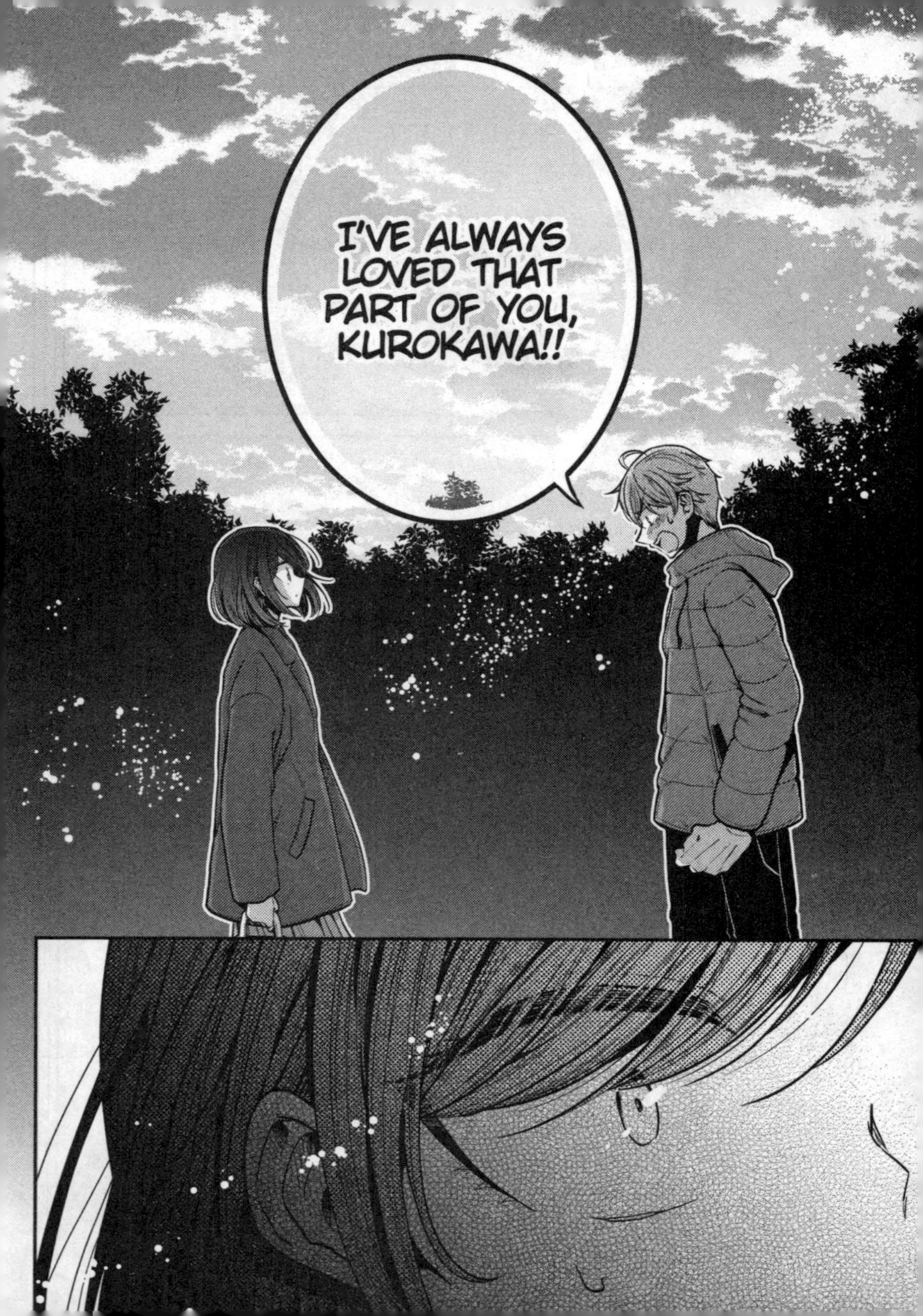
I'VE ALWAYS LOVED THAT PART OF YOU, KUROKAWA!!

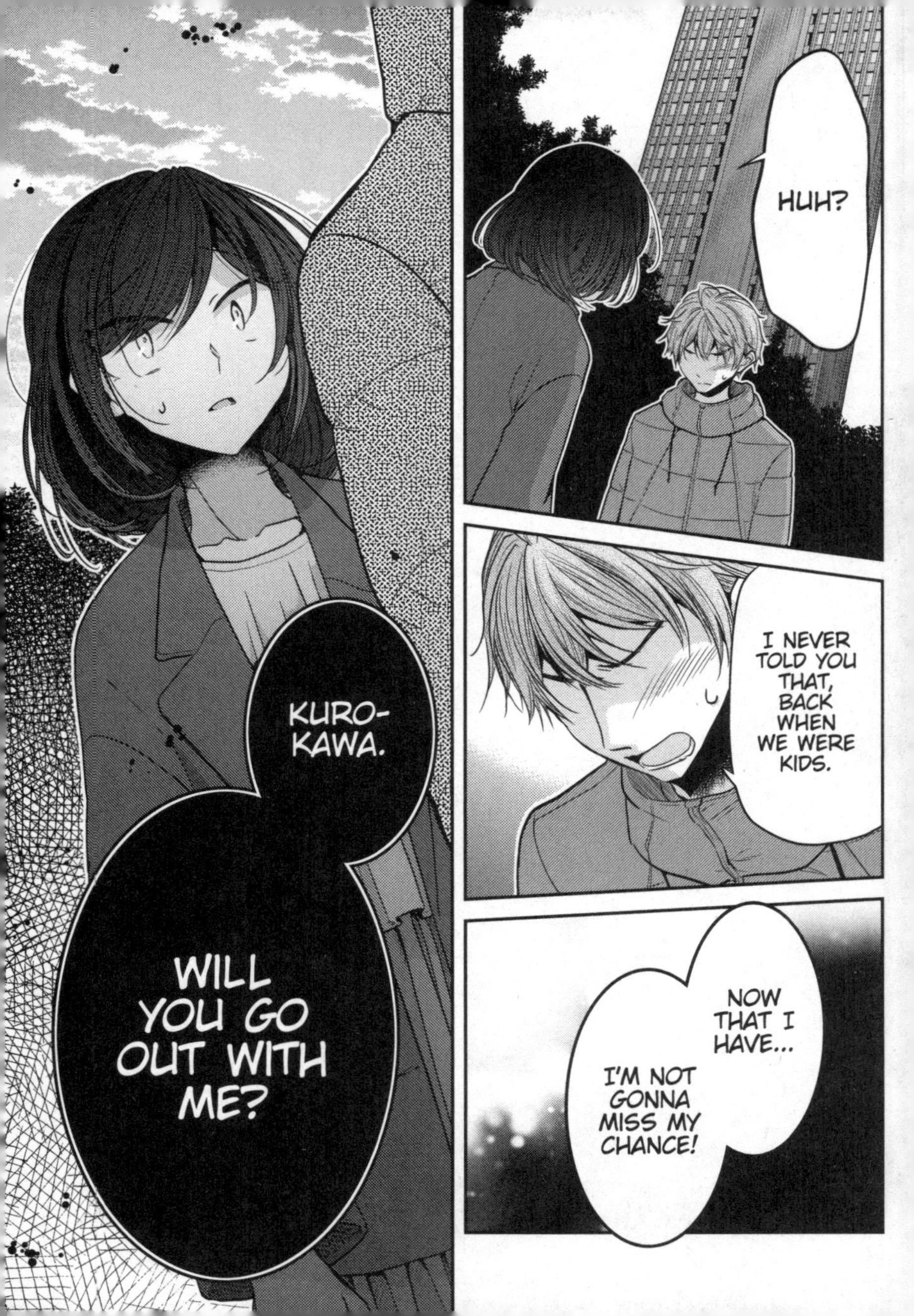
HUH?
I NEVER TOLD YOU THAT, BACK WHEN WE WERE KIDS.
NOW THAT I HAVE...
I'M NOT GONNA MISS MY CHANCE!
KURO-KAWA.
WILL YOU GO OUT WITH ME?

Failed Princesses

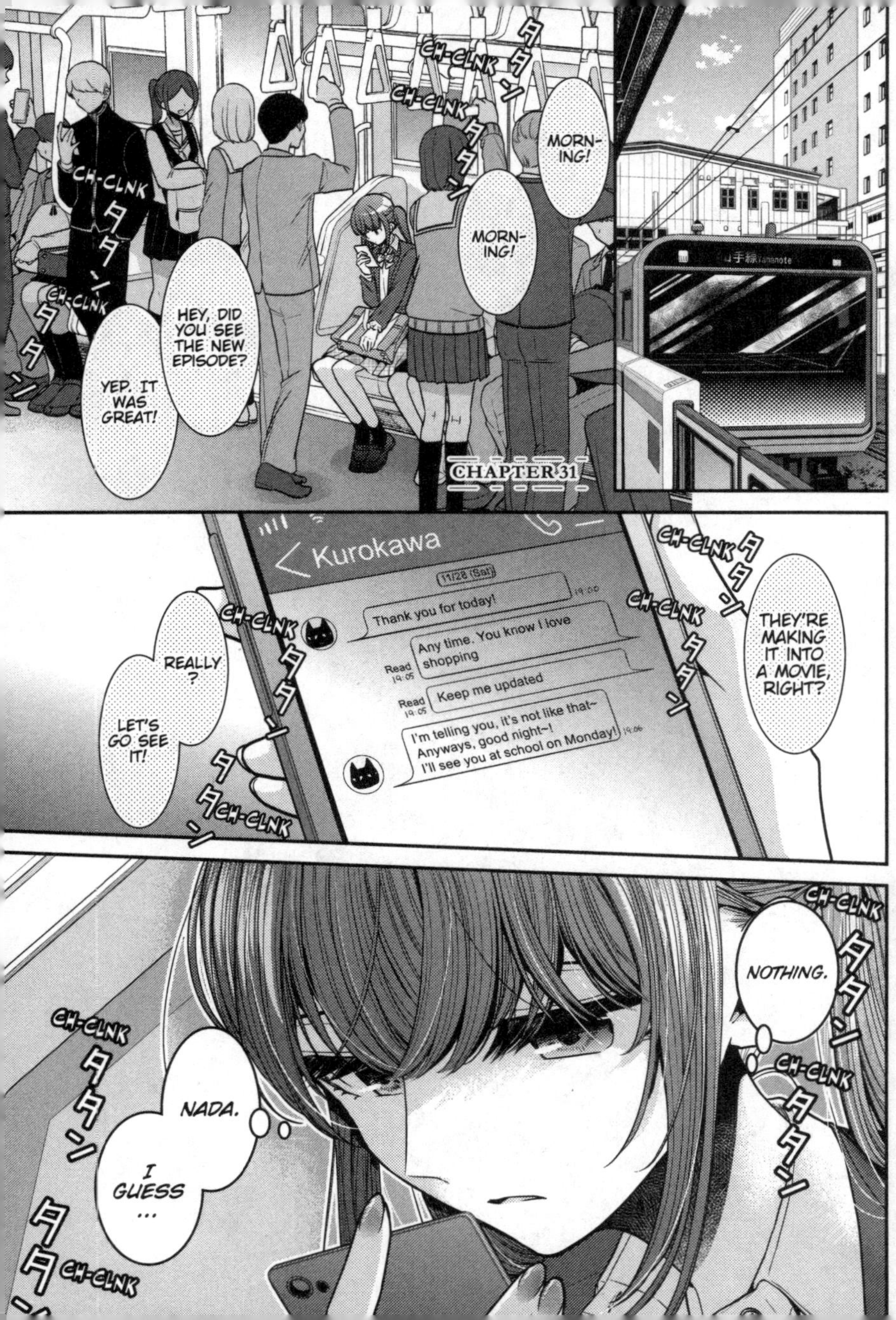
CH-CLNK タタン
CH-CLNK タタン
MORNING!
MORNING!
CH-CLNK タタン
CH-CLNK タタン
HEY, DID YOU SEE THE NEW EPISODE?
YEP. IT WAS GREAT!
CHAPTER 31
CH-CLNK タタン
THEY'RE MAKING IT INTO A MOVIE, RIGHT?
CH-CLNK タタン
Kurokawa
11/28 (Sat)
Thank you for today! 19:00
Read 19:05 Any time. You know I love shopping
Read 19:05 Keep me updated
I'm telling you, it's not like that~ Anyways, good night~! I'll see you at school on Monday! 19:06
CH-CLNK タタン
REALLY?
LET'S GO SEE IT!
タタ CH-CLNK ン
CH-CLNK タタン
NOTHING.
CH-CLNK タタン
CH-CLNK タタン
NADA.
I GUESS...
タタ CH-CLNK ン

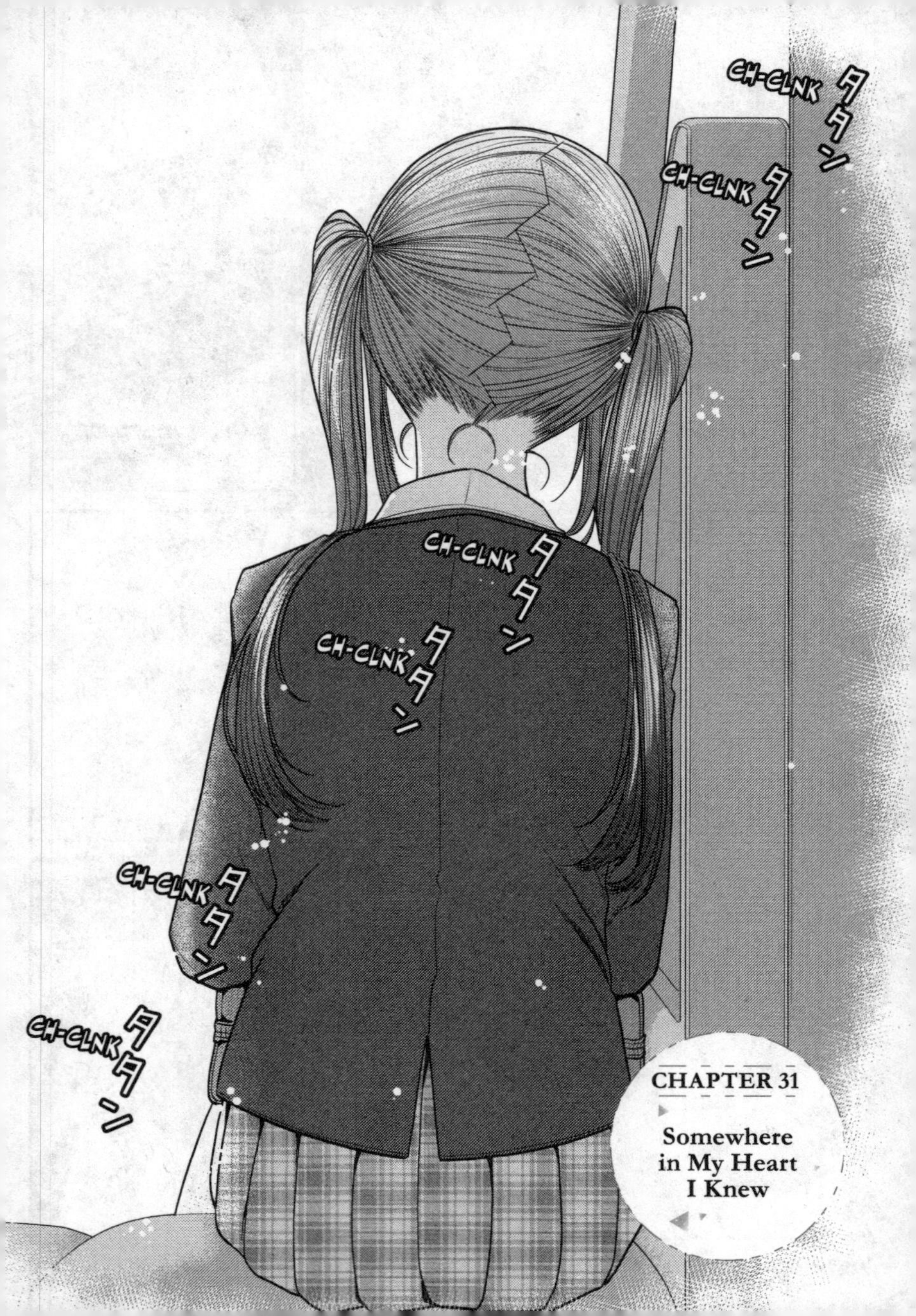
CH-CLNK
タターン
CH-CLNK
タターン
CH-CLNK
タターン
CH-CLNK
タターン
CH-CLNK
タターン
CH-CLNK
タターン

CHAPTER 31

Somewhere in My Heart I Knew

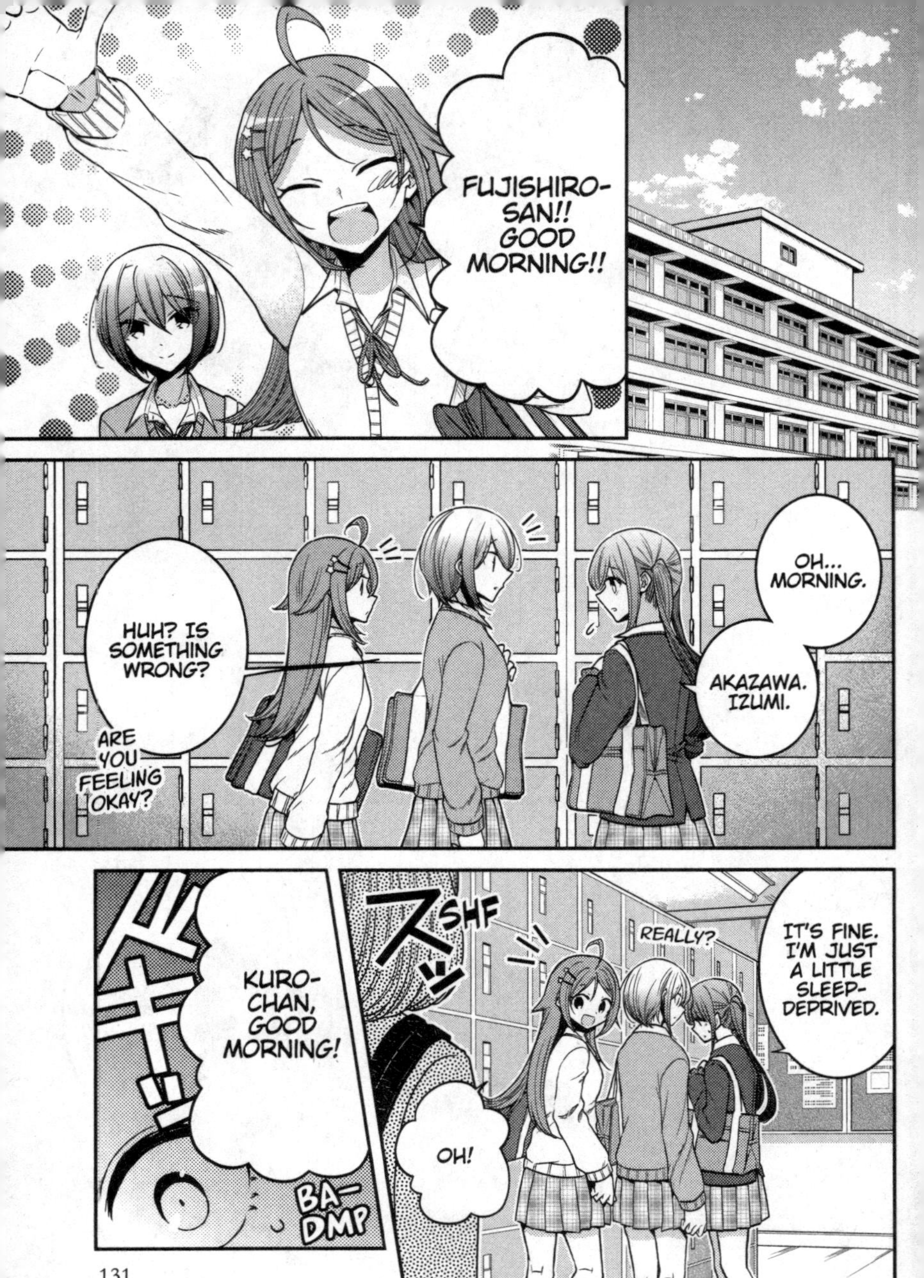
FUJISHIRO-SAN!! GOOD MORNING!!
OH... MORNING.
AKAZAWA. IZUMI.
HUH? IS SOMETHING WRONG?
ARE YOU FEELING OKAY?
IT'S FINE. I'M JUST A LITTLE SLEEP-DEPRIVED.
REALLY?
SHF
OH!
KURO-CHAN, GOOD MORNING!
BA-DMP

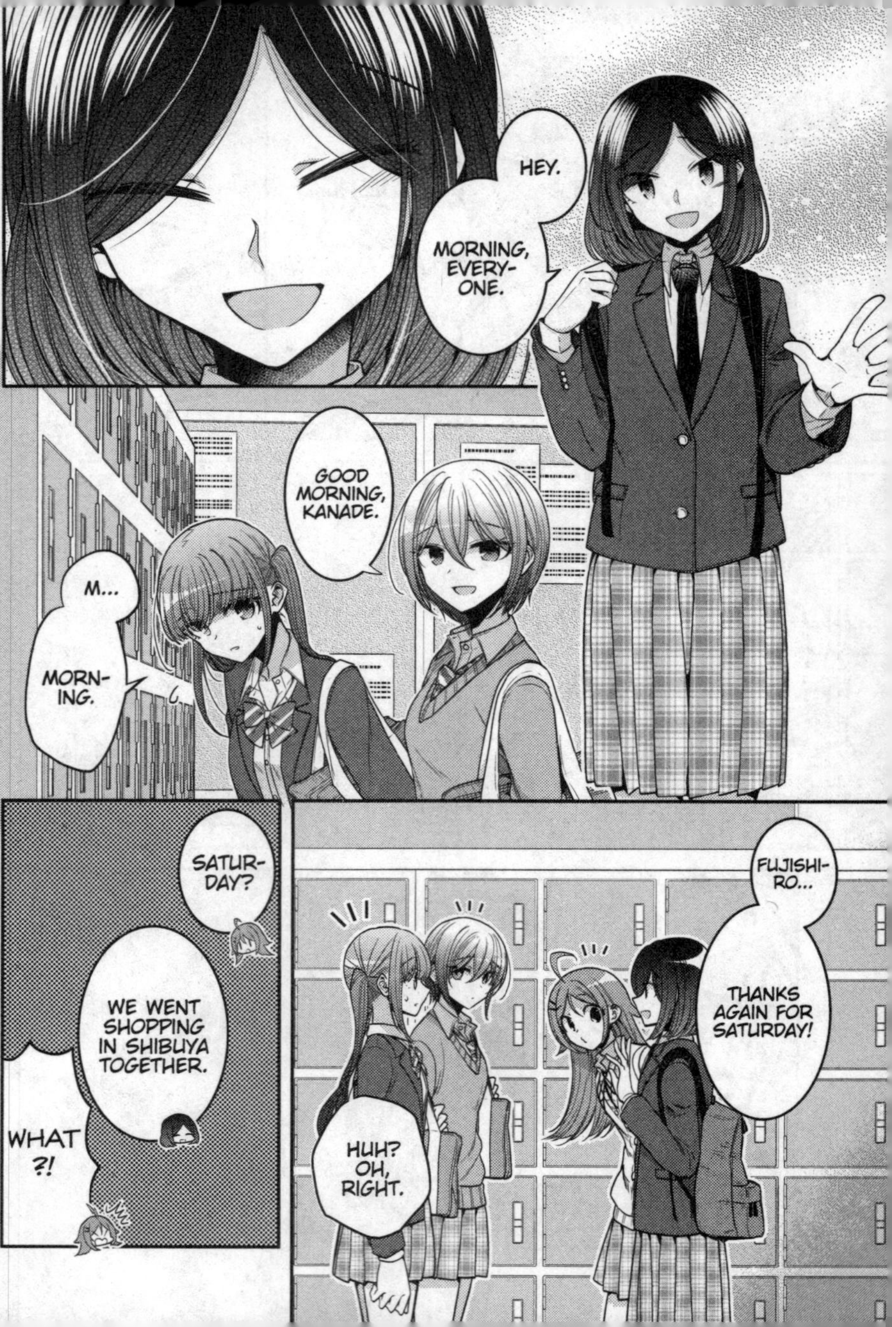
HEY.
MORNING, EVERY-ONE.
GOOD MORNING, KANADE.
M...
MORN-ING.
FUJISHI-RO...
THANKS AGAIN FOR SATURDAY!
HUH? OH, RIGHT.
SATUR-DAY?
WE WENT SHOPPING IN SHIBUYA TOGETHER.
WHAT?!

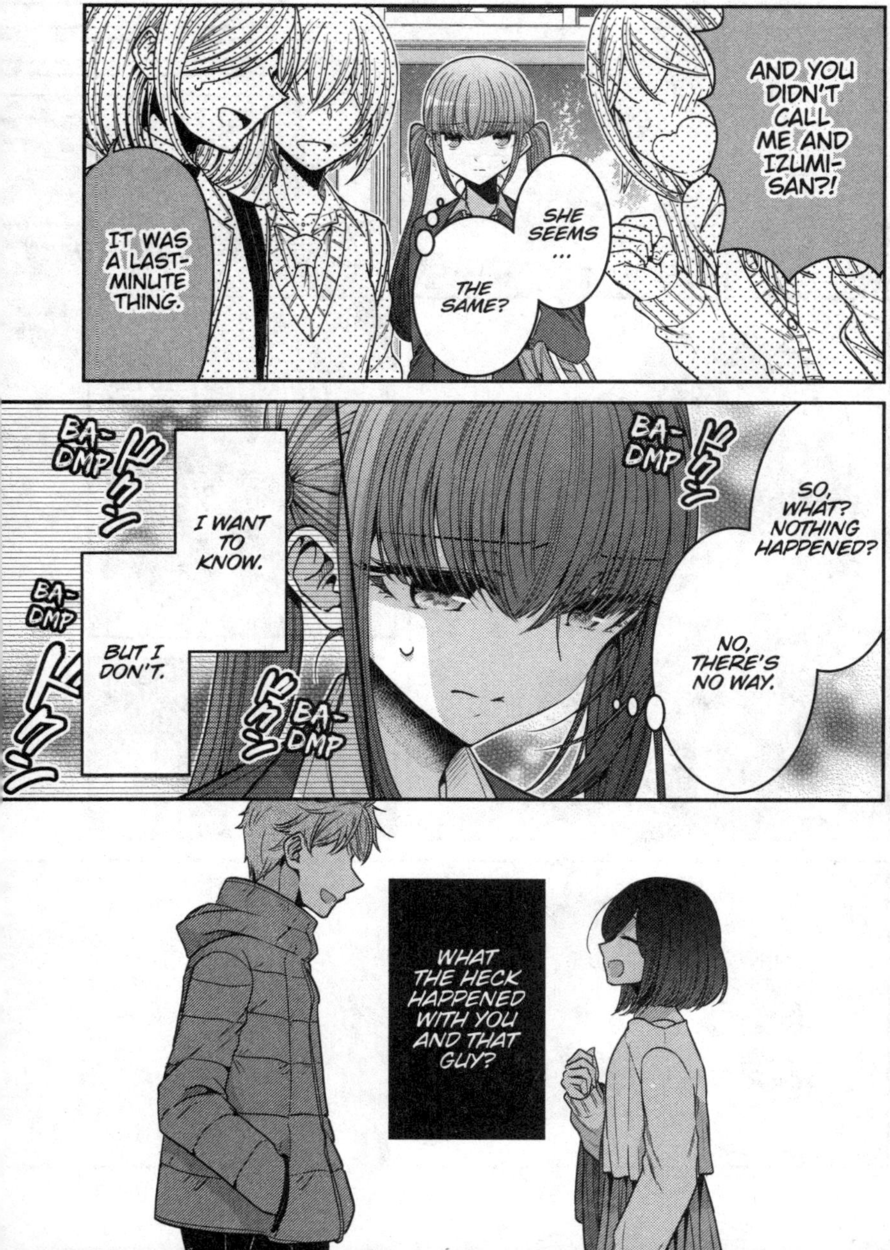
AND YOU DIDN'T CALL ME AND IZUMI-SAN?!
SHE SEEMS ...
THE SAME?
IT WAS A LAST-MINUTE THING.
BA-DMP
SO, WHAT? NOTHING HAPPENED?
NO, THERE'S NO WAY.
BA-DMP
I WANT TO KNOW.
BUT I DON'T.
BA-DMP
BA-DMP
WHAT THE HECK HAPPENED WITH YOU AND THAT GUY?

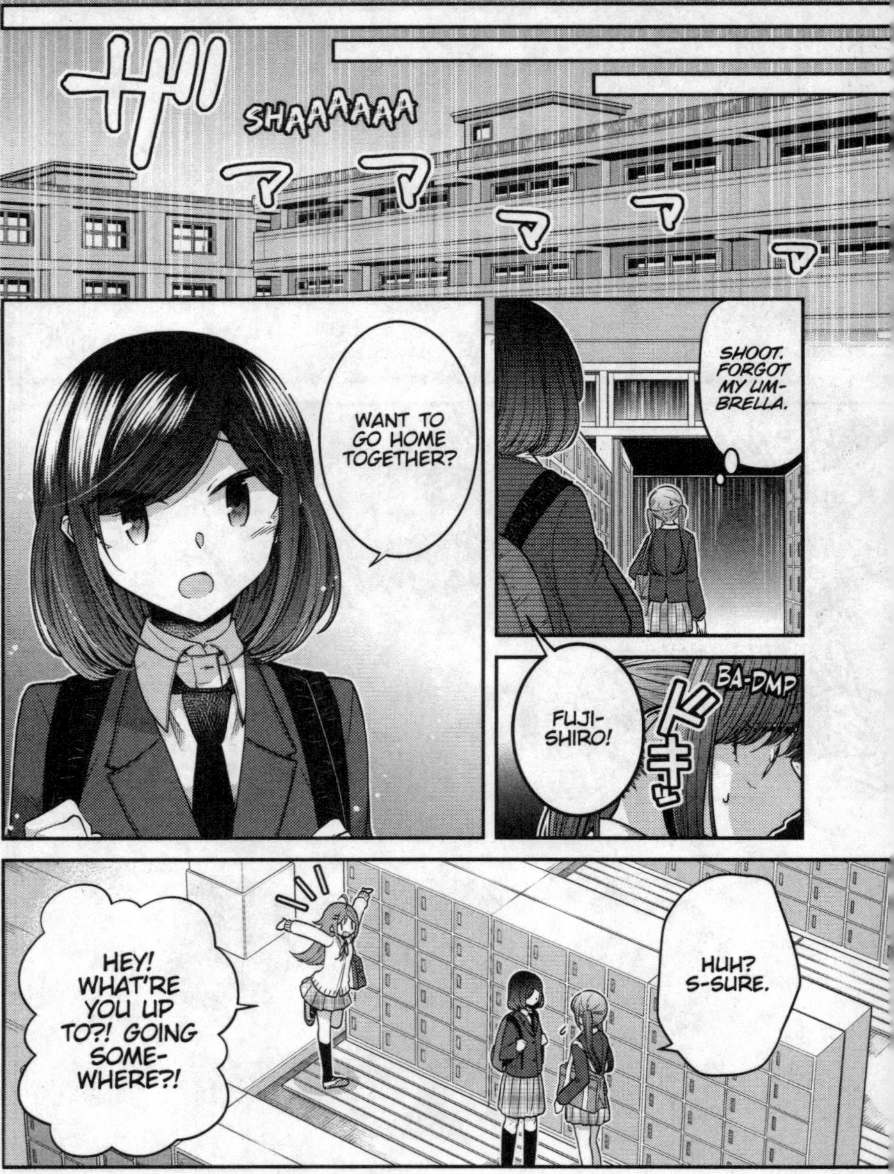
SHAAAAAA
SHOOT. FORGOT MY UM-BRELLA.
BA-DMP
FUJI-SHIRO!
WANT TO GO HOME TOGETHER?
HUH? S-SURE.
HEY! WHAT'RE YOU UP TO?! GOING SOME-WHERE?!

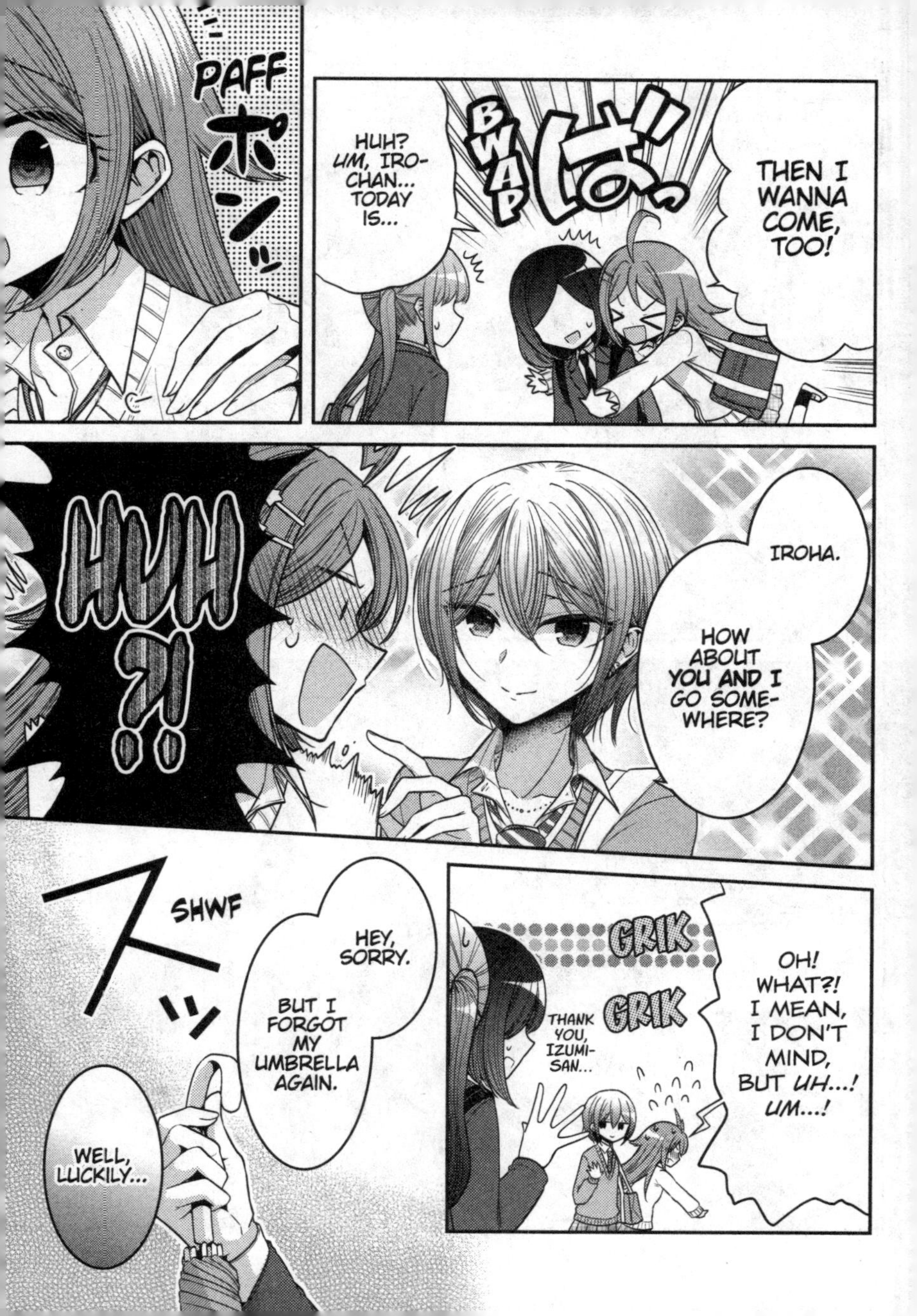
THEN I WANNA COME, TOO!
BWAP
ばっ
HUH? UM, IRO-CHAN... TODAY IS...
PAFF
ポーンッ
IROHA.
HOW ABOUT YOU AND I GO SOME-WHERE?
HUH?!
OH! WHAT?! I MEAN, I DON'T MIND, BUT UH...! UM...!
GRIK
GRIK
THANK YOU, IZUMI-SAN...
SHWF
スッ
HEY, SORRY.
BUT I FORGOT MY UMBRELLA AGAIN.
WELL, LUCKILY...

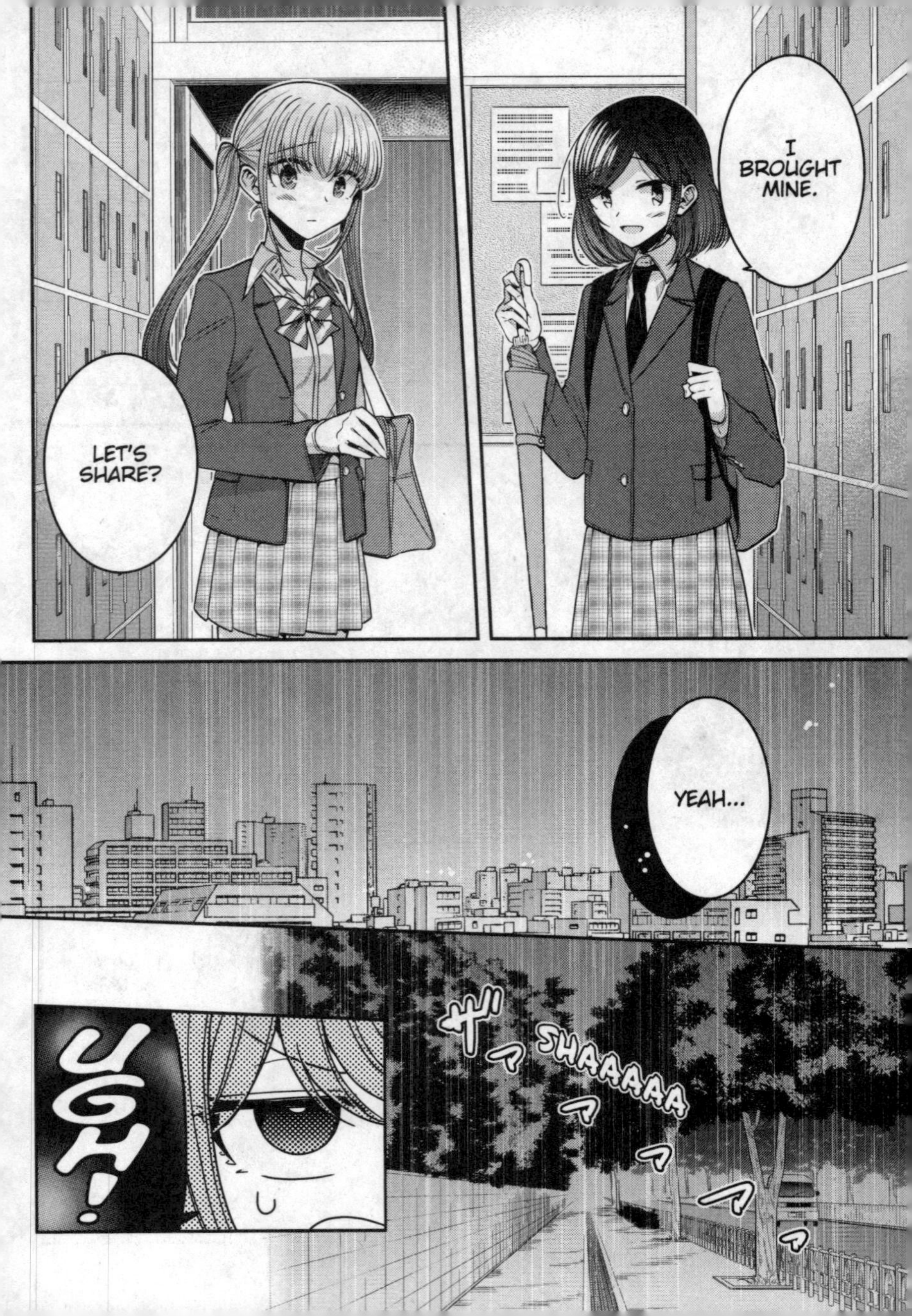
I BROUGHT MINE.
LET'S SHARE?
YEAH...
ザァァァァァ
SHAAAAAA
UGH!

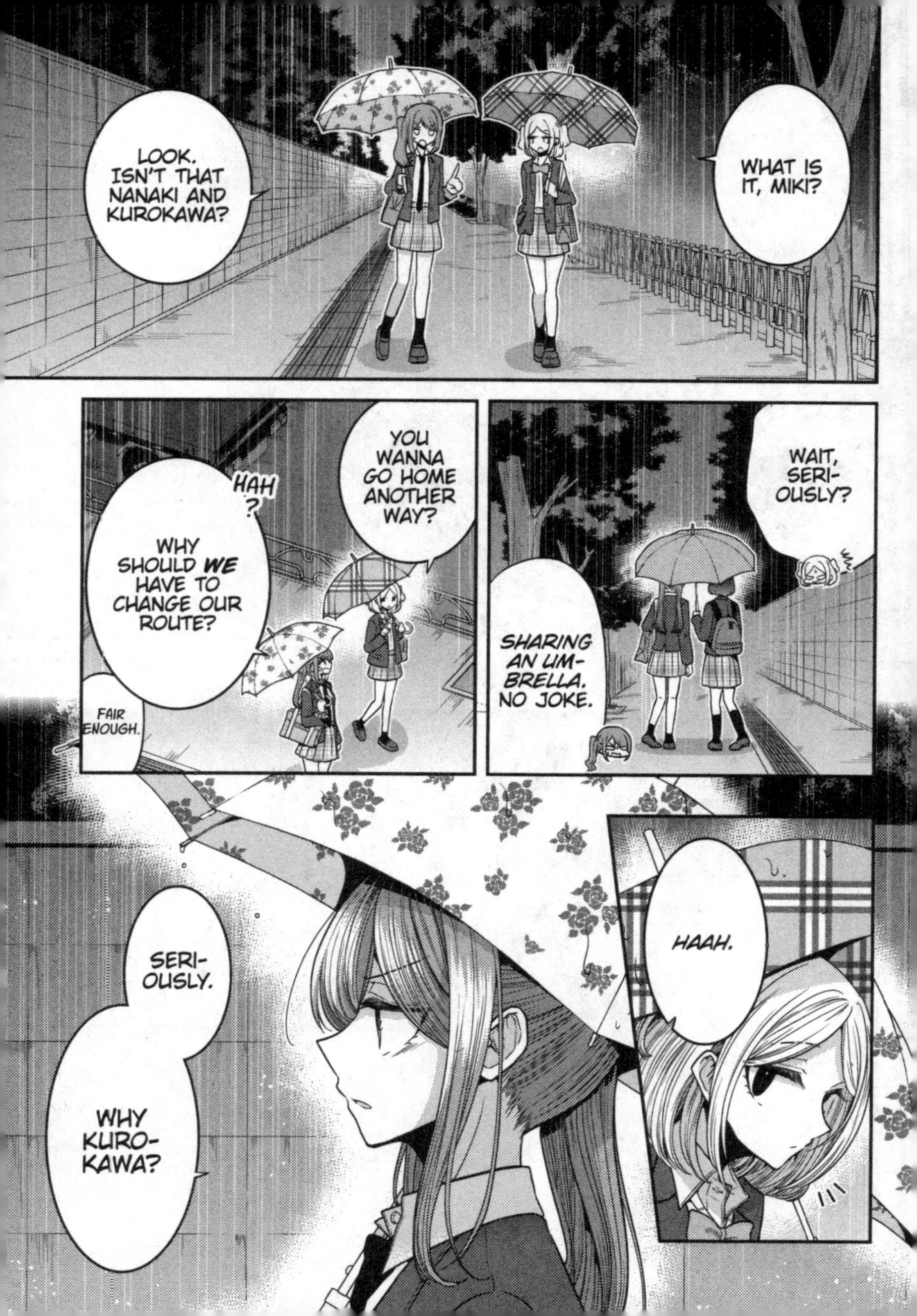
WHAT IS IT, MIKI?
LOOK. ISN'T THAT NANAKI AND KUROKAWA?
WAIT, SERI-OUSLY?
SHARING AN UM-BRELLA. NO JOKE.
YOU WANNA GO HOME ANOTHER WAY?
HAH?
WHY SHOULD *WE* HAVE TO CHANGE OUR ROUTE?
FAIR ENOUGH.
HAAH.
SERI-OUSLY.
WHY KURO-KAWA?

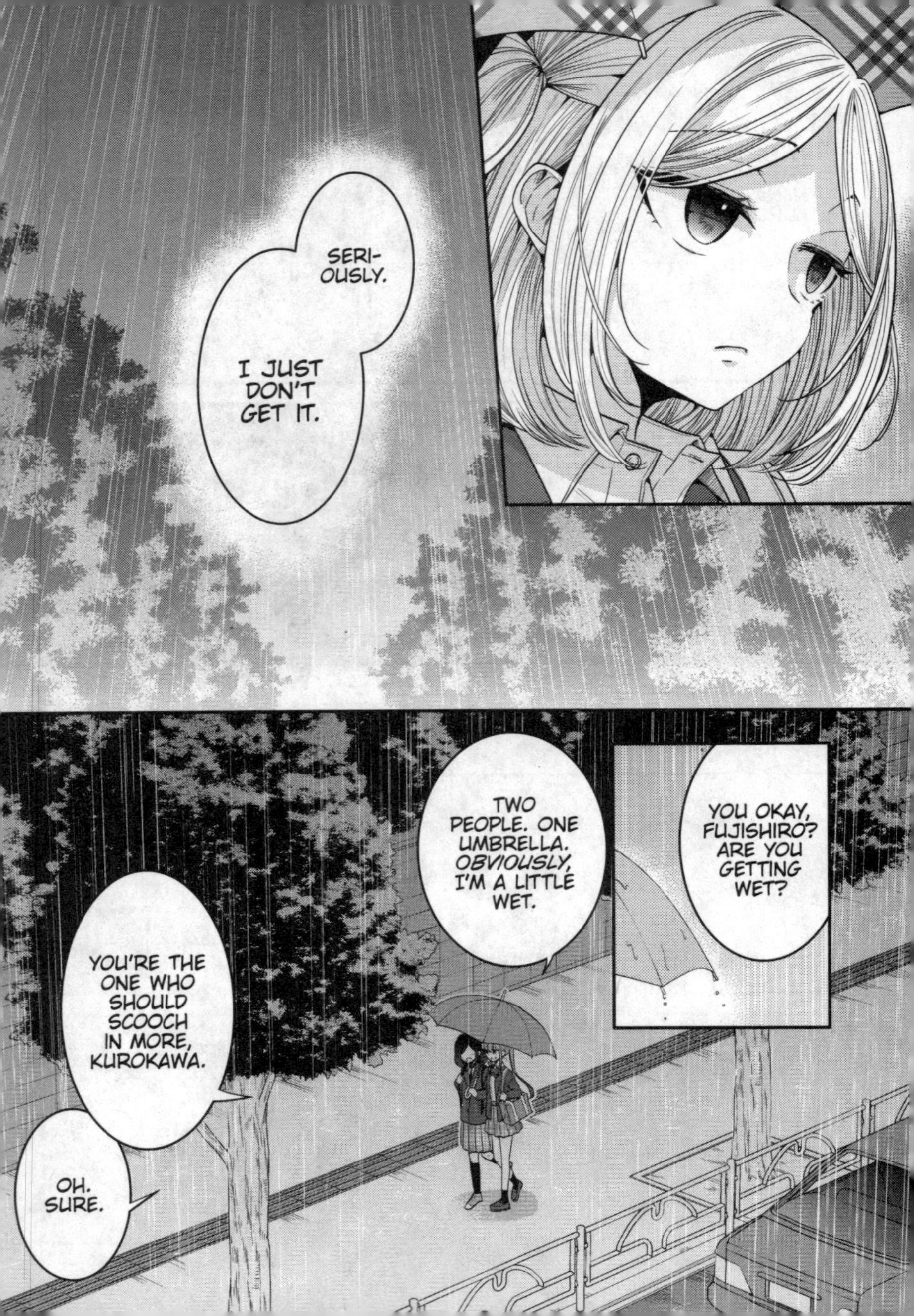
SERI-OUSLY.
I JUST DON'T GET IT.
YOU OKAY, FUJISHIRO? ARE YOU GETTING WET?
TWO PEOPLE. ONE UMBRELLA. OBVIOUSLY, I'M A LITTLE WET.
YOU'RE THE ONE WHO SHOULD SCOOCH IN MORE, KUROKAWA.
OH. SURE.

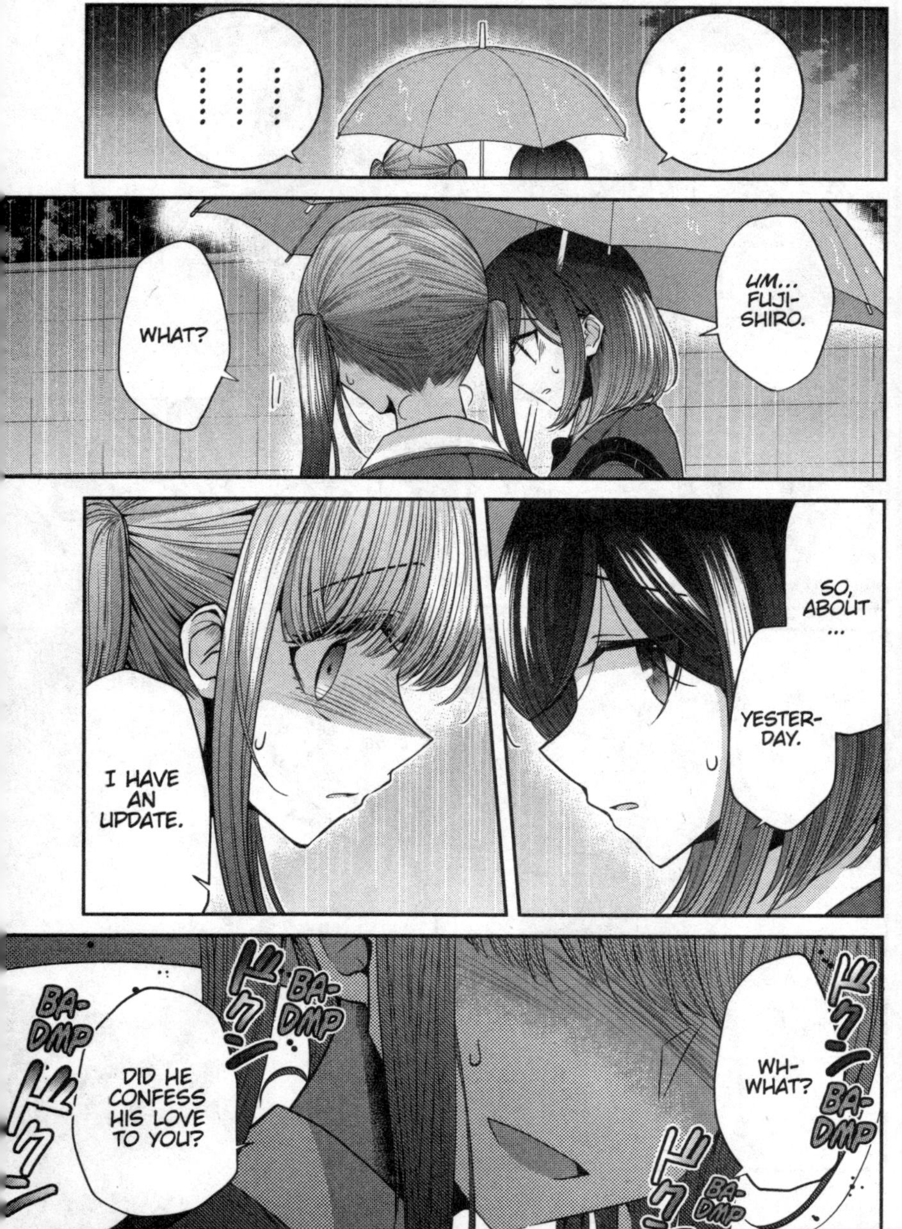
......
......
UM... FUJI-SHIRO.
WHAT?
SO, ABOUT ...
YESTER-DAY.
I HAVE AN UPDATE.
BA-DMP
WH-WHAT?
BA-DMP
BA-DMP
BA-DMP
BA-DMP
DID HE CONFESS HIS LOVE TO YOU?

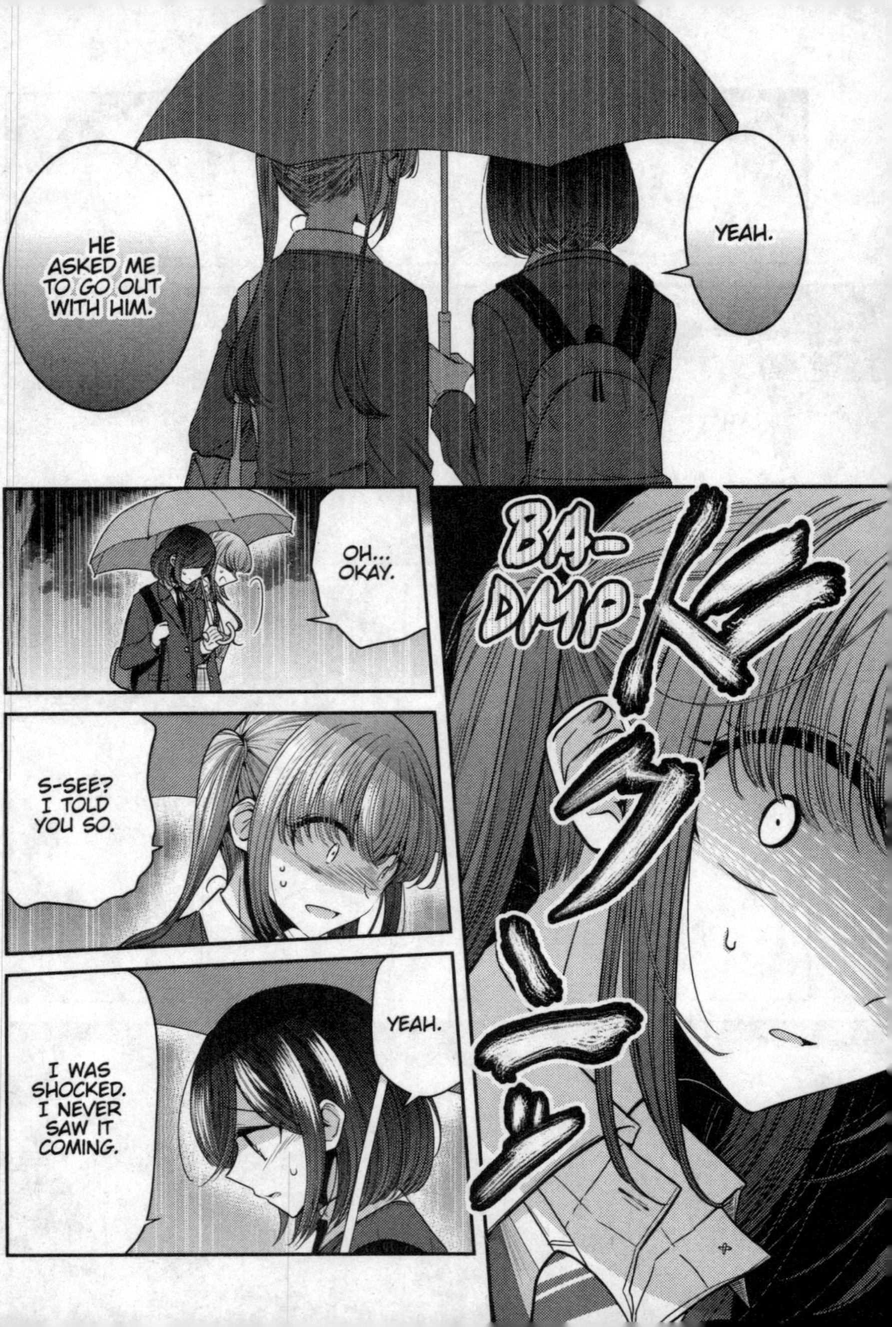
YEAH.
HE ASKED ME TO GO OUT WITH HIM.
BA-DMP
OH... OKAY.
S-SEE? I TOLD YOU SO.
YEAH.
I WAS SHOCKED. I NEVER SAW IT COMING.

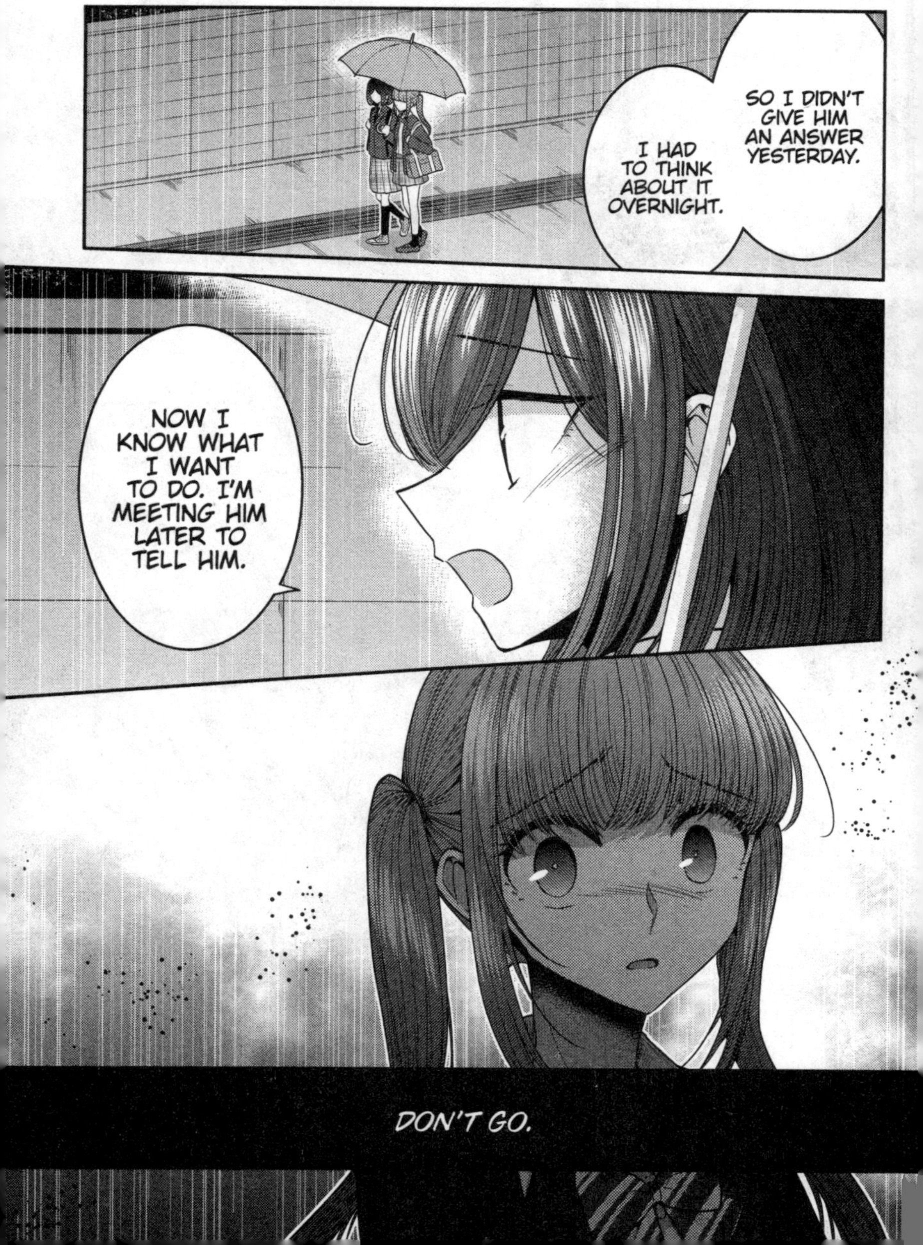
SO I DIDN'T GIVE HIM AN ANSWER YESTERDAY.
I HAD TO THINK ABOUT IT OVERNIGHT.
NOW I KNOW WHAT I WANT TO DO. I'M MEETING HIM LATER TO TELL HIM.
DON'T GO.

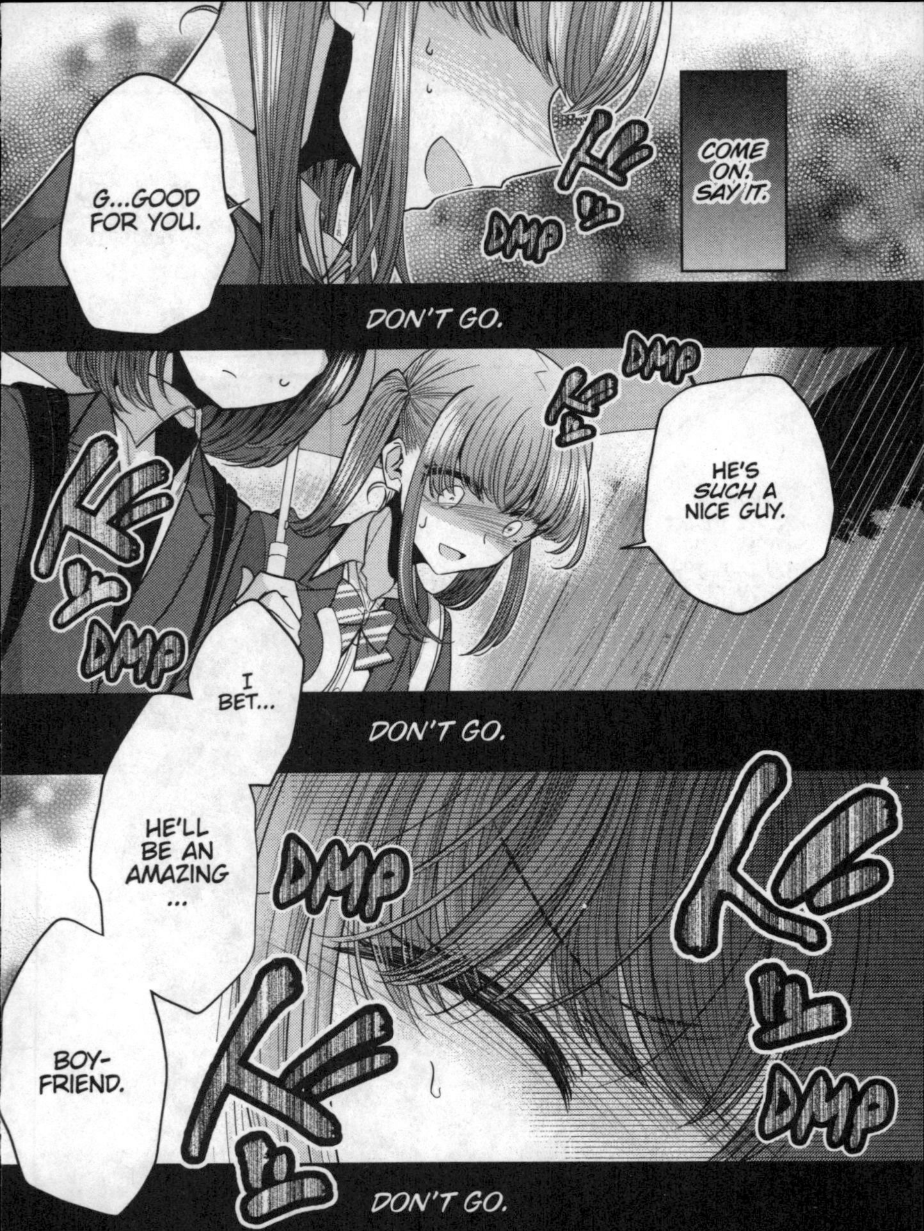

COME ON. SAY IT.
DMP
G...GOOD FOR YOU.
DON'T GO.
DMP
HE'S SUCH A NICE GUY.
DMP
I BET...
DON'T GO.
DMP
HE'LL BE AN AMAZING ...
DMP
BOY-FRIEND.
DON'T GO.

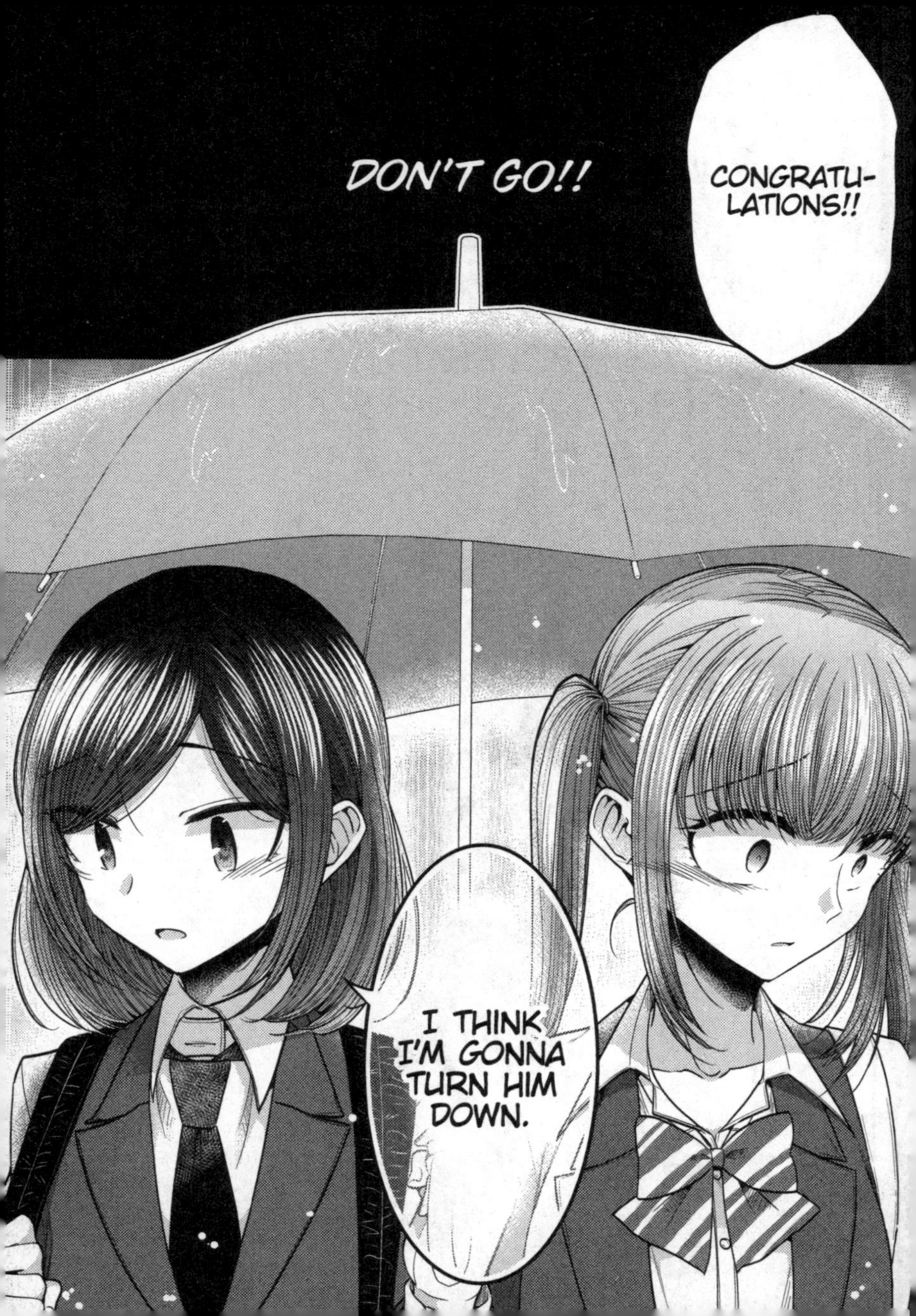
CONGRATU-
LATIONS!!
DON'T GO!!
I THINK I'M GONNA TURN HIM DOWN.

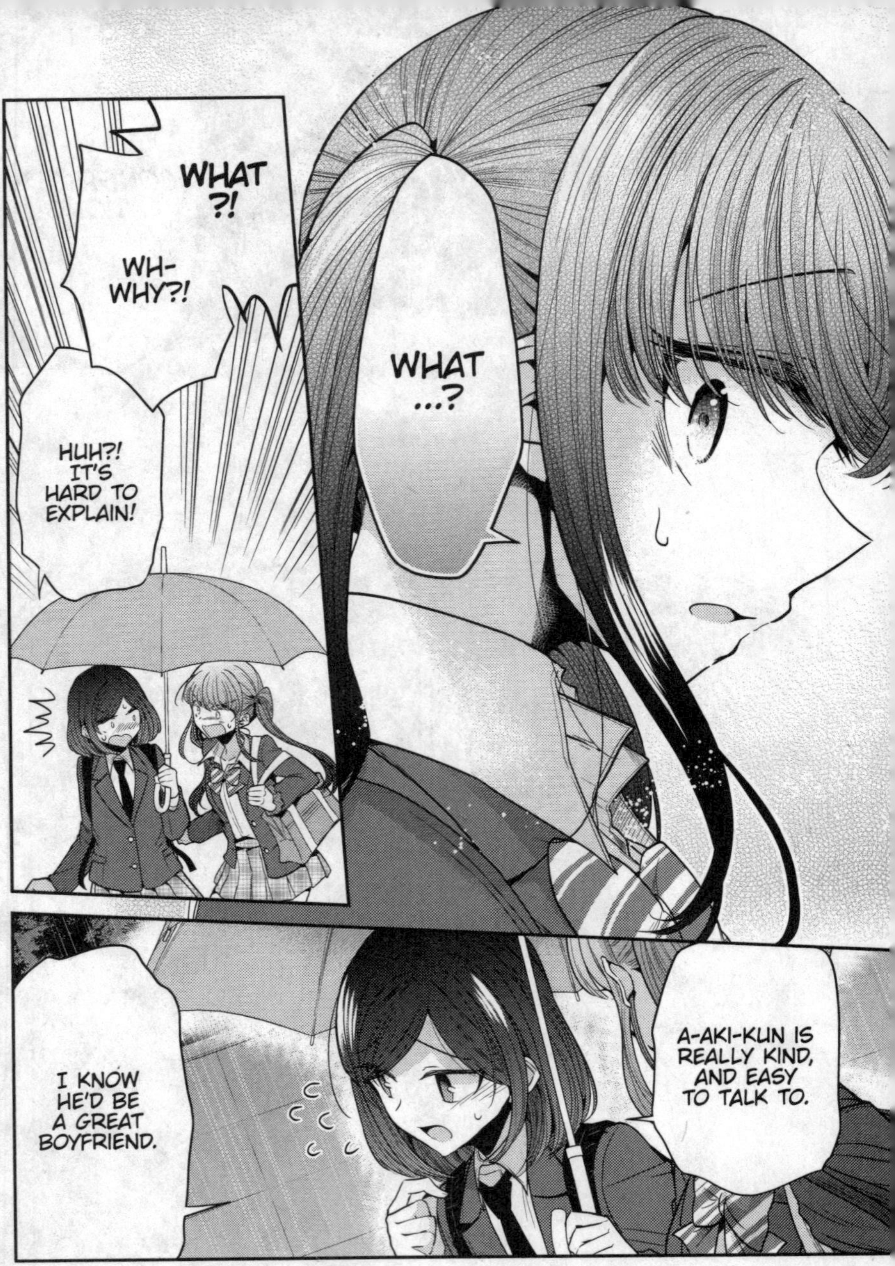
WHAT ...?
WHAT ?!
WH- WHY?!
HUH?! IT'S HARD TO EXPLAIN!
A-AKI-KUN IS REALLY KIND, AND EASY TO TALK TO.
I KNOW HE'D BE A GREAT BOYFRIEND.

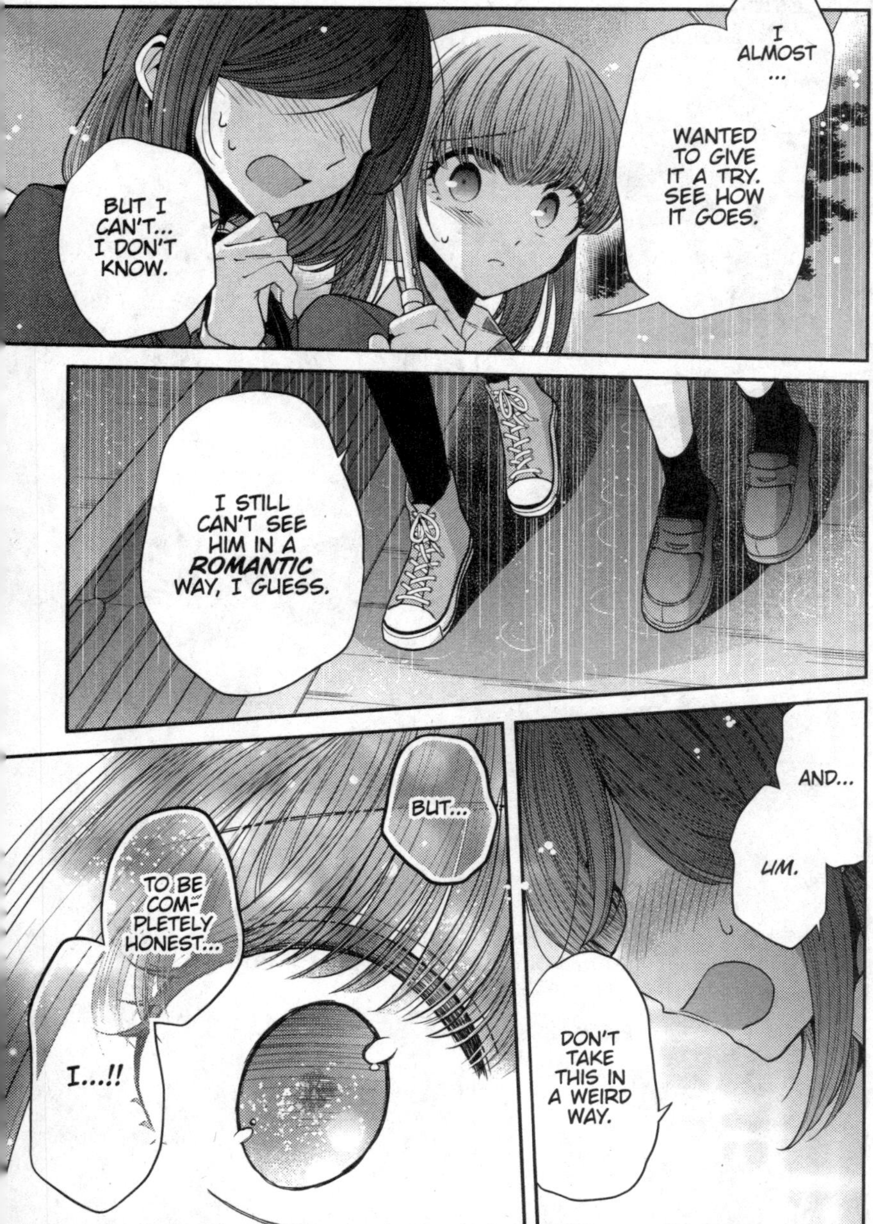
I ALMOST ...
WANTED TO GIVE IT A TRY. SEE HOW IT GOES.
BUT I CAN'T... I DON'T KNOW.
I STILL CAN'T SEE HIM IN A *ROMANTIC* WAY, I GUESS.
AND...
UM.
DON'T TAKE THIS IN A WEIRD WAY.
BUT...
TO BE COM-PLETELY HONEST...
I...!!

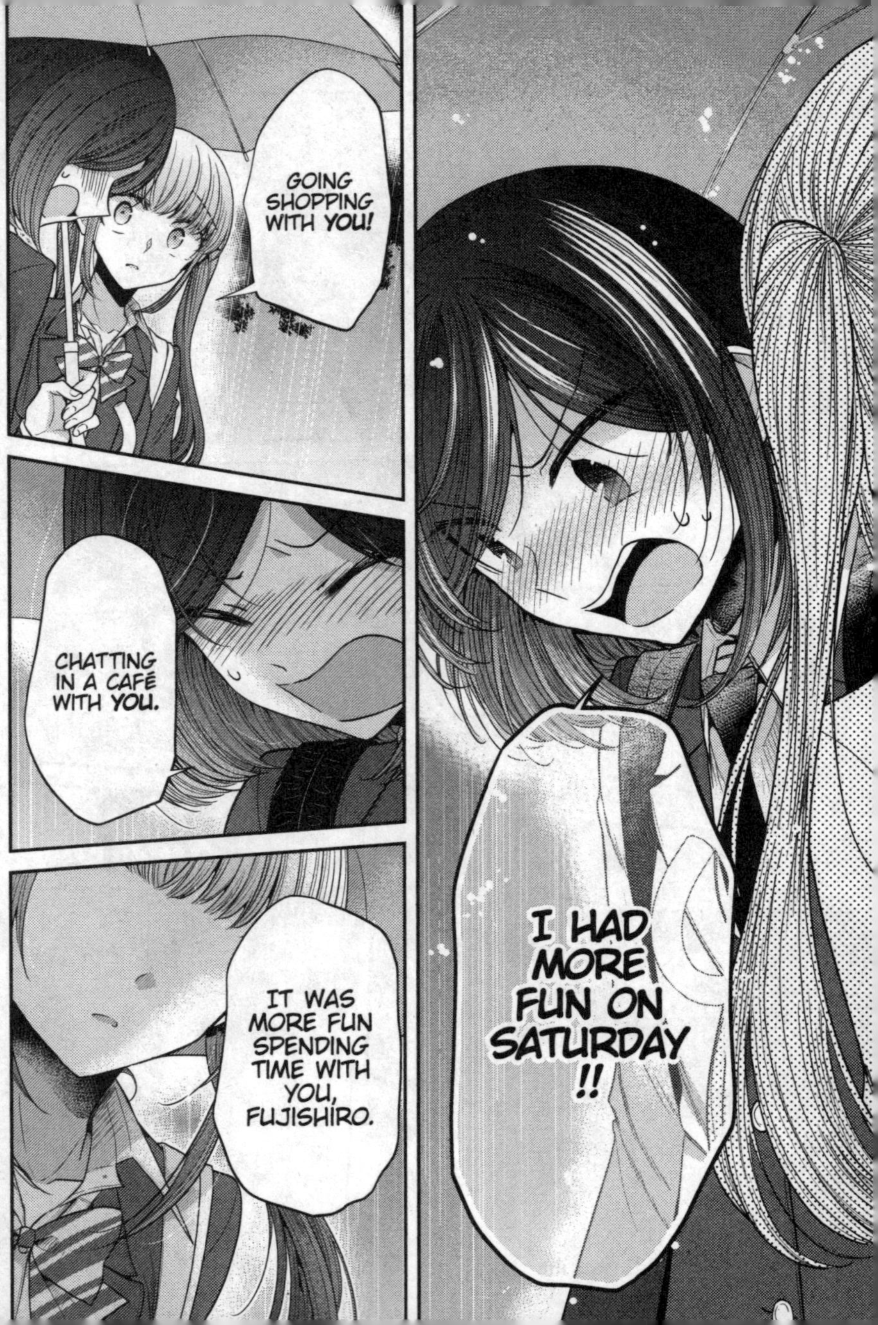
I HAD MORE FUN ON SATURDAY!!
GOING SHOPPING WITH YOU!
CHATTING IN A CAFÉ WITH YOU.
IT WAS MORE FUN SPENDING TIME WITH YOU, FUJISHIRO.

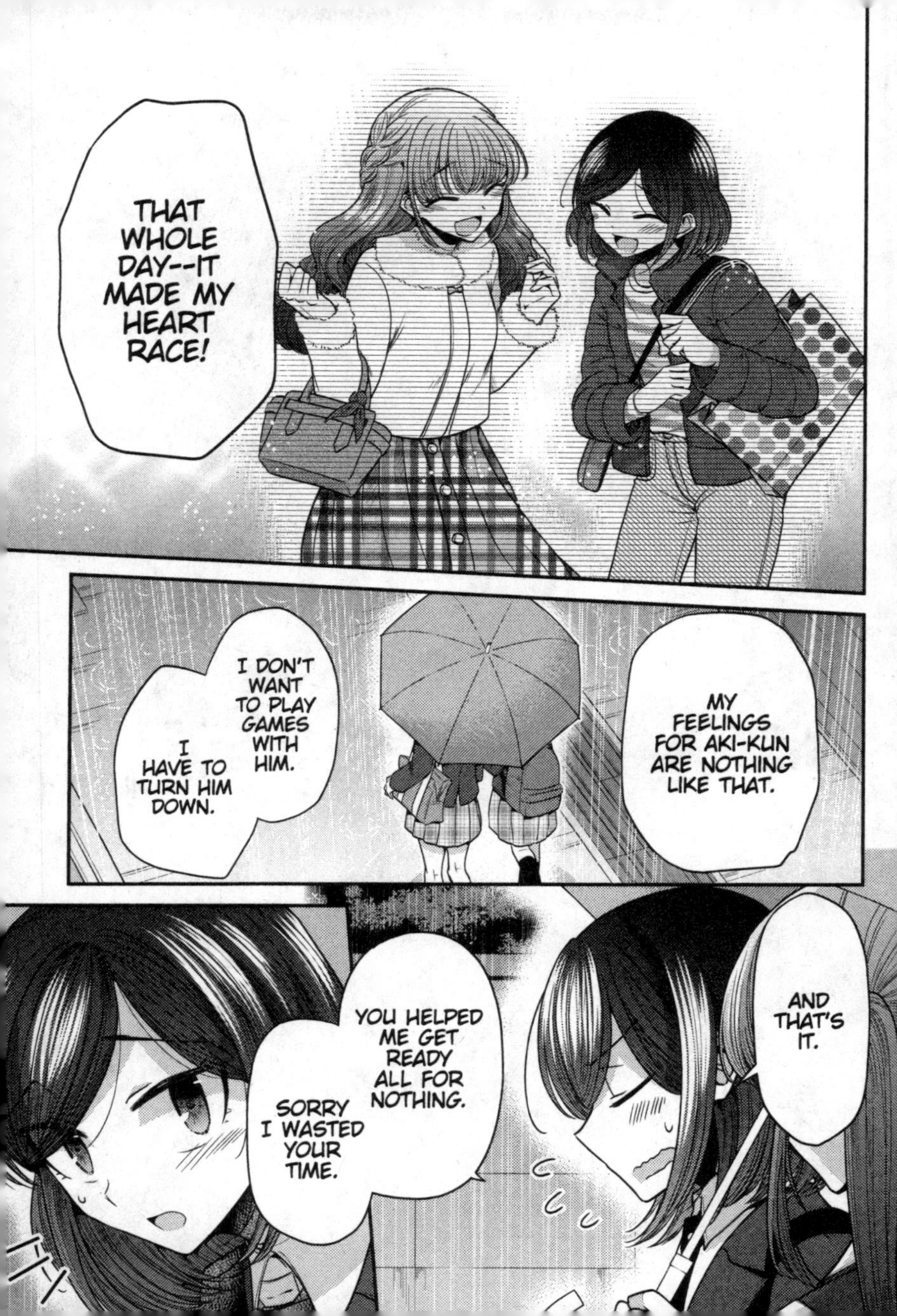
THAT WHOLE DAY--IT MADE MY HEART RACE!
MY FEELINGS FOR AKI-KUN ARE NOTHING LIKE THAT.
I DON'T WANT TO PLAY GAMES WITH HIM.
I HAVE TO TURN HIM DOWN.
AND THAT'S IT.
YOU HELPED ME GET READY ALL FOR NOTHING.
SORRY I WASTED YOUR TIME.

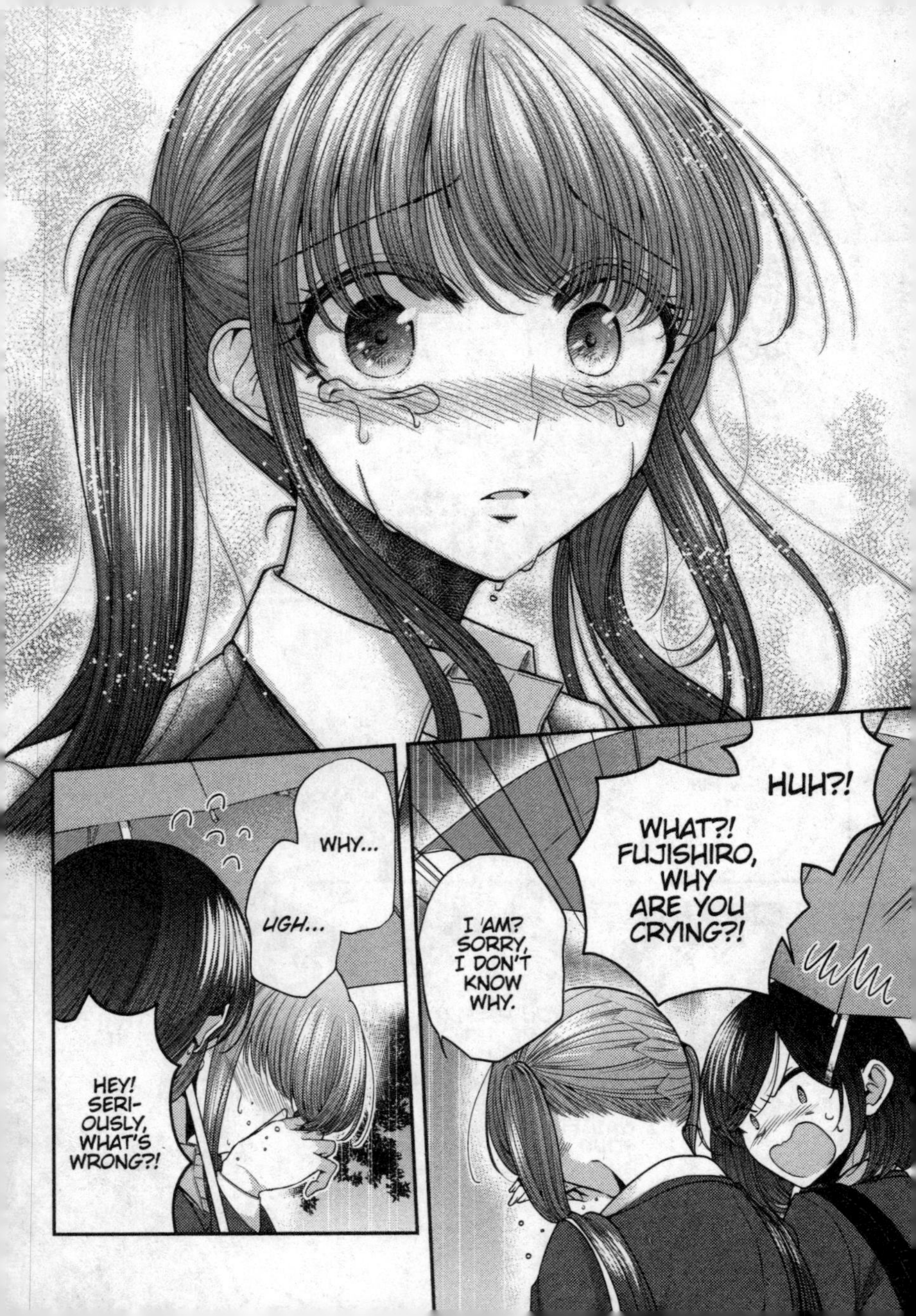
HUH?!
WHAT?! FUJISHIRO, WHY ARE YOU CRYING?!
I AM? SORRY, I DON'T KNOW WHY.
WHY...
UGH...
HEY! SERI-OUSLY, WHAT'S WRONG?!

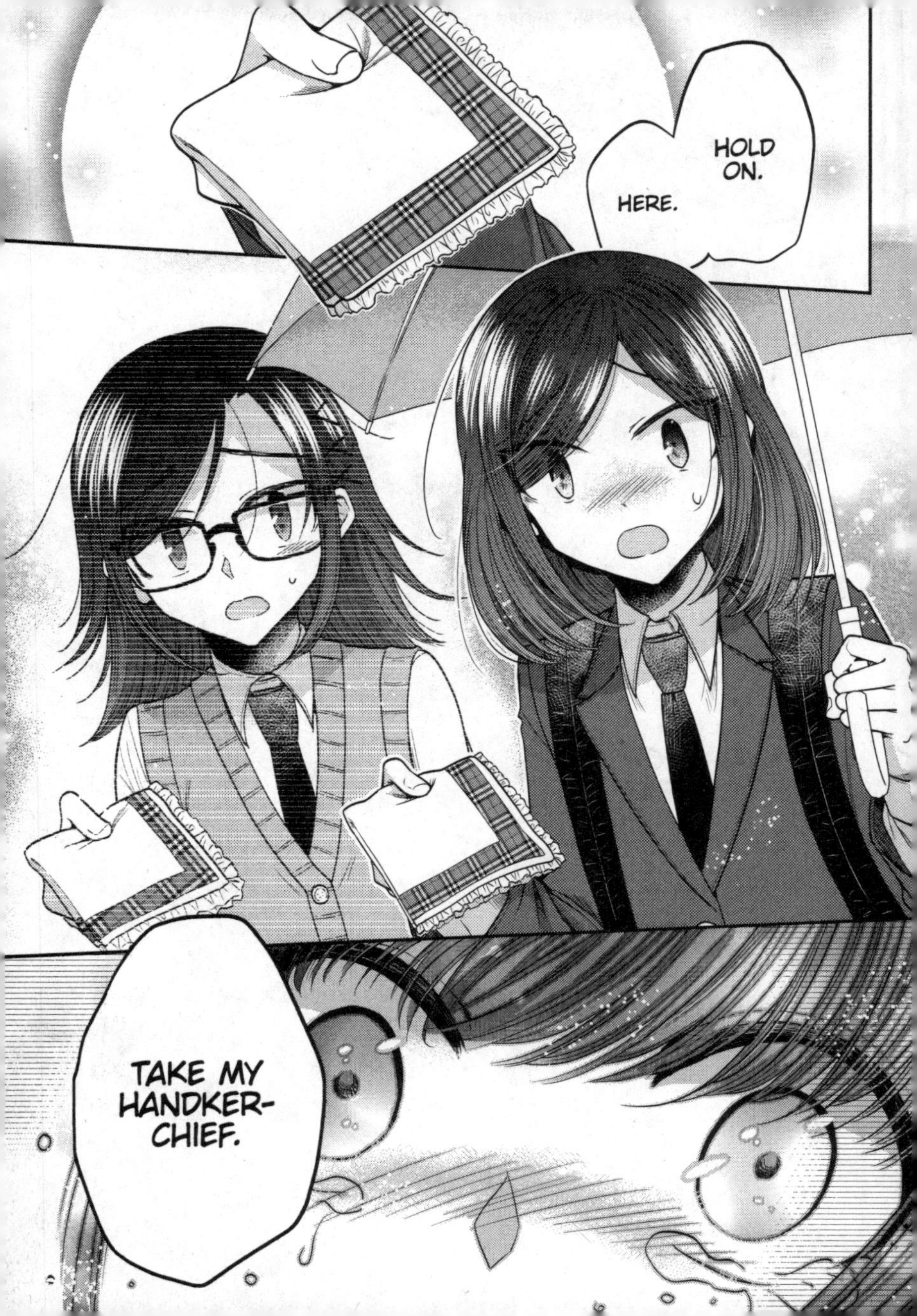
HOLD ON.
HERE.
TAKE MY HANDKER-CHIEF.

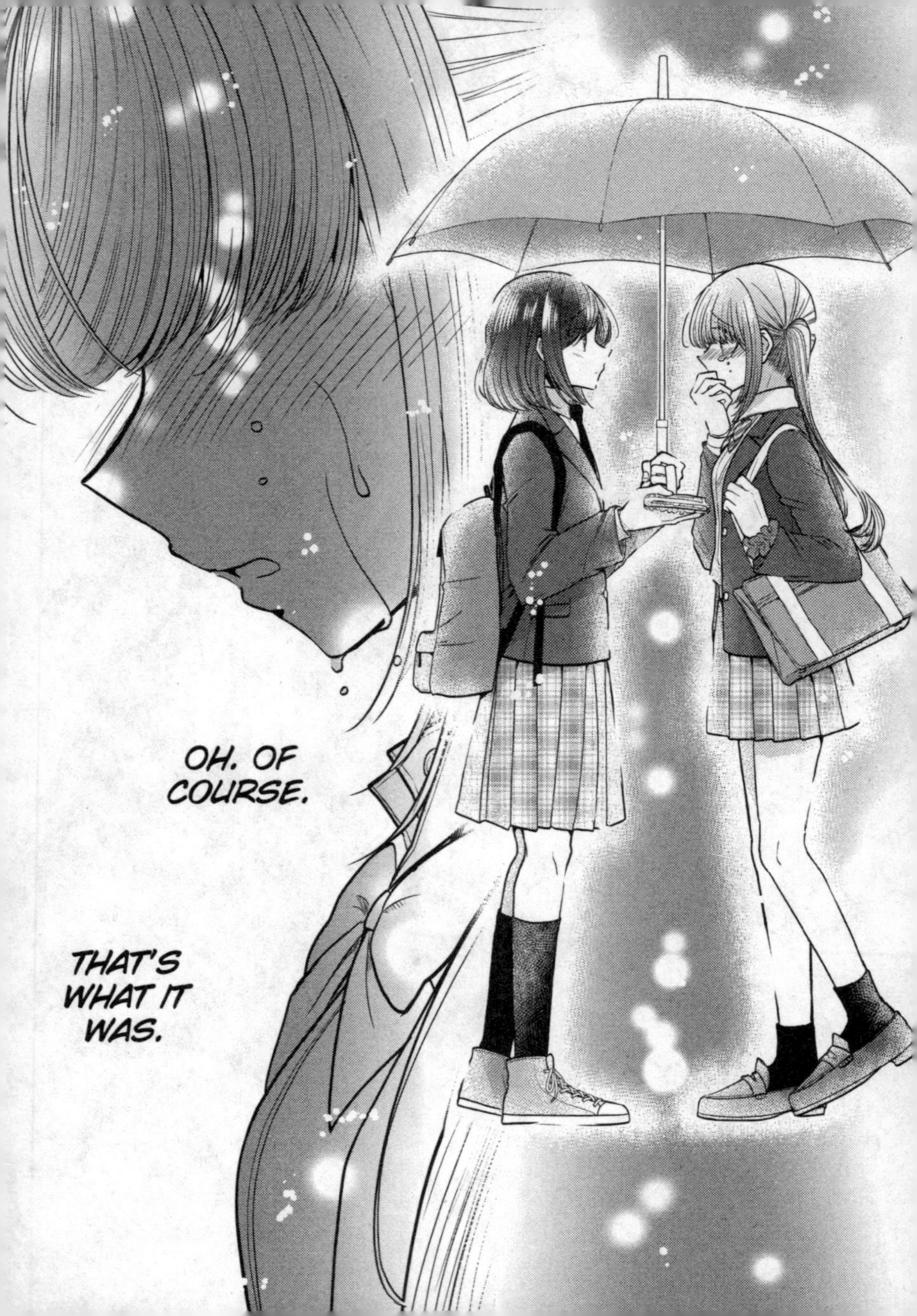
OH. OF COURSE.
THAT'S WHAT IT WAS.

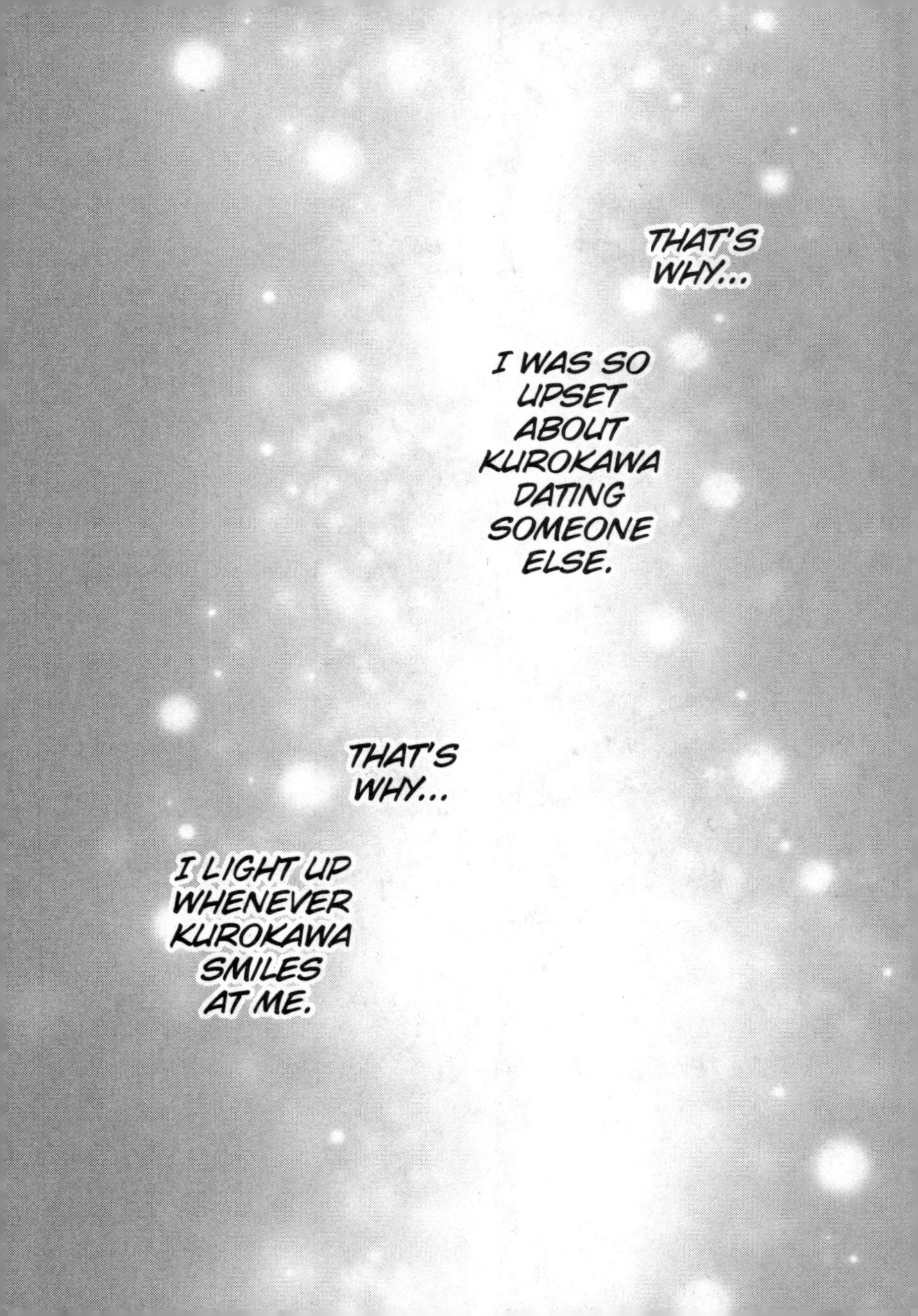
THAT'S WHY...
I WAS SO UPSET ABOUT KUROKAWA DATING SOMEONE ELSE.
THAT'S WHY...
I LIGHT UP WHENEVER KUROKAWA SMILES AT ME.

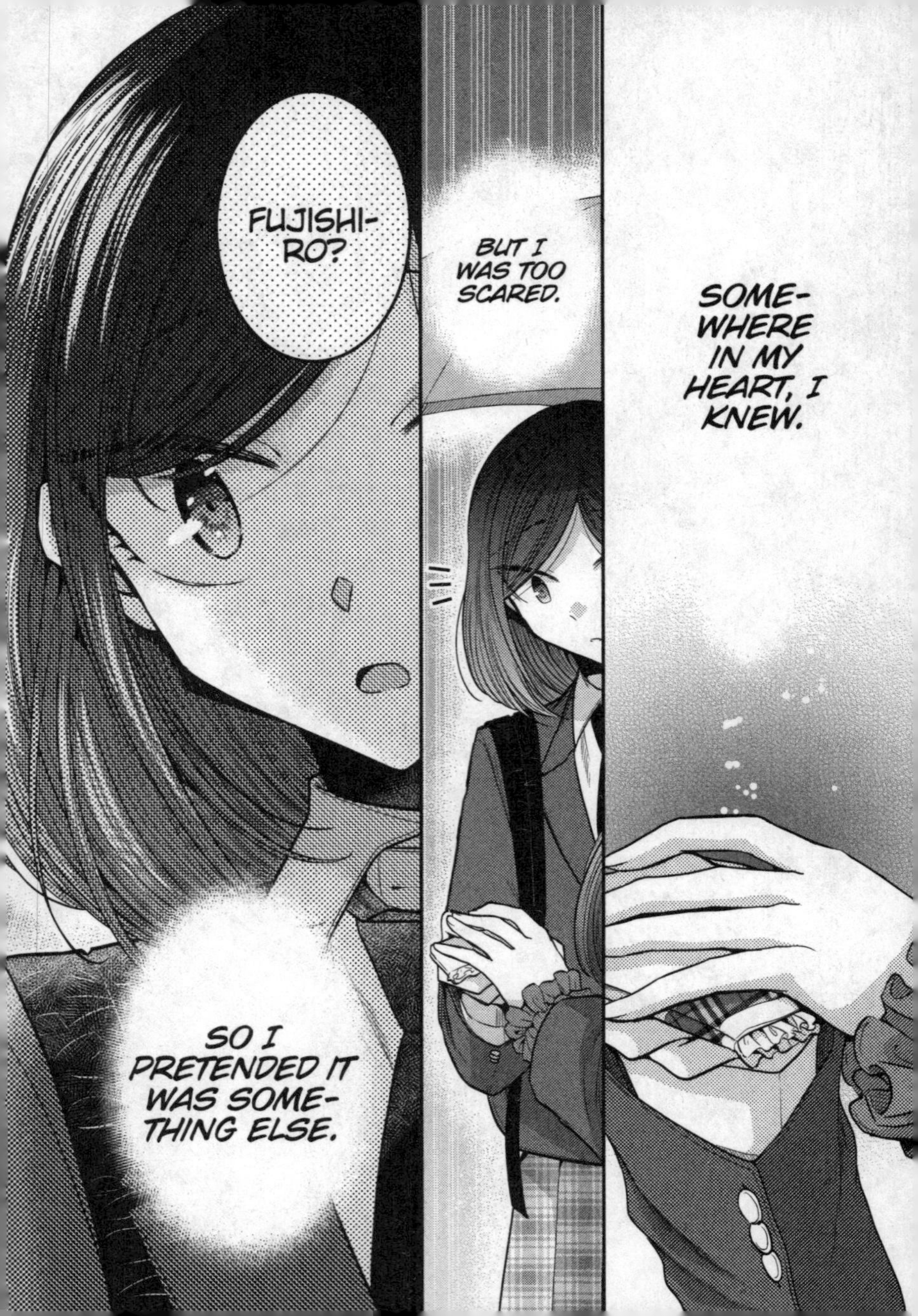
SOME-WHERE IN MY HEART, I KNEW.
BUT I WAS TOO SCARED.
FUJISHI-RO?
SO I PRETENDED IT WAS SOME-THING ELSE.

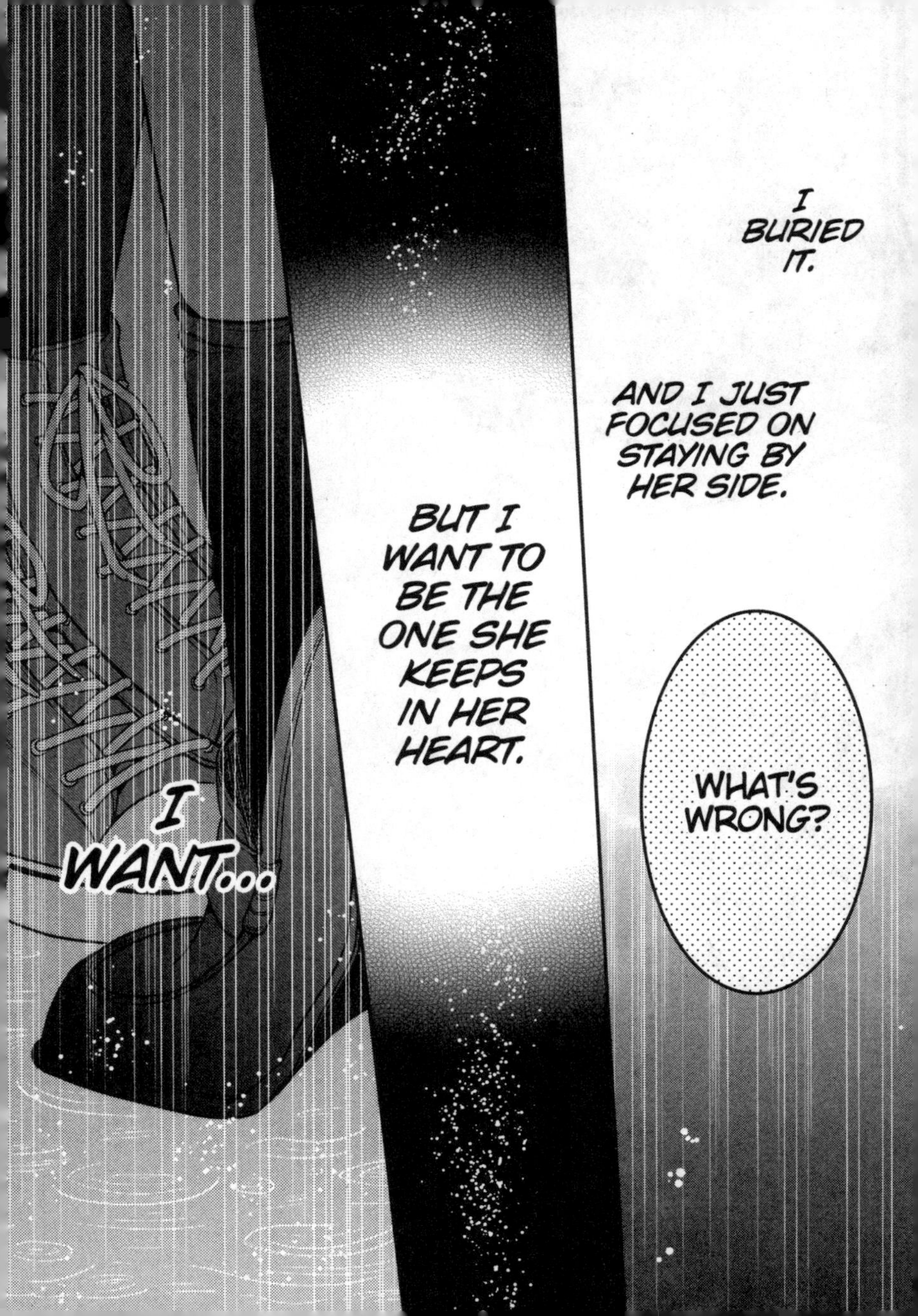

I BURIED IT.
AND I JUST FOCUSED ON STAYING BY HER SIDE.
WHAT'S WRONG?
BUT I WANT TO BE THE ONE SHE KEEPS IN HER HEART.
I WANT...

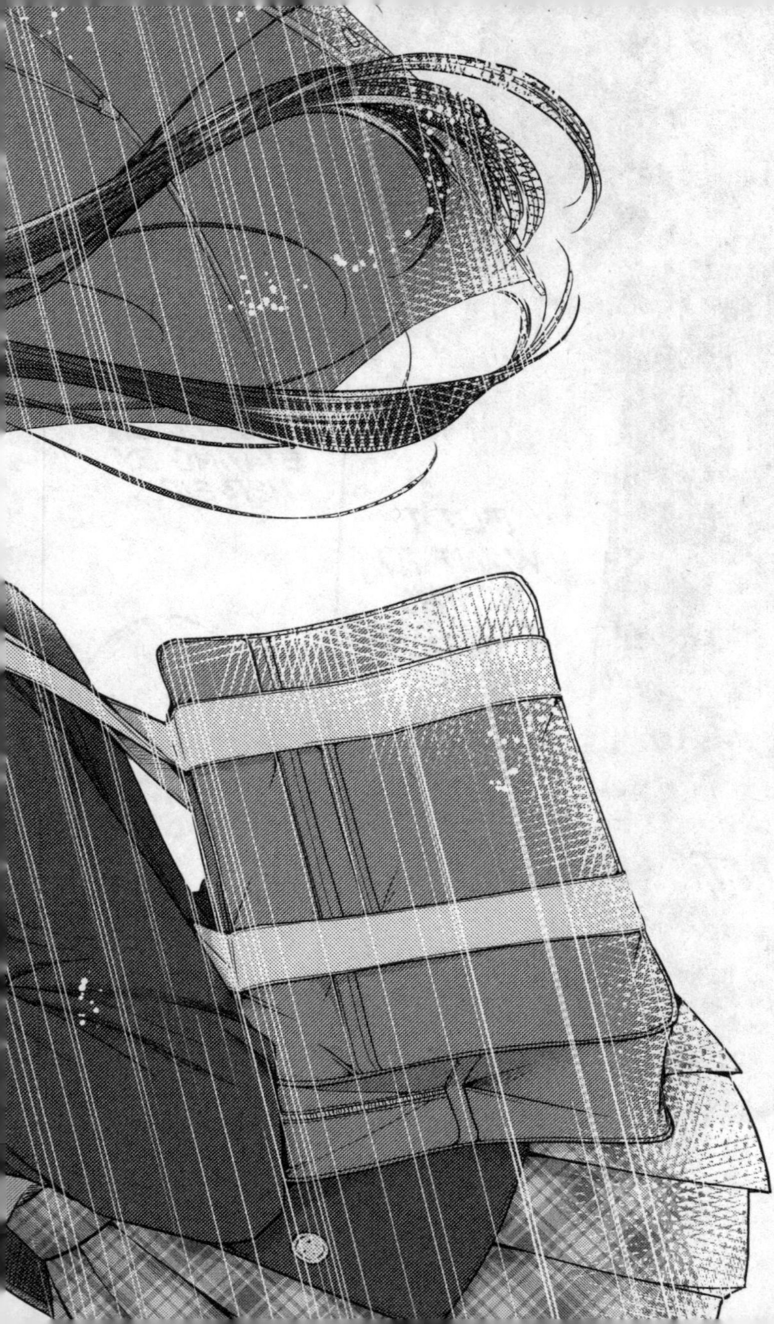

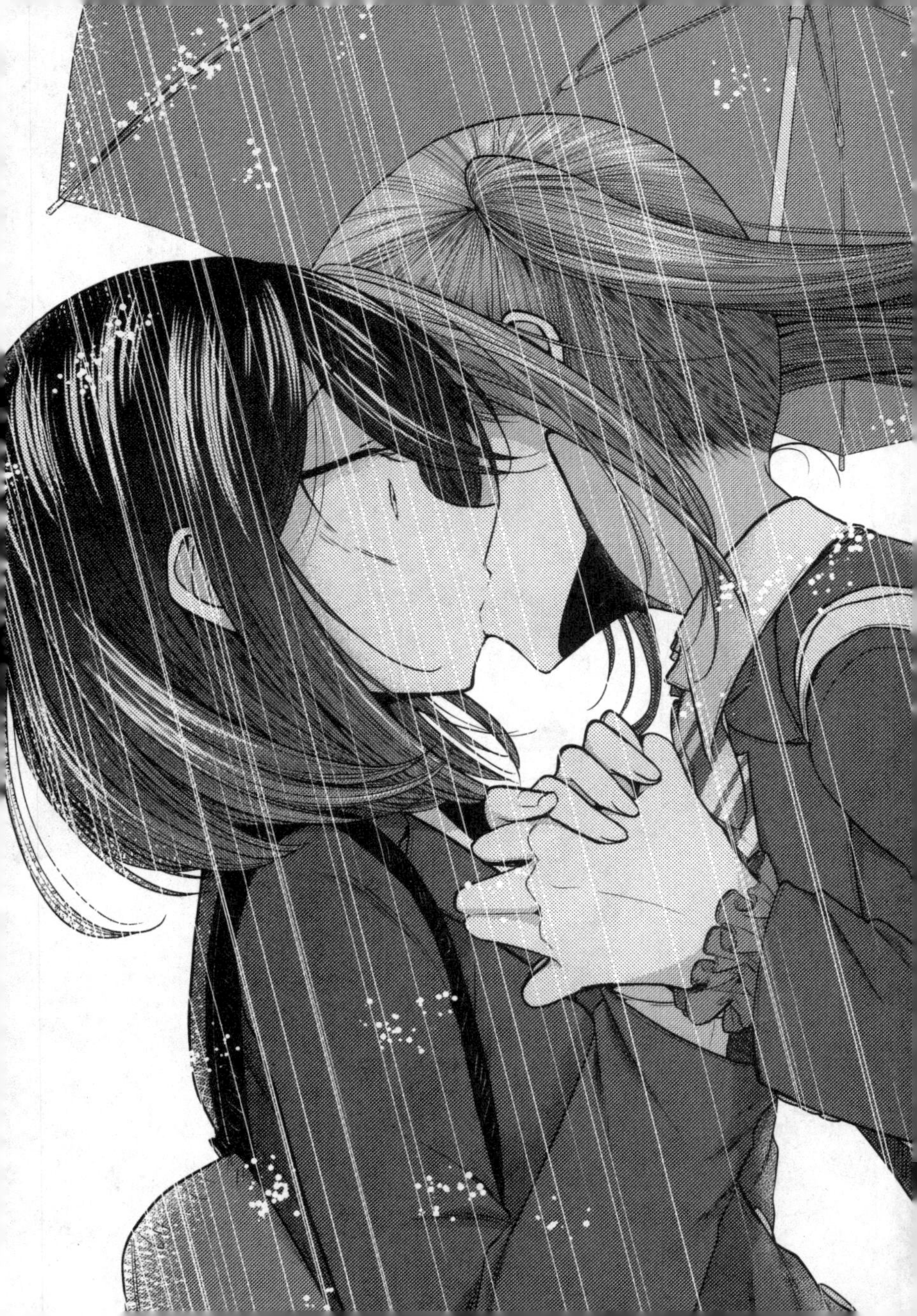

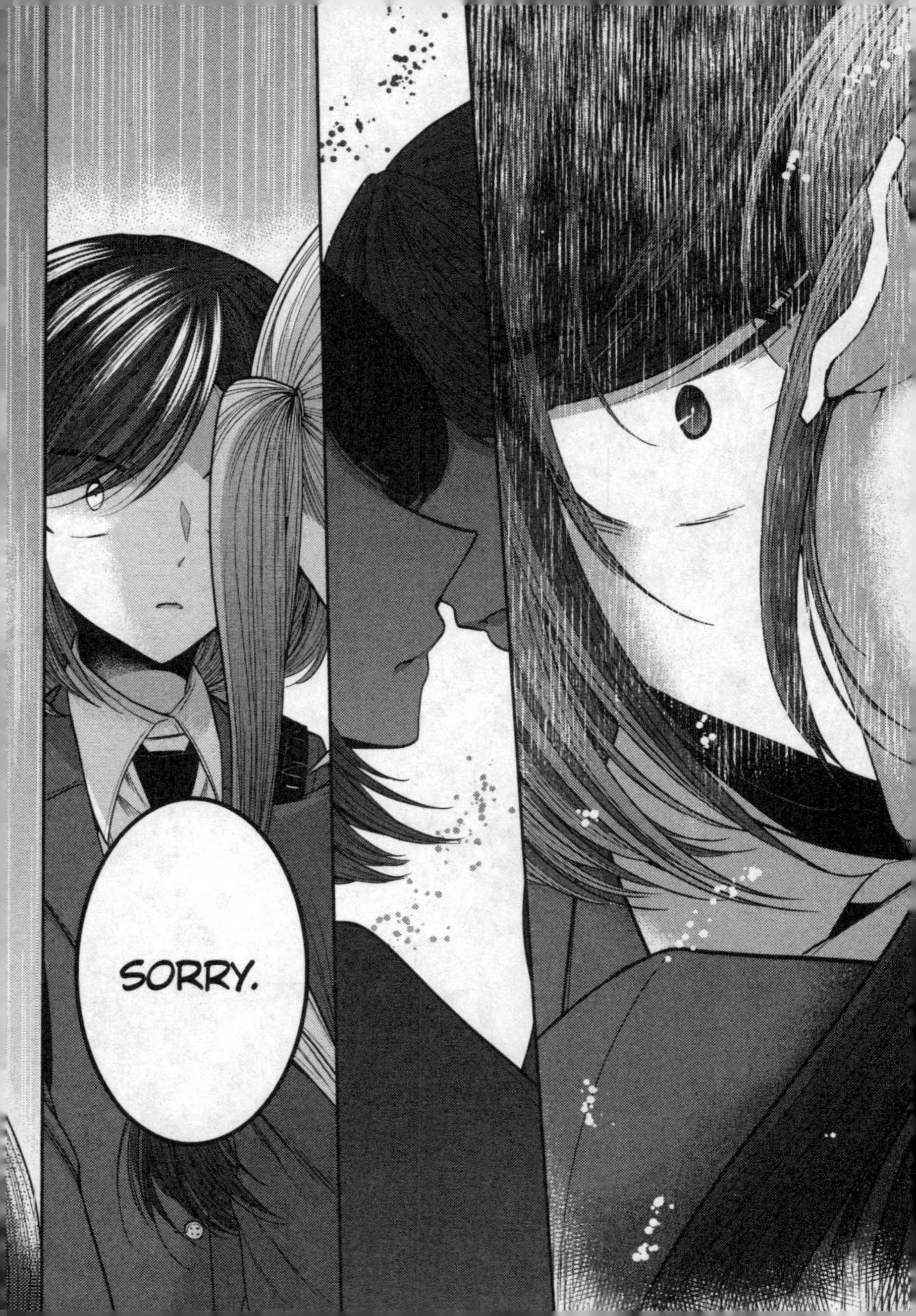
SORRY.

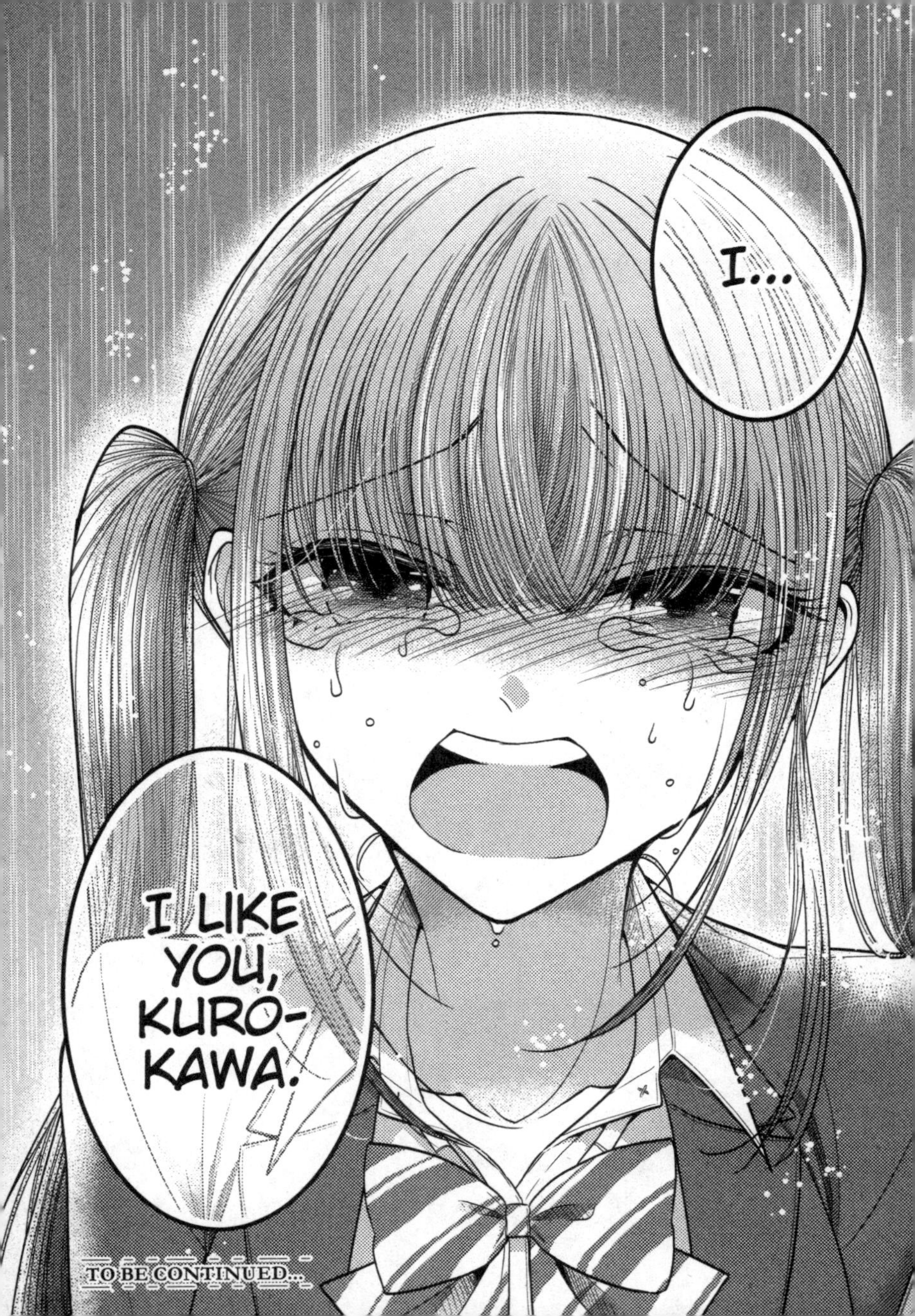
I...
I LIKE YOU, KURO-KAWA.
TO BE CONTINUED...

NEXT VOLUME PREVIEW

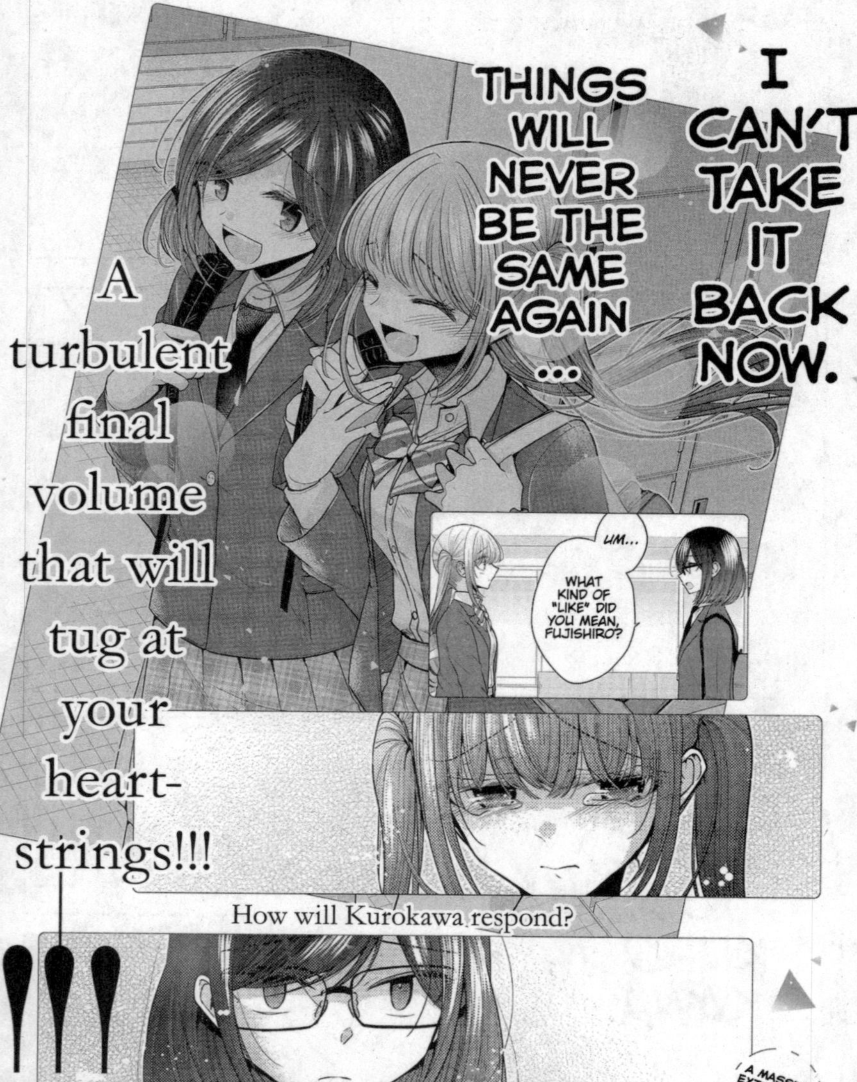
I CAN'T TAKE IT BACK NOW.
THINGS WILL NEVER BE THE SAME AGAIN...
A turbulent final volume that will tug at your heart-strings!!!
UM...
WHAT KIND OF "LIKE" DID YOU MEAN, FUJISHIRO?
How will Kurokawa respond?
!!!...
A MASSIVE, EXTRA-LONG VOLUME!!

SERIES FINALE COMING SOON!!

AFTERWORD

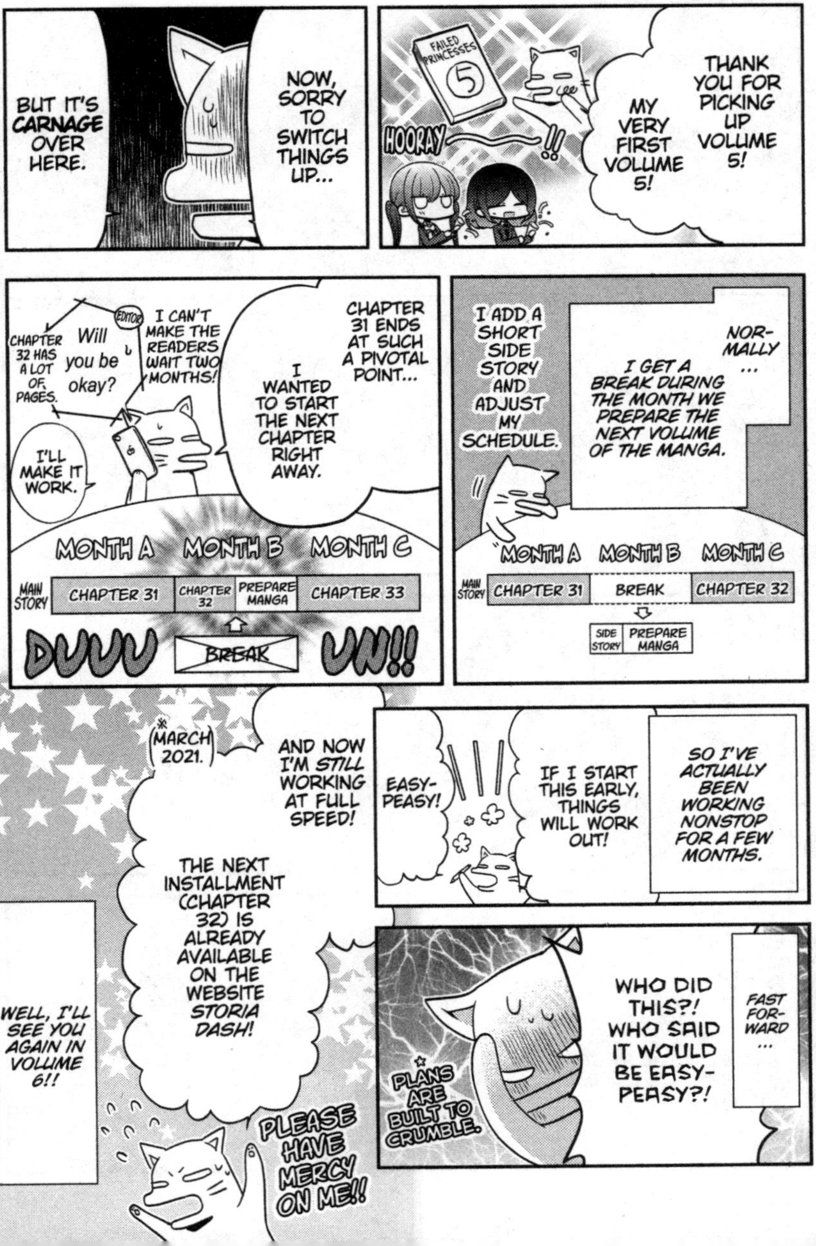

THANK YOU FOR PICKING UP VOLUME 5!
MY VERY FIRST VOLUME 5!
FAILED PRINCESSES
5
HOORAY!!
NOW, SORRY TO SWITCH THINGS UP...
BUT IT'S CARNAGE OVER HERE.
NORMALLY...
I GET A BREAK DURING THE MONTH WE PREPARE THE NEXT VOLUME OF THE MANGA.
I ADD A SHORT SIDE STORY AND ADJUST MY SCHEDULE.
MONTH A
MONTH B
MONTH C
MAIN STORY
CHAPTER 31
BREAK
CHAPTER 32
SIDE STORY
PREPARE MANGA
CHAPTER 31 ENDS AT SUCH A PIVOTAL POINT...
I WANTED TO START THE NEXT CHAPTER RIGHT AWAY.
I CAN'T MAKE THE READERS WAIT TWO MONTHS!
EDITOR
Will you be okay?
CHAPTER 32 HAS A LOT OF PAGES.
I'LL MAKE IT WORK.
MONTH A
MONTH B
MONTH C
MAIN STORY
CHAPTER 31
CHAPTER 32
PREPARE MANGA
CHAPTER 33
DUUU
BREAK
UN!!
SO I'VE ACTUALLY BEEN WORKING NONSTOP FOR A FEW MONTHS.
IF I START THIS EARLY, THINGS WILL WORK OUT!
EASY-PEASY!
AND NOW I'M STILL WORKING AT FULL SPEED!
※(MARCH 2021.
FAST FORWARD...
WHO DID THIS?! WHO SAID IT WOULD BE EASY-PEASY?!
☆PLANS ARE BUILT TO CRUMBLE.
THE NEXT INSTALLMENT (CHAPTER 32) IS ALREADY AVAILABLE ON THE WEBSITE STORIA DASH!
PLEASE HAVE MERCY ON ME!!
WELL, I'LL SEE YOU AGAIN IN VOLUME 6!!

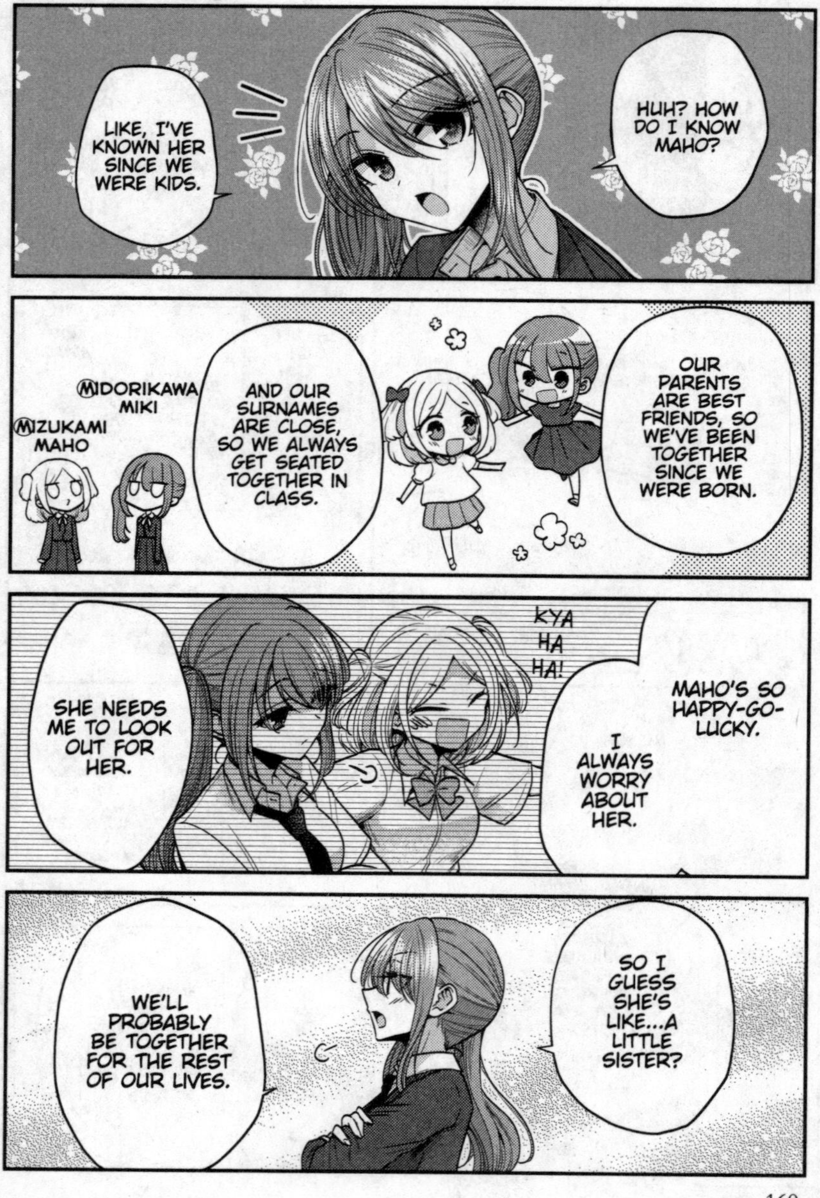
HUH? HOW DO I KNOW MAHO?
LIKE, I'VE KNOWN HER SINCE WE WERE KIDS.
OUR PARENTS ARE BEST FRIENDS, SO WE'VE BEEN TOGETHER SINCE WE WERE BORN.
AND OUR SURNAMES ARE CLOSE, SO WE ALWAYS GET SEATED TOGETHER IN CLASS.
ⓂIDORIKAWA MIKI
ⓂIZUKAMI MAHO
MAHO'S SO HAPPY-GO-LUCKY.
KYA HA HA!
I ALWAYS WORRY ABOUT HER.
SHE NEEDS ME TO LOOK OUT FOR HER.
SO I GUESS SHE'S LIKE...A LITTLE SISTER?
WE'LL PROBABLY BE TOGETHER FOR THE REST OF OUR LIVES.

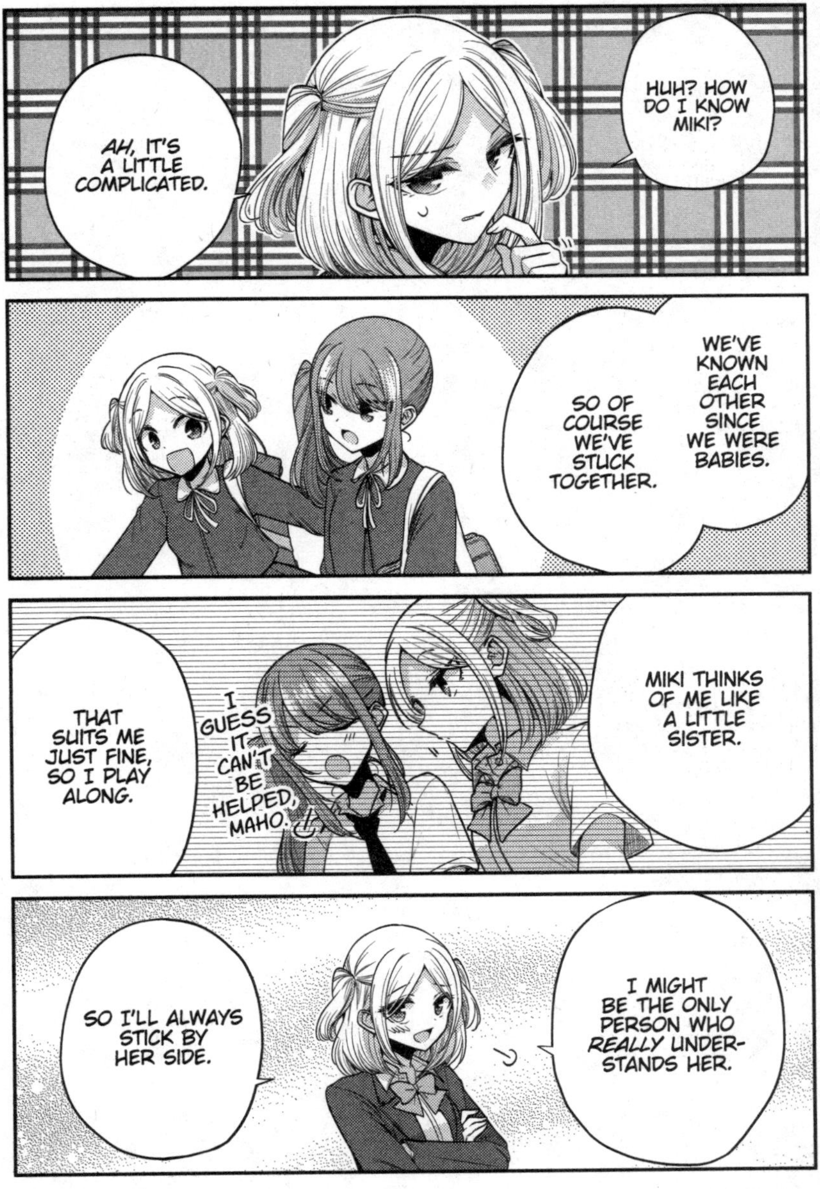
HUH? HOW DO I KNOW MIKI?
AH, IT'S A LITTLE COMPLICATED.
WE'VE KNOWN EACH OTHER SINCE WE WERE BABIES.
SO OF COURSE WE'VE STUCK TOGETHER.
MIKI THINKS OF ME LIKE A LITTLE SISTER.
I GUESS IT CAN'T BE HELPED, MAHO.
THAT SUITS ME JUST FINE, SO I PLAY ALONG.
I MIGHT BE THE ONLY PERSON WHO *REALLY* UNDER-STANDS HER.
SO I'LL ALWAYS STICK BY HER SIDE.

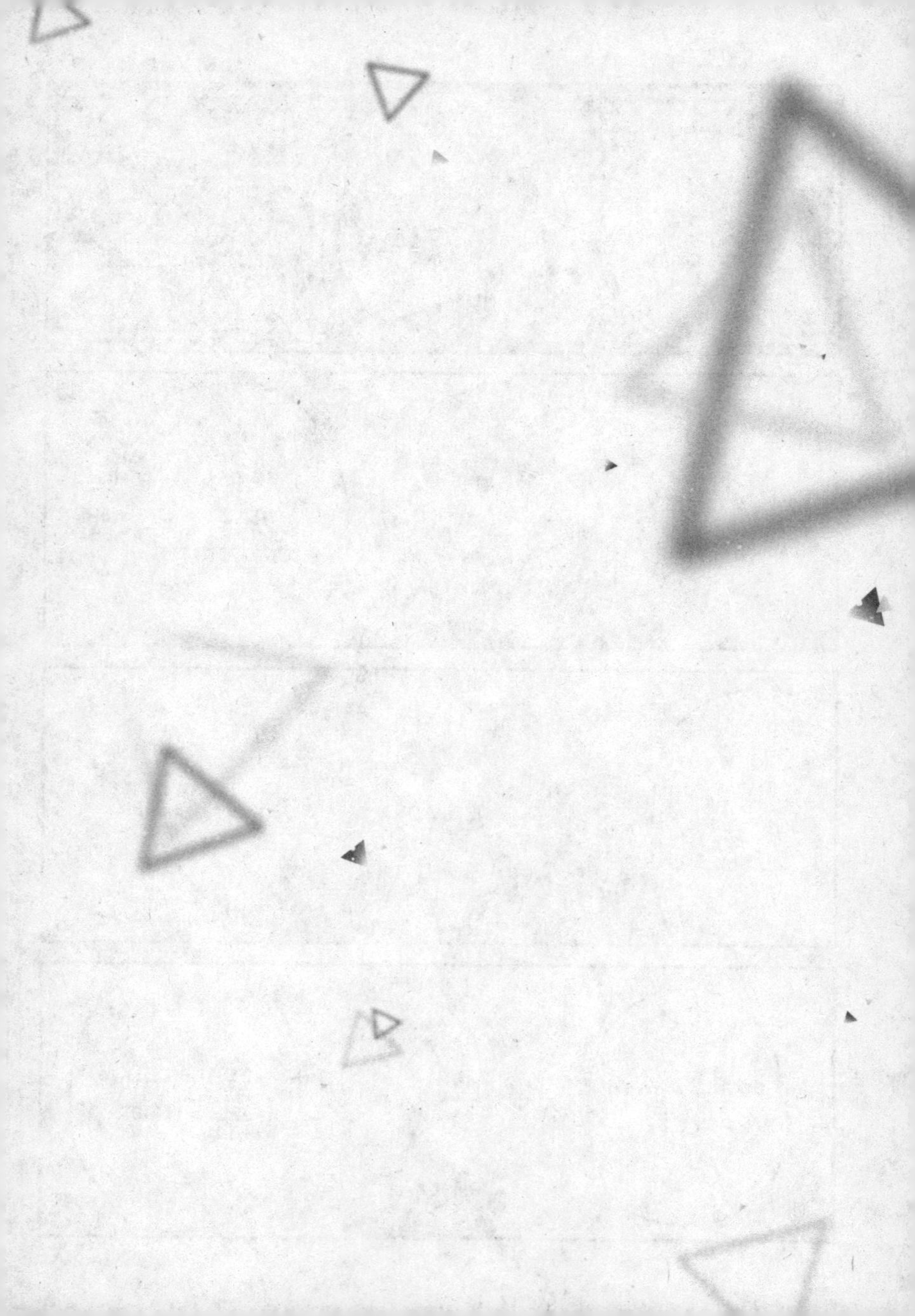

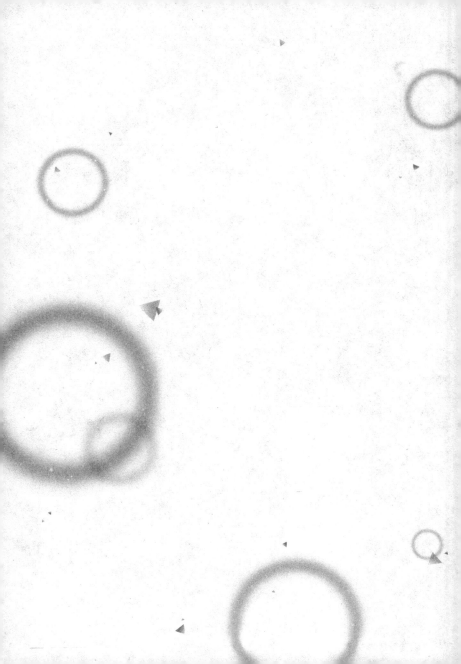

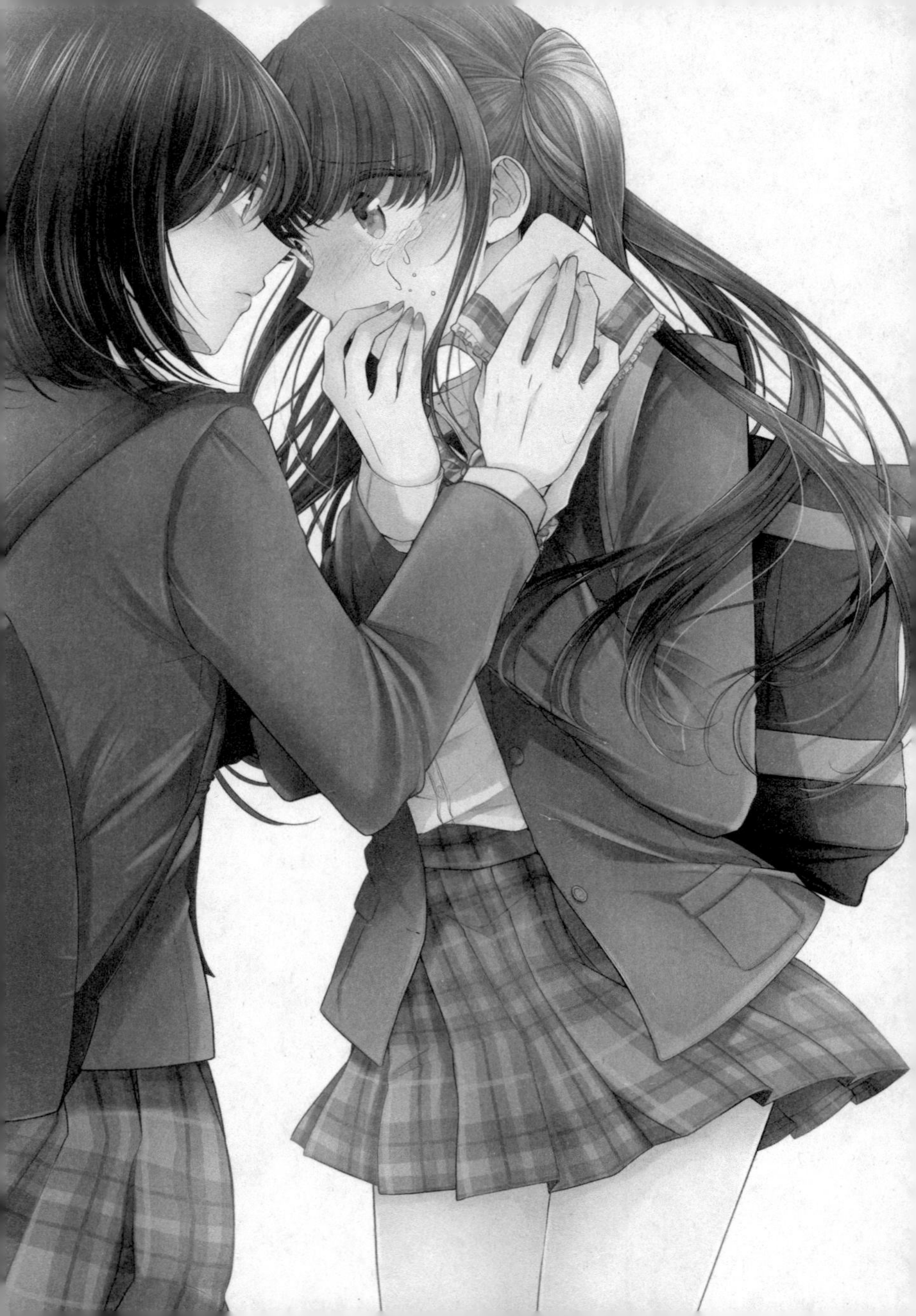

Failed Princesses

SEVEN SEAS ENTERTAINMENT PRESENTS

Failed Princesses

VOLUME 5

story and art by AJIICHI

TRANSLATION
Angela Liu

ADAPTATION
Marykate Jasper

LETTERING AND RETOUCH
Rina Mapa

COVER DESIGN
Nicky Lim

PROOFREADING
Leighanna DeRouen

SENIOR EDITOR
Jenn Grunigen

PREPRESS TECHNICIAN
Rhiannon Rasmussen-Silverstein

PRODUCTION ASSOCIATE
Christa Miesner

PRODUCTION MANAGER
Lissa Pattillo

EDITOR-IN-CHIEF
Julie Davis

ASSOCIATE PUBLISHER
Adam Arnold

PUBLISHER
Jason DeAngelis

Seven Seas press and purchase enquiries can be sent to Marketing Manager
Lianne Sentar at press@gomanga.com. Information regarding the distribution
and purchase of digital editions is available from Digital Manager CK Russell
at digital@gomanga.com.

Seven Seas and the Seven Seas logo are trademarks of
Seven Seas Entertainment. All rights reserved.

ISBN: 978-1-63858-175-8

Printed in Canada

First Printing: March 2022

10 9 8 7 6 5 4 3 2 1

FOLLOW US ONLINE: *www.sevenseasentertainment.com*

READING DIRECTIONS

This book reads from *right to left*, Japanese style.
If this is your first time reading manga, you start
reading from the top right panel on each page and
take it from there. If you get lost, just follow the
numbered diagram here. It may seem backwards at
first, but you'll get the hang of it! Have fun!!

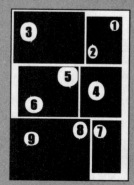